A/70

D Ⅱ

Hilary A. Taylor
September, 1971.

The Sociology of Education

Foundations of Modern Society

The Sociology of Education

OLIVE BANKS
Research Lecturer, Department of Social Science
University of Liverpool

B. T. BATSFORD LTD London

First published 1968
Reprinted 1969 (twice)
Reprinted 1970

© Olive Banks 1968

Made and printed in Great Britain by
Fletcher & Son Ltd, Norwich
for the publishers B. T. Batsford Ltd
4 Fitzhardinge Street, London W.1

7134 0952 5

Contents

1 Introduction

1 *The development of the subject*

The sociology of education, like the sociology of the family or of politics, is no more, but at the same time no less, than the application of socio-logical perspectives to one of the major institutions of society, and for this reason needs no special justification as the subject matter of a text for sociology students. At the same time the history of the subject, especially in the United States, has been unusual enough to warrant some account of its development as a discipline. Although depending for its advance upon the development of sociological concepts and research findings, the subject for many years remained outside the main stream of sociology, being conceived in the main as a part of the study of education. The interest of educationalists like John Dewey ensured the subject an early start, and it soon became a popular subject in colleges and universities in the U.S.A. Between 1910 and 1926 the number of colleges offering a course in educational sociology increased from 40 to 194, and 25 textbooks were published between 1916 and 1936.[1] Yet by the 1940s the number of colleges offering it had declined and the subject generally had fallen into disrepute. Only very recently has the work of rescue really begun.

Both Orville Brim[2] and Ronald G. Corwin[3] have analysed the weak-nesses of the early attempts to develop the subject, and their arguments will only be summarized here, since in essence all the faults arise from the same source, its separation from the main stream of sociology. Many of the courses in the subject were developed in colleges or schools

[1] Corwin, R. G. *A Sociology of Education*, New York: Appleton-Century-Crofts, 1965, p. 56.
[2] Brim, O. *Sociology in the Field of Education*, New York: Russell Sage Foundation, 1958.
[3] Corwin, R. G. *op. cit.*, ch. 3.

of education and few of those who taught them were sociologists by training. Some of the teachers undoubtedly had little knowledge of or interest in developments in sociology itself, and were interested in the subject primarily, if not indeed wholly, as an applied discipline. This tendency was further encouraged by the predominance, amongst the students, of teachers in training. In consequence there was a strong emphasis on a programmatic and polemic approach. Research techniques remained at a primitive level, and there was a focus on a limited area of problems of interest to the practising teacher. Even in 1963 James Conant, making a plea that educational sociology should be taught by sociologists, was able to write: 'As to whether the present group of professors who consider themselves educational sociologists, should perpetuate themselves, I have the gravest doubts. I would wish that all who claim to be working in sociology would get together in the graduate training and appointment of professors who claim to use sociological methods in discussing school and youth problems.'[1]

These criticisms are not to be taken to imply that the preoccupation with practical problems was wrong in itself. Indeed educationalists have a right to ask the practical help of sociology in the solving of certain basic educational problems. But no discipline can hope to provide such assistance if the development of basic concepts and methods is neglected. Moreover, all applied studies are interdisciplinary and it seems that too much hope was put in sociology to solve all the problems of society and the schools.

The increasing disillusion with the old approach has in recent years been challenged by new developments in the subject which are bringing it back into departments of sociology, and this is symbolized by a change in nomenclature. It is now becoming customary to refer to the sociology of education rather than the old and now suspect terminology of educational sociology. On the whole, too, this new emphasis has come about because sociologists themselves have started to take an interest in education as a field of study. Significantly, also, a number of distinguished sociologists have recently made outstanding contributions in general theoretical sociology which have taken the form of studies in educational institutions. It is true that this development is very new, and in spite of a number of brilliant individual contributions the sociology of education, viewed as a body of organized knowledge, is

---

[1] Conant, J. B. *The Education of American Teachers*, New York: McGraw-Hill, 1963, p. 131.

still more of a hope than a realization. Nevertheless, as Corwin has recently pointed out, 'Perhaps the early limitations of the sociology of education do not lie so much in the inadequacy of its conclusions as in the sterility of the questions that it asked.'[1]

This brief account of the early history and subsequent development of the subject does not, however, apply at all to Britain. In Britain, generally, educational sociology failed to capture the interest of educationalists and even after the Second World War it was rare to find it taught in either Teacher Training Colleges or University Education Departments. Only in the 1960s has it become recognized, on any scale, as a valuable part of a teacher's education. In consequence the sociological study of education, in so far as it has existed at all, has taken place in departments of sociology rather than in departments of education, and although, at the present time, there is something of a boom in sociology, including the sociology of education, in the teacher-training field there is no evidence at present either that the subject will be taken over by the educationalists or that it will become divorced from the main body of sociology.

On the other hand, although quite a number of British sociologists, largely under the influence of David Glass, have worked in this field, there is no doubt that the approach used has been a limited one. Research has tended to concentrate on the demographic aspects of education and in particular on its relationship to social class and social mobility. While this is clearly an important part of the subject it is not adequate on its own, and in particular it ignores the study of educational institutions themselves. Nevertheless there are signs that more recently greater attention is being paid to studies in the sociology of the school. At the present time the weaknesses arise from causes which are common to all British sociology, notably shortages of financial and manpower resources, rather than from any neglect of the subject by sociologists themselves. Moreover, a consideration of the approach to the subject suggests that there is considerable convergence of interest on both sides of the Atlantic. This also appears to be true for Western Europe generally.[2] It would seem, therefore, that the future of the subject as a branch of sociology rather than of education is now assured.

---

[1] Corwin, R. G. *op. cit.*, p. 65.
[2] See, for example, Floud, J. and Halsey, A. H. 'The Sociology of Education. A Trend Report and Bibliography', *Current Sociology*, vol. VIII (3), 1958.

2 The structural–functional framework

It remains now to give a more precise definition of the scope of the subject as it is to be defined in this volume, and in particular to introduce some of the more important concepts around which it has been organized. The traditional conceptual framework in the subject is that of functionalism, and derives primarily from the writings of the French sociologist Emile Durkheim. The functionalist approach, as Durkheim used it, is to seek for the social function performed by an institution; that is to say the part played by the institution in the promotion and maintenance of social cohesion and social unity. All of the major institutions studied by Durkheim are conceived in this way and education is no exception. Its special task is defined by him as 'the methodical socialization of the young generation'. By this he means the development in the child of certain values and certain intellectual and physical skills 'which are demanded of him by both the political society as a whole and the special milieu for which he is specifically destined'.[1] Only in this way can the cohesion and survival of the society be assured.

This requirement is a basic necessity of all societies, however simple, and many anthropological studies have described the socialization process at work within primitive societies. The sociology of education, however, is more usually confined to studies of industrial societies, which offer certain distinctive and challenging problems. Most fundamental perhaps is the increasing importance in advanced industrial societies of specialized educational agencies which share with, and in certain circumstances replace, the pre-industrial socializing agencies, of which normally the family is the most important. Immediately, as Floud and Halsey have pointed out, this creates a fresh set of problems, since the specialized agencies themselves enter the situation as relatively independent factors, 'promoting or impeding change and producing unintended as well as intended, and dysfunctional as well as functional consequences'.[2] For example, there may be prolonged resistance to changes in curricula, teaching methods or entrance requirements, especially on the part of long-established institutions like grammar schools or universities, with consequences that may be disadvantageous

---

[1] Durkheim, E. *Education and Sociology*, Glencoe, Illinois: Free Press, 1956, p. 71.
[2] Floud, J. and Halsey, A. H. *op. cit.*, p. 168.

for the economy. On the other hand, teachers can, and often do, act as a powerful pressure group to promote educational change.

At the same time the process of socialization itself becomes more complex. It is no longer simply a matter of the transmission of skills and values; the educational process itself must take on the role of the allocation and selection as well as the training of individuals for their adult role. Increasingly, in all advanced industrial societies, educational qualifications become important not simply as a sign or symbol of high status but as a necessary prerequisite of the majority of highly rewarded occupations. Indeed, the problems to which this gives rise have pre-occupied the attention of sociologists in Britain and to a large extent also in the United States, to the almost virtual exclusion of the problems of social integration and social control with which Durkheim was so concerned.

One of the major strengths of the structural functional approach to education is the placing of educational institutions firmly in their relationship with the wider social structure. In any consideration of either the socializing or the selective function of education regard must be had to the context in which the educational institutions operate and the influences at work upon them. Of these, the economy is obviously of paramount importance, determining as it does the complexity of the skills required according to the level of technology. At the same time its differentiating and selective functions bring education inevitably into close relationships with the demographic aspects of society and with the stratification system. The controlling and integrating functions of education and its role in the transmission of values also necessitate close ties with the value system of society, with religious institutions and with the State itself as an instrument of control. Moreover, in so far as the educational process is a shared one, other socializing agencies, of which the family is the most important, must be recognized for the part they play, and their relationship with the more specialized educational agencies must be explored. Consequently, within the general framework of a structural functionalist approach the sociology of education has developed as a largely macrocosmic study of educational institutions.

Yet, as Floud and Halsey have pointed out, structural functionalism has certain methodological faults which have contributed to the weaknesses of the sociology of education. 'The structural functionalist is preoccupied with social integration based on shared values—that is, with consensus—and he conducts his analysis solely in terms of the motivated actions of individuals. For him, therefore, education is a means of motivating individuals to behave in ways appropriate to maintain the society in a state of equilibrium. But this is a difficult notion to apply to developed, especially industrialized societies, even if the notion of equilibrium is interpreted dynamically. They are dominated by social change, and "consensus" and "integration" can be only very loosely conceived in regard to them.'[1]

Briefly, the structural functional approach tends to overlook not only the extent of differentiation in a modern complex society but also the fact that differentiation implies at least some degree, and often a considerable degree, of actual or contained conflict. It was one of the major errors of Durkheim to minimize the amount of conflict consequent upon the division of labour,[2] and this same error continues within the structural functional school. Yet even a brief glance at some of the educational controversies in our own society reveals that there is no common value system with regard to educational goals, but a series of opposing ideologies put forward by certain pressure groups which include, amongst others, the major political parties. The wider social structure in which the educational institutions are enmeshed must, therefore, be seen not as the result of any single or unified set of values, but as the expression of manifest or latent ideological conflict. The concept of ideology, including both its cognitive and evaluative aspects,[3] is indeed of fundamental importance in any understanding of the educational process, and it is unfortunate that it should have been so seriously neglected in the study of education.

Although it is often argued that the functional approach tends to neglect social change, this is not altogether a fair criticism since many of the major thinkers in this field have attempted to find a place for change in their theory. So far as education is concerned, however, there has been a very widespread tendency to treat it as a wholly adaptive institution. That is to say, change in the educational system tends to be seen as a response to changes in the other parts of the social structure. This contrasts with the prevailing viewpoint of educationalists

---

[1] *Ibid.*, p. 171.

[2] Consider, for example, his relegation of conflict to pathological types of the division of labour. Durkheim, E. *The Division of Labour in Society*, Glencoe, Illinois: Free Press, 1933.

[3] Ideology includes both popularly accepted ideas about the nature of society and popularly approved values and goals for the society. See Johnson, H. M. *Sociology: A Systematic Introduction*, London: Routledge & Kegan Paul, 1961, pp. 587-8.

like John Dewey, who have seen the educational system as a direct agency of social change, and who have enthusiastically looked to the schools to reform society. It is, of course, not difficult to prick the rather facile optimism of the educationalists who have sometimes hoped to produce major social reforms by simple changes in educational organization. Moreover, educational institutions have often been largely adaptive in their functioning, as can be seen in even a cursory examination of their response to the technological requirements of the economy in many advanced industrial societies. On the other hand, there is no evidence for any simple theory of technological determinism. Educational institutions are shaped by many aspects of the social structure including the dominant value system. We need only consider in this context the ideological barriers to the development of technical education in Britain, and in particular the influence on the educational system and elsewhere of the support for the amateur rather than the expert.

Nor can it be asserted with confidence that education can never initiate change. There is an absence of concrete studies in this field but work is now being done on such topics as the part played by education in economic growth, and the effect of education in changing attitudes. It is clear, too, that education may well have unintended consequences of some importance as, for example, on the composition of new and old elites. Most important of all, in an age when change has itself become institutionalized, the pursuit of innovation rather than the maintenance of the social order becomes one of the major goals of the educational process.

3 *The theory of organization*

Although there have been many studies of schools and colleges using a variety of methods and theoretical approaches, there has until very recently been very little development of a genuine sociology of the school. In particular there has been a very considerable neglect of the school as an organization and the effect of its organizational setting on the educational process. 'Too many sociological studies of schools are, in fact, studies of the social life of adolescents, and little account is taken of the more or less tacit demands and pressures of the formal organization of school life and work.'[1]

[1] Floud, J. and Halsey, A. H. *op. cit.*, p. 186.

In the last few years, however, a growing interest in organizational theory in general, and the increasing application of this theory to an educational setting, has provided us with some of the main dimensions for a framework of analysis. The attempt to construct a general theory of organizations derives initially from the study of industry, and the typologies and theories in this area have been developed primarily to explain industrial rather than educational organizations where the kind of task and the type of personnel are very different. Nevertheless, there are certain basic concepts which appear to be useful in the analysis of all types of organization. Hoyle[1] has argued that two of the most widely used concepts in organization theory are authority and bureaucracy, both of which stem from Max Weber's treatment of authority in his political sociology. Weber defined power as 'the possibility of imposing one's will upon the behaviour of other persons',[2] and in this general sense power is an aspect of most social relationships. The power which is derived from established authority is, however, of a very special kind, arising as it does from the authoritarian power of command. Bureaucracy is a particular kind of authority found in several types of society but developing particular importance in modern complex organizations. In its most typical form modern bureaucracy is characterized by a hierarchical structure of power, in which each individual in each level of the organization has a clearly defined position and a clearly defined set of duties, according to a set of written rules.

The question as to how far a school as an educational system can be described as a bureaucracy is still an open one, yet it is clear that educational systems do contain many bureaucratic elements, which are increasing in importance in modern societies. School and college administration, for example, usually takes a hierarchic form and there are many highly centralized procedures even in an educational system as decentralized as it is in the United States.

An alternative set of concepts basic to organizational theory revolves around the concept of role which, as used by most sociologists, refers to a set of norms relating to a specific activity or relationship. Corwin defines a role as a 'shorthand way of referring to related norms'.[3] A set

[1] Hoyle, E. 'Organizational Analysis in the Field of Education', *Educational Research*, vol. VII (2), 1965.
[2] Quoted in Bendix, R. *Max Weber: an Intellectual Portrait*, New York: Doubleday, 1960, p. 294.
[3] Corwin, R. G. *op. cit.*, p. 36.

of roles that is consistently related is defined as a social position. For example, the position of teacher comprises his role relationships with pupils, head teacher, parents, committee members, officials, inspectors, and so on. Frequently in practice, however, the word role is used when role position would be more accurate, and it is indeed quite common to refer simply to the teacher's role.

Role conflict occurs when there are inconsistencies between the roles expected of a person in a particular position, or alternatively there may be incompatibility within a single role, or between two positions held by a single person. Roles conceived as sets of norms have, of course, an essentially prescriptive character; they relate to expectations about the rights and obligations comprising a particular set of relationships. On the other hand, recent studies by Gross and his associates have shown that there is frequently a considerable amount of discrepancy with respect to role expectations. They found, for example, frequent disagreements about their responsibilities between school superintendents and their school boards, as well as disagreements amongst the school board members themselves.[1] Consensus about role expectations must therefore be shown rather than assumed to exist, and dissensus must be regarded as a possible source of conflict.

At the same time it must not be assumed that role expectations and behaviour are one and the same. We have to take into account the concept of role performance, which allows for the deliberate or unwitting breaking of norms, even where they are accepted by the individuals as part of the role prescription. Studies of certain kinds of unconscious discrimination against particular groups of children are thus essentially studies in role performance, and so are some of the studies of teacher effectiveness.

The concept of authority and bureaucracy, and the cluster of concepts centring upon role, are obviously of great potential value for the study of educational organizations. Yet as late as 1959 Gross was able to argue that 'a critical examination of the sociological literature reveals that there have been few significant advances in our knowledge of the social and cultural structure of the school, and of the impact it exerts on the functioning of educational systems, since the publication of Waller's *Sociology of Teaching* in 1932'.[2] Since then, however,

---

[1] Gross, N., Mason Ward, S. and McEachern, Alexander W. *Explorations in Role Analysis: Studies of the School Superintendency Role*, New York: Wiley, 1958.
[2] Gross, N. 'The Sociology of Education', in Merton, R.K. (ed.) *Sociology Today*, New York: Basic Books, 1959, p. 131.

interest in organizational theory and the school as an organization have continued to grow, and a recent review of the literature by Bidwell,[1] although still leaning heavily on Waller, is also able to make use of a number of recent sources. Moreover Corwin's textbook on the sociology of education specifically sets out to view school systems as 'complex bureaucratic organizations'. The sociology of the school may therefore be said to have begun; although, as its more detailed treatment in subsequent chapters will show, it has not as yet attracted the attention of researchers to the same extent as the more traditional structural functional approach.

4 *Aims and limitations*

In preparing this outline of the growing body of knowledge on the sociology of education, the needs of the sociology student rather than the intending teacher have been chiefly in mind. Consequently some familiarity with sociological concepts and, even more important, some knowledge of comparative social institutions has been assumed. The text, that is to say, is intended to follow on from an introductory course in sociology rather than to act as a substitute for it. This is to break away from tradition both in Britain and in the United States where until recently textbooks in this field have been aimed at the student of education rather than of sociology and the general slant of the subject matter has been to introduce sociology to teachers rather than to explore the sociological dimensions of educational institutions. Gross has claimed that Brookover's textbook, published in 1955,[2] constitutes the first effort in more than a quarter of a century to examine the school system from a consistently sociological rather than an 'applied education' frame of reference.[3]

Even the best and most recent textbooks in this field tend to a very definite insularity in their approach. In particular American textbooks give only a minimum of attention to other educational systems than their own. This is understandable enough in view of the enormous difficulties in the way of a genuinely comparative approach to educa-

[1] Bidwell, C., 'The School as a Formal Organization', in March, J. G. (ed.) *Handbook of Social Organization*, Chicago: Rand McNally, 1965.
[2] Brookover, Wilbur A. *A Sociology of Education*, New York: American Book Co., 1955.
[3] Gross, N. *op. cit.*, p. 129.

tional systems which is at the same time sociological in its aims. Nevertheless it is the present writer's contention that, without some attempt to be comparative, it is very difficult to treat a number of important areas in the subject. Accordingly, although the main emphasis in this book is on the educational system in Britain, and indeed primarily in England and Wales, material from the United States has been introduced very freely, and wherever possible the United States and Britain are compared. In addition, information from a number of other European countries, and especially from the U.S.S.R., has been included from time to time. Unfortunately it has not been possible to include more than a brief reference to educational systems outside Europe and the United States, so that the place of education in developing societies has not been given the attention that the importance of the subject deserves. However, a short survey of the main problems in the area has been included in the final chapter.

The general plan of the book is to proceed from a consideration of education in its societal setting to a discussion of the sociology of the school itself. The final chapter—on social change—is, however, an exception. It has been left to the last, partly because of the difficulties inherent in the subject, and partly because it cannot be adequately treated without an attack at the level of both society and the school. The book begins therefore with a consideration of educational systems in their relationship to such major social institutions as the economy, social stratification and social mobility. At this stage, considerable attention is given to the concept of ideology, and to the relationship between ideology, values, social structure and educational systems. A consideration at this point of the effect of social class on school performance leads into a study of education and the family, and a review of research into the effect of home environment on the educability of the child. This is followed by a chapter on the control of education, and involves an examination in the light of such data as are available of the external pressures on schools and universities from the state, the churches and the local community. From here the focus begins to turn more directly on to the school itself, although there is a preliminary chapter on the teachers as a professional group. This is followed by an attempt to bring together studies on the school as a social system, which treats the school both as an organization and a set of informal relationships. The final chapter is concerned with a discussion of the way in which the educational system relates to social change.

This particular approach to the subject, and especially the order in which the topics have been introduced, is inevitably a somewhat personal one and no claim is made that this is the only or indeed the best approach. It is presented in the hope that this particular version of the sociology of education will prove to be interesting to others besides the author.

2 Education and the economy

1 *The education explosion*

A consideration of the theoretical scheme outlined in the previous chapter makes it clear that in any society the educational system will be linked to the economy, in so far as it must train its young people in the skills they will require as adult members of the society. It by no means follows, however, that these skills will be taught wholly or even mainly within the school system, even where such a system exists. In pre-industrial societies all such skills are taught 'on the job' either within the family itself or at the work place. Even after industrialisation, 'on the job' training has retained its importance, until recently, for many of the lower levels of industrial skill. What characterizes an advanced industrial society is the extent to which skills at all levels of the occupational hierarchy are increasingly acquired within formal educational institutions.

The new tools, new techniques and new materials which transformed nineteenth-century Britain, were only the start of a continuous process of technical development which has, in the twentieth century, accelerated rather than declined. Contemporary innovations, particularly in the field of automation, are so far-reaching that it is customary to talk and write of a second industrial revolution. At the same time innovation itself has become institutionalized, and research in pure science and in technology is harnessed to the needs of higher productivity. It is no wonder, then, that corresponding changes in the scope and the content of education are so often seen in terms of the needs of the economy. The purpose of this chapter will be to describe the relationship between these two aspects of society, and to consider in particular how far changes in modern educational systems can be explained in economic terms. Schelsky[1] has described the way in which science and technology have influenced the amount and kind of skill required of the labour force, and the changes which the future is likely to bring. He shows that the proportion engaged in manual work has declined and the proportion in white-collar and professional and managerial work has risen. Many new professional and semi-professional occupations have grown up, based upon the developing sciences and technologies. Within manual work itself the nature of skill has gone through many changes, as the traditional craft skills of a pre-industrial society gave way to new skills appropriate to new and changing technologies. Moreover, in recent years, especially where automation has been introduced, the traditional distinction between skilled and semi-skilled manual workers and clerical and technical staff is practically being obliterated. As a result of these changes the formal educational system of school and college, hitherto required mainly for an elite group of professional occupations, has expanded to provide for the needs, not only of a growing number of professional and semi-professional occupations, but also a skilled labour force which increasingly needs to be literate, adaptable and mobile.

The consequence has been what can only be regarded as an educational explosion. The establishment of universal literacy has been followed by a lengthening of school life, a widening and deepening of the curriculum and the gradual extension of higher education to a wider section of the community. This expansion of education has not followed the same pattern everywhere, and is considerably more advanced in some industrial societies than in others, but the general lines of the educational explosion can be traced in all advanced industrial societies.

At the same time the attitude to education has changed. An abundant and increasing supply of highly educated people has become the absolute prerequisite of social and economic development in our world. It is rapidly becoming 'a condition of national survival', Drucker argues,[2] and increasingly educational expenditure is seen as a vital investment in human beings. A growing interest in the economics of education have produced efforts not only to reach a more precise measurement of the cost of education but also a more accurate estimate

---

[1] Schelsky, H. 'Technical Change and Educational Consequences', in Halsey, A. H., Floud, J. and Anderson, C. A. (eds.) *Education, Economy and Society*, 1961, p. 33.

[2] Drucker, P. T. 'The Educational Revolution', in Halsey, Floud, Anderson, *op. cit.*, p. 15.

of the contribution that education can make to economic growth.[1] So far, however, no general agreement has been reached on this issue and there is still considerable debate on the extent of education's contribution, particularly in the developing societies.[2]

This association between the development of an educational system and the growth of the economy carries, perhaps misleadingly, the implication of a mechanistic relationship. It is indeed quite reasonable to imply that an advanced economy 'needs' literate workers and educated scientists and technicians if it is to maintain its efficiency. It is, however, easy to show that the 'response' to this need by the educational system is far from automatic, and many other factors can be shown to have an influence on educational expansion, some of which may operate to inhibit its growth. At the same time some of the educational expansion that has occurred can be shown to be the consequence of influences which are ideological rather than economic.

One important limiting factor on educational expansion is, however, itself an aspect of the economy, for it is only an advanced economy that can afford a highly developed educational system. In counting the cost of such a system, moreover, it is not enough to estimate only the provision of buildings and the salaries of teachers; it is also necessary to include the cost of training and foregone earnings during the years spent at school and college when the student entry to the work force is delayed. Another hidden cost is the drain on skilled personnel that the provision of teachers represents, and this can be particularly important when there is a general shortage of educated manpower.[3]

The age-structure of the population is another highly relevant factor. When the child population rises, the cost of educational expansion is high, and even the maintenance of existing standards will entail an increase in expenditure. When the child population falls, however, educational standards may rise even if expenditure remains the same. Consequently a fall in the birth-rate may have very considerable advantages for educational provision, just as a 'baby-boom' can lead to over-crowded classes and inadequate school provision.

[1] Bowman, M. J. 'The Human Investment Revolution in Economic Thought', *Sociology of Education*, vol. XXXIX (2), 1966.

[2] Hoselitz, B. I. 'Investment in Education', in Coleman, James S. (ed.) *Education and Political Development*, Princeton University Press, 1965. We shall return to a consideration of this issue in chapter 10.

[3] Vaizey, J. and Debeauvais, M. 'Economic Aspects of Educational Development', in Halsey, Floud, Anderson, *op. cit.*, p. 37.

EDUCATION AND THE ECONOMY

Another highly important aspect of the cost of education is its *quality*. The standard of accommodation and equipment, the level of teachers' salaries, the teacher/student ratio are all highly variable items, and their provision on a generous scale can make any considerable educational expansion a costly venture. It would, for example, be exceedingly difficult to maintain the teacher/student ratio customary in British university education if the proportions of the age-group entering it were as high as in the United States.

Apart from considerations of cost, such factors as the supply of teachers may also have an important influence on educational provision, especially in the short run. This is particularly likely to occur if expansion has been rapid or if the salaries paid to teachers are below those available in competing employment. Shortage of teachers combined with a shortage of buildings have seriously delayed the raising of the school-leaving age in Britain since the Second World War.

It is, however, likely that the most important factor influencing educational development lies in the field of social and educational policy. National differences in ideology can be shown to lie behind many of the variations in educational expansion both within Europe and between Western Europe and the United States. It is necessary therefore to look at ideological differences in some detail and to consider in particular some of the ways in which they may actually impede the response of the educational system to economic needs.

The ideological conflict between elitist and populist theories of education is found in all industrial societies and is the source of much current educational controversy. It can also be shown to have considerable influence on the rate of educational expansion. The elitist ideology, as its name implies, is traditionalist in its orientation, looking back to the time when education was the prerogative of a small elite. The attitude to education to which it gives rise tends therefore to be exclusive and emphasizes the needs of the few rather than the many. Such an educational philosophy can be seen very clearly in early nineteenth-century England, where the provision of free elementary education was made by charitable and religious bodies whose aim was primarily moral, and whose conception of the amount of education necessary for this purpose was of a very limited kind. The children of the poor needed to be taught Christian principles and to be able to read their Bibles, but writing was suspect and even dangerous. Moreover, although ideas on what was necessary grew gradually more liberal, the anxiety that the poor would be over-educated and made unfit for their station in life, continued at least until the end of the century. Indeed, in spite of the reforms of the early twentieth century which widened the curriculum and postponed the school-leaving age, the elementary system remained in being until 1944, providing a cheaper and more limited schooling for the children of the poor.

At the same time secondary education was conceived as a distinct system, providing for the needs of the middle and upper classes. Even the recognition by the end of the century of an educational ladder from the elementary school to the university did not really alter the conception of secondary education as a distinct system, linked to the elementary system by scholarships and free places, but separate from it administratively and socially. Moreover, attempts from within the elementary system to extend into secondary education were severely curbed.[1]

The 1944 Education Act, as is well known, abolished the elementary school and introduced free secondary education for all, and the secondary school became a stage in the educational process for every child. On the other hand, in spite of the attempts to achieve parity of esteem between the different types of secondary education, the secondary modern school has retained at least some of the traditions of the old elementary system, and it is at the secondary modern school that the great majority of working-class children complete their formal education.[2] It is for this reason that the tripartite system of secondary education since 1944 has frequently been linked with the three grades of secondary education described by the Newcastle and Bryce Commissions of the nineteenth century. Moreover, 'If the ladder between elementary and secondary education as a whole has been abandoned,' Glass has argued, 'it has been replaced by a ladder from the primary school to the grammar school.'[3] At the same time selection by ability has replaced, within the maintained grammar school, the right to entry on the payment of fees. An aristocracy of brains is not, however, any less of an elite than an aristocracy of birth, and in so far as the grammar school selects an able minority of children and prepares them for

[1] See, for example, Banks, O. *Parity and Prestige in English Secondary Education*, London: Routledge & Kegan Paul, 1955.

[2] Taylor, W. *The Secondary Modern School*, London: Faber & Faber, 1963, ch. 3.

[3] Glass, D. V. 'Education and Social Change in Modern England', in Halsey, Floud, Anderson, *op. cit.*, p. 402.

middle-class occupations it is still fulfilling an elite function and representing an elite philosophy of secondary education.

Evidence that the elite conception of education is out of line with the needs of the labour market is provided very graphically by Taylor's study of the secondary modern school. He shows how full employment and the creation of new jobs which require both a high level of skill and a good educational background have deeply influenced the direction of development of the schools. Not only has there been a widespread provision of extended courses of both an academic and a vocational nature, but the modern schools have been able 'to break the examination monopoly of other types of secondary school, and to participate in, rather than contract out of the process of vocational competition and the promotion of social mobility through education'.[1] Developments within the secondary modern school since 1944 are therefore a particularly interesting example of the sensitive interplay between economic and ideological factors in educational change.

It is true, of course, that the elite concept of secondary education has to a very considerable extent remained the dominant ideology in Britain, but it has by no means gone unchallenged. The emergence of a genuine populist ideology can be seen very clearly as far back as the controversy over the high-grade schools in the 1890s. At the same time the need for skilled manpower, particularly for clerks and school teachers, made possible not only the expansion of secondary education, but the development of higher forms of elementary education. In the years between the two world wars, for example, many local authorities experimented with selective central schools, providing what amounted to a secondary education within the elementary system.[2] The effect has been a compromise in which the elite ideology, populist pressures towards equality, and the needs of the economy have together produced an expansion of secondary education to include all children, but within the framework of an elite system.

The elite ideology in secondary education is at present severely challenged both in Britain and in other parts of Western Europe[3] by the idea of the comprehensive school, and it may be that the selective system of secondary education will eventually give way to some form of unselected school. If, however, we wish to see the effect on secondary

[1] Taylor, W. *op. cit.*, pp. 53-4.
[2] Banks, O. *op. cit.*
[3] See, for example, Halsey, A. H. *Ability and Educational Opportunity*, O.E.C.D., 1962.

education of an educational philosophy in which the populist ideology has long been the major influence we must look to the United States. The controversy between what has come to be called the Jeffersonian and Jacksonian principles of educational provision resulted in an early and almost complete victory for Jacksonian principles, which has expressed itself in the belief that education for all was essential in a democratic society, irrespective of social origins or even learning ability. This has been combined with strong popular support for the value of education.

Unlike the situation in Britain where the education of the masses has been imposed or withheld by powerful elite groups in Church or State, the common school in the United States was founded by 'relatively untutored farmers who established one-room district schools in rural neighbourhoods as they moved across the continent'.[1] In consequence, except in certain regions and neighbourhoods, there is a great deal of public enthusiasm for education, and parents on the whole are eager to take advantage of what the schools have to offer. As a result of this, not only is the common high school the normal type of secondary school in the United States, but graduation from high school at the age of 17 or 18 has now become the generally accepted level of educational achievement.

It is, however, in the field of higher education that we find the biggest consequences of differing ideological approaches to educational opportunity. The universities, as Halsey has pointed out, are 'intrinsically inequalitarian',[2] but this tendency is considerably enhanced when they are restricted to a very small section of the community. The symbolic value of the higher learning has always conferred high status on those who are admitted to it, and in addition it has had functional value, in so far as it has been a limited but possible avenue to positions of wealth and power in Church or State.

The effect of industrial development is to link the university to the economy through the market for professional and scientific manpower, and the benefits of higher education are inevitably extended to cover a higher proportion of the community. At the same time there are wide differences between countries in the actual amount of expansion, and

[1] Counts, G. S. *Education and American Civilization*, New York Teachers' College, 1952, p. 454.
[2] Halsey, A. H. 'The Changing Functions of Universities', in Halsey, Floud, Anderson, *op. cit.*, p. 457.

the form the expansion takes—differences, moreover, which cannot be explained solely in terms of economic development. Anderson, for example, using data from a large number of countries in Eastern and Western Europe and the United States showed that, for males only, there is some relationship between a nation's type of economy and the rate of university attendance, but that this relationship is a limited one. 'The underlying factors explaining national contrasts must', he argues, 'be sought in values, customs and public educational policies.' Moreover, for women, none of the differences can be explained in economic terms.[1] Ben-David has also reached similar conclusions using, this time, a world-wide range of data. Even though there is some correlation between the production of graduates and the level of economic development, 'there still remain obvious and glaring exceptions'.[2]

Ben-David distinguished 'three influential academic systems, the European, the American and the Soviet, each of which produces different ratios and kinds of graduates. The positions of the other countries seem to be, at least superficially, the function of respective spheres of influence. The developing countries of the Middle East and Latin America whose academic traditions were imported from Europe, are situated close to and below the European countries, while the Philippines, which used to be an American dependency, are trailing the United States. The position of Canada and that of Japan reflect the replacement of European influence by American. Among the communist countries of Eastern and Central Europe there is a tendency to approach the U.S.S.R.'[3]

The European pattern of higher education is strongly influenced by the dominant elite ideology. Only a very small proportion of the age-group enter any form of higher education, and the universities, at the apex of the hierarchically organized system, are particularly narrow in their recruitment. Table One gives particulars from several countries in Western Europe, and shows that in spite of some variations, the general picture is fairly similar.

[1] Anderson, C. Arnold. 'Access to Higher Education and Economic Development', in Halsey, Floud, Anderson, *op. cit.*, pp. 253–5.
[2] Ben-David, J. 'Professions in the Class System of Present-day Societies', *Current Sociology*, vol. XII (3), 1963–4, pp. 256–61.
[3] *Ibid.*, p. 261.

Table One[1]

Percentage of age-group entering higher education
in selected countries, 1958-9

	Full-time courses only		All methods of study	
	Courses of British degree level %	All levels of higher education %	Courses of British degree level %	All levels of higher education %
Great Britain	4·6	7·7	6·6	12·4
France	8	9	8	9
Germany (F.R.)	4	6	4	8
Netherlands	3	7	3	8
Sweden	7	10	8	11
Switzerland	5	10	5	11

In the United States in contrast higher education is open to a wide range of ability and to a very wide sector of the age-group. There is no attempt to restrict it to a minority of the population. Already, in 1958-9, 35 per cent of the relevant age-group entered college, and by 1970 it is expected to be almost half. At the same time the distinctions within higher education are much less clear-cut than they are in Europe. In Britain, for example, there are clear differences between universities and other institutions providing higher education, and this is true of Europe generally. In the United States, however, there are no formal barriers between institutions and the system is 'in a state of constant flux. The Junior Colleges tend to develop into liberal arts colleges. Professional schools tend to develop general arts and science faculties. The liberal arts colleges themselves, if publicly controlled, seek to become State universities, and the latter soon begin to award Doctorates.'[2] The whole system indeed is one of open competition, an academic procession, as Riesman has called it, in which it is not always easy to decide on a single scale of rank or prestige.[3] This openness of the American system is an important element in the populist ideology and is one to which it will be necessary to return in more detail in the following chapter.

[1] Adapted from *Report on Higher Education* (Robbins Report), London: H.M.S.O., Cmnd 2154 – V, 1963, Appendix 5, Table 3, p. 9.
[2] *Ibid.*, p. 171.
[3] Riesman, D. 'The Academic Procession', in Halsey, Floud, Anderson, *op. cit.*, pp. 477-501.

In the U.S.S.R., too, a populist ideology has led to a rapid expansion of both secondary and higher education. Moreover, in order to appreciate the Russian achievement it is necessary to recall how much needed to be done both educationally and technologically to bring standards even up to those in Western Europe. 'In a country where in 1917 the large majority of people were illiterate there had come by 1958 (when the last major reorganization of education occurred) a system under which a third of the younger people completed a full secondary education.'[1] The development of higher education has also been very rapid and although it has not reached the same level as in the United States it compares very well with many countries in Western Europe, including Great Britain.

2 The content of education

So far the discussion has been concerned with educational expansion, but any consideration of educational development must take into account changes in content as well as in scale. As the demands of the economy have required higher levels of skill, so the nature of that skill has changed, and with it the perception of the educated man. This is not the place to trace these changes in detail, but rather to indicate something of their general scope and direction.

It is sometimes argued that the changes in curriculum which have characterized the development of educational systems as a consequence of industrialization have been mainly a trend towards vocationalism. In fact this is true only in a very special sense. The process of education, whatever the agency that has charge of it, is always in part vocational, in so far as it must be concerned with the transmission of skills and values. This was no less true of the schools and universities of the past than of the schools and universities of today. Hofstadter and Metzger make this point very clearly when they write, of the universities of the middle ages, that their work 'was as relevant to the ecclesiastical and political life of the thirteenth and fourteenth centuries as the modern university is to the scientific and industrial life of our time. They provided vocational training for the clerical functionaries of church and state—for notaries, secretaries, legates and lawyers.'[2] This link

---

[1] Robbins Report, *op. cit.*, p. 189.
[2] Hofstadter, Richard, and Metzger, Walter P. *The Development of Academic Freedom in the United States*, Columbia University Press, 1955, p. 6.

between the formal educational system and the two great professions, the Law and the Church, has been of vital importance, determining as it has the content of schools and universities for many centuries.

If we are to understand the process by which the classical and literary curriculum—the traditional vocational training of the professions—became the very essence of non-vocational or general education, it is necessary to consider the extent to which the schools and universities have stood apart from the needs of the economy, focused as they were upon the needs of the Church and the State. Training in practical skills, at all levels, has traditionally taken place at home and in the work-place. Moreover, this tradition remained all but unbroken up to and indeed into the nineteenth century.

It is true that science had a place, if only a small one, in some schools and universities, but this had almost always been divorced from the practical processes of industry. So extreme indeed was the separation of the formal educational process from the development of the economy that Ashby could write that 'in the rise of British industry the English Universities played no part whatever'.[1]

The extent to which a modern industrial economy makes demands upon the educational system is not in question. An advanced technology can no longer depend upon the traditional 'on the job' training. New and more complex skills require not only a literate work force but, in the higher echelons, a formal training in science and technology. At the same time the concomitant expansion in trade and commerce gave rise to a demand for commercial skills both at the practical and the more theoretical level. Finally the education explosion itself, with its need for more and more teachers, had a profound effect on the secondary and higher stages of the educational process.

On the other hand the extent to which these pressures are accepted or resisted varies very greatly from country to country. In particular, America and Russia have moved further and faster in this direction than Western Europe. Moreover the reasons for these differences are very complex, including not only the acceptance or otherwise of an elite ideology but the nature of the elite itself. In addition, as Ben-David points out, the rate of expansion of educational provision is itself related in several important ways to changes in educational curricula.

---

[1] Ashby, Sir Eric. *Technology and the Academics*, London: Macmillan; New York: St Martin's Press, 1958, ch. III.

For this reason it is necessary to look in some detail at the social processes involved in harnessing the educational system to the needs of the economy, and in particular to the means by which these processes have been delayed.

A number of studies have shown how the development of scientific and technical education in Britain has been handicapped by the association of the universities with the training of an elite. 'University education was a matter of luxury, part of the way of life of the upper classes. Originally the clergy was the only profession for which people were trained at universities. Higher civil service and secondary school teaching were added to this during the second part of the last century. All these professions, or important parts of them, were closely connected to the upper class, or were upper-class callings.'[1] As a result, a university education was in itself a powerful status symbol, indicating membership of the community of the educated, and giving the rank of gentleman.

Moreover, the Industrial Revolution, as Ashby has pointed out, was not accomplished by the educated classes. 'Men like Bramah and Maudslay, Arkwright and Crompton, the Darbys of Coalbrookdale and Neilson of Glasgow, had no systematic education in science or technology. Britain's industrial strength lay in the amateurs and self-made men: the craftsman-inventor, the mill-owner, the iron-master. It was no accident that the Crystal Palace, that sparkling symbol of the supremacy of British technology, was designed by an amateur.'[2] In consequence for a long time technical education in Britain was seen as appropriate to the artisan and foreman level, rather than at the level of higher education, and there was little appreciation of the practical application of science to industry.

Cotgrove in his study of the development of technical education in England and Wales, has attempted to explain the late start in the nineteenth century and the slow progress in the inter-war years largely in terms of 'the 50 years or more of industrial pre-eminence which had established industrial traditions in which science and research were absent'.[3] This long period of pre-eminence induced a mood of com-

---

[1] Ben-David, J. *op. cit.*, p. 275.

[2] Ashby, Sir Eric. 'On Universities and the Scientific Revolution', in Halsey, Floud, Anderson, *op. cit.*, p. 466.

[3] Cotgrove, S. *Technical Education and Social Change*, London: Routledge & Kegan Paul, 1958, p. 27.

placency among British industrialists and businessmen which has lasted, to some extent, until recent years.

A second factor which Cotgrove also believes to be of considerable importance, is the lack of scientific and technical qualifications on the part of the proprietors and managers in industry. Either they had risen from the ranks with only a modicum of elementary education or they had been educated in the mainly classical and literary tradition of the middle-class secondary school. Consequently they were not themselves in a position to appreciate the potential value of a scientific or technical education to industry and might even be prejudiced against it. As a result there has not been, until recent years, a demand for men with scientific or technical qualifications, and in much of top industrial management the arts graduate has been preferred.

The same points have been made by Musgrave in a recent study of the British and German iron and steel industries, and their relationship to the labour force. He, too, lays stress on the cleavage between industry and higher education which arose partly out of the tradition of the self-made man, partly because of a belief in the practical rather than the theoretical approach. The general belief was that 'every workshop or factory in the kingdom' was a technical school in which trades could be 'learned with far more efficiency than under the most learned professors'.[1] At the same time the dislike of science and industry on the part of the upper classes and the universities meant that 'many able men were diverted from industry to politics, the professions and the Civil Service'.[2]

Musgrave contrasts the situation in Britain with that of Germany, where science was given a very high place, both in secondary and higher education, and in industry itself. Consequently, by 1900 German boards of management in large firms consisted of highly paid specialists, who were constantly watching for scientific discoveries helpful to their business; under them was a large staff of men trained to university level to develop such discoveries. In the iron and steel industry, mainly large integrated firms, the salaries of such experts ran into thousands of pounds.[3] As a consequence, Germany's technical and scientific development was rapid and, in spite of her late start, was able not only

[1] *The Economist*, 25 January 1868, p. 87, quoted in Musgrave, P. W. *Technical Change, the Labour Force and Education*, Oxford: Pergamon, 1967, p. 62.

[2] Musgrave, P. W. *op. cit.*, p. 200.

[3] *Ibid.*, p. 80.

to catch up with Britain but even in some instances to surpass her.

This is not to suggest that there has been no change in higher education in Britain. The new university colleges founded at the end of the nineteenth century were much more utilitarian in their outlook than were the ancient foundations at Oxford and Cambridge with their elitist traditions. Indeed, representing middle-class rather than aristocratic attitudes, the provincial universities and university colleges were willing enough to accept the task of training for the newer technological professions as well as for the growing needs of the secondary-school teaching profession. Nevertheless, although technology has gradually taken its place in British universities, its expansion has been only gradual. Even into the twentieth century, industry has continued to be apathetic and State support has been 'reluctant and inadequate'.[1] Only since 1945 has there been any real willingness to provide money for expansion, and a demand from industry for the large-scale employment of science and technology graduates. Government plans have included the expansion of science and technology faculties at the universities, the setting up of new technological institutions, including technological universities, and the provision of more advanced work in technical colleges below university level.[2]

In the secondary grammar schools, too, there has been a major swing over to science teaching since the end of the war. According to the Crowther Report, 'among the maintained boys' schools the proportion of science specialists among boys in the sixth form has risen between 1952 and 1959 from 52 to 65 per cent, leaving out of account for both years boys in a general sixth. In 1956, in those independent and direct grant schools which are members of the Headmasters' Conference, the proportion of science specialists was 47 per cent in independent schools and 54 per cent in direct grant schools, while the proportions which had gone on to full-time courses of university standing in the previous year showed an even stronger bias towards science.'[3]

Nevertheless, in spite of a period of rapid development in the facilities for higher scientific and technological education, the rate of expansion is still much less than in the United States and in Russia. Nor has the

[1] Ashby, Sir Eric. *op. cit.*, p. 471.
[2] For details of changes in Government policy since 1945 see Cotgrove, S. *op. cit.*, ch. 12.
[3] Crowther Report, pp. 254-5.

rate of change been sufficient to meet the increasing demands of industry. Even more serious is an apparent unwillingness on the part of potential university entrants to take up the places that are offered in science and technology. In the last few years some university faculties in these subjects have not been able to fill all the places offered because of a dearth of suitable candidates. Moreover, this has happened even though many such faculties have been prepared to consider applicants with lower qualifications than those asked for in arts faculties, and in social science faculties and departments. At the same time there has been something of a swing away from science subjects in the schools. According to the Universities Central Council on Admissions, 'Entries at advanced level in the G.C.E. for mathematics, physics, chemistry and the biological sciences have shown a tendency to shrink when considered as proportions of the rising total number of advanced level candidates each year.'[1]

It is, of course, possible that these recent trends reflect the shortage of good science and mathematics teachers in the schools.[2] Nevertheless they do indicate something of the complexity of the relationships between economic pressure and educational response, especially in a society where occupational choice is a matter for individual decision. Moreover, there are clear signs that technology as a career does not enjoy the prestige of pure science—a reflection, almost certainly, of its very recent admission as a full academic discipline, and its still un-certain social status as a profession.[3]

At the lower levels of industry there was also for a long time a failure to develop specific technical education. The traditional 'on the job' training for craft and allied manual skills was still, throughout the nineteenth and into the twentieth century, the preferred method, and formal technical education was seen as subsidiary to training on the job. It was, in Cotgrove's words, a 'theoretical supplement to the practical experience of the artisan',[4] desirable perhaps but not essential. In consequence it had of necessity to be provided in the evenings. Moreover, since it was regarded as a venture in self-improvement on the part of the ambitious artisan, attendance was voluntary, although success might be rewarded by higher pay or perhaps promotion.

[1] *Report of the Universities Central Council on Admissions*, 1965.
[2] Taylor, G. 'School Science Crisis', *New Society*, 23 February 1967.
[3] For a full discussion see Prandy, K. *Professional Employees, a Study of Scientists and Engineers*, London: Faber & Faber, 1965, chs. 1 and 2.
[4] Cotgrove, S. *op. cit.*, p. 201. See also Musgrave, P. W. *op. cit.*

This preference for a mixture of learning and earning has influenced not only craft training but also and even more significantly the whole new range of technical and professional employment opened up by changes in industry in the twentieth century. To meet the needs of these students a profusion of courses have developed, leading to a variety of qualifications ranging from a predominantly craft level, like the City and Guilds courses, to the National Certificate Courses catering for largely non-manual occupations such as draughtsmen, quantity surveyors and similar occupations. The whole recruitment and training policy in many industries has also been geared to these part-time qualifications. Such firms have preferred an early entry, at or about the statutory school-leaving age, followed by on-the-job training, and part-time study. These courses have consequently been the route not only to technician level but even, for the determined and lucky student, to full professional status. This part-time route to professional employment has been an important one in Britain in the history of the professions and has indeed in some cases provided a good proportion of its recruits in the past.[1] 'Even now many engineers have learned their skill by some form of apprenticeship with part-time further education, and only about half are graduates.'[2] There is some evidence, however, that those who achieve professional status by this route are at some disadvantage, at least in financial terms.[3] Moreover, even the successful achievement of a Higher National Certificate does not necessarily lead to commensurate promotion. Cotgrove, for example, cites a government enquiry which found that 48 per cent of those obtaining Higher National Certificate in 1952 were in posts in 1958 which did not require H.N.C. as a necessary qualification.[4]

Since students attend evening classes in the hope of occupational reward it is not surprising to find that the popularity of certain types of course is closely related to the expectation of rewards for such studies. In the inter-war period the lack of interest shown by employers in technical education is reflected in the predominance in technical colleges of classes in professional and commercial subjects. Enrolment in professional and commercial classes in 1931 comprised 21 per cent

[1] Ben-David, J. *op. cit.*, pp. 274–5.
[2] Prandy, K. *op. cit.*, p. 20.
[3] *Ibid.*, p. 57.
[4] Cotgrove, S., 'Education and Occupation', *British Journal of Sociology*, vol. XIII, 1962, pp. 34–5. See also Lee, D. 'Industrial Training and Social Class', *Sociological Review*, vol. XIV, 1966, p. 271.

of total enrolments, compared with 13 per cent in classes related to industry. Since the war, however, the growing prestige and security of the technically and scientifically qualified worker in industry is reflected in a relative increase in the number of students enrolling in classes preparing for such occupations. By 1955 enrolments in industrial classes had increased 66 per cent over 1931 while enrolments in professional and commercial classes had not increased at all.[1]

This change in emphasis in technical college enrolments has a close parallel in the field of secondary education. The greater willingness of clerical and professional employment to recognize the General and Higher School Leaving Certificates and Matriculation exemption, was a powerful incentive to turn the grammar school leaver away from industrial employment, especially when so many firms actively discouraged grammar school recruits by their apprenticeship requirements.[2] Since the Second World War, conditions have changed considerably. Firms are now more flexible in their entrance requirements and the larger firms in particular have frequently made provision for several grades of apprenticeship to meet the needs of the 16- or even the 18-year-old leaver from grammar school.[3] There is also more opportunity in industry for the graduate with a scientific or technological degree. Although, as we have seen, the grammar school boy appears still to have some resistance to technical employment there is evidence, not least in the overall shift to science subjects since the war, of a genuine response to changed industrial conditions.

In recent years there has been considerable dissatisfaction with the present structure of technical education. Cotgrove, for example, points out that 'the application of science to industry requires the widespread dissemination of scientific knowledge, rather than the production of an aristocracy of learning'.[4] He alleges that the present system not only results in a restricted output of men trained at the highest levels, but prevents necessary improvements in the education of the technician. In particular criticism has focused on the part-time route because of the lack of time it allows for study, even when evening classes are supplemented by periods of day release. Wastage is high and is not necessarily related to ability, the attitude of the firm and the motivation

[1] Cotgrove, S. *Technical Education and Social Change, op. cit.*, pp. 112-3.
[2] Banks, O. *op. cit.*, ch. 12.
[3] See, for example, Hordley, I. and Lee, D. 'Technical Education—an Alternative Route?', *Technical Education*, vol. VIII, September 1966.
[4] Cotgrove, S. *op. cit.*, p. 204.

of the individual student being perhaps the most important factors. Present government policy favours a rationalization of the courses available, more care in selecting students for courses, and in particular more time for study during the day, including periods of block release, and, particularly at the level of professional training, more full-time courses. Such schemes are, however, still largely dependent on the good will of the firms concerned, and there are many who doubt whether they go far enough to meet national needs.[1]

The United States, on the other hand, has been characterized not only by the rate of expansion but by the breadth of the curriculum in both secondary and higher education. 'In Europe students pursued more or less the same kinds of study in the thirties as they did in the early years of this century, and the variety is still limited. In the United States, on the other hand, growth of higher education took place through a process of constant differentiation. Fields of intellectual and occupational interest which elsewhere remained outside the academic framework became academic subjects in the United States.'[2] It must also be borne in mind that in the United States there is not the sharp distinction customary in Europe between universities and other institutes of higher education. 'In American universities, besides the liberal arts and sciences and the traditional professional schools of law, medicine and theology found in Europe since medieval times, there appeared schools of journalism, librarianship, business methods, nursing and later, practical arts, home economics, physiotherapy. In Europe few, if any of these schools are to be found in universities, but usually in separate institutions of sub-university standard.'[3]

Undoubtedly this variety in higher education has been of vital significance in making possible the high rate of expansion in the United States. If, as in Europe, the scope of higher education tends to be restricted to the traditional subjects, expansion on any scale is impossible without overcrowding in the traditional professions. This overcrowding did of course actually occur in many European countries in the inter-war period and is a feature of twentieth-century India and China.[4] The outstanding feature of the system in the United States

[1] See, for example, Cotgrove, S. *op. cit.*, pp. 200–6, and Venables, E. 'The Further Education of the Young Worker', *Educational Review*, vol. XIII, 1960–1.

[2] Ben-David, J. *op. cit.*, p. 270.

[3] Stewart, C. 'The Place of Higher Education in a Changing Society', in Sanford, N. (ed.) *The American College*, New York: Wiley, 1962, p. 930.

[4] Ben-David, J. *op. cit.*, p. 273.

is the way in which this overcrowding has been averted. Under the influence of pragmatic and equalitarian ideologies the original elitist conception of higher education has been transformed. Universities and colleges in the United States are essentially middle-class rather than aristocratic in their outlook, serving the needs of the new professional middle classes created by the economy.

The situation in the U.S.S.R. is sociologically even more interesting. The traditional elites have been destroyed and the new power group, the Party, has deliberately attempted to fashion the educational system as an instrument for social and economic change. 'The role of Soviet education is to assist in the building of a communist society, in shaping the materialist world outlook of the students, equipping them with a good grounding in the different fields of knowledge and preparing them for socially useful work.'[1] This aim is pursued by the central authority, the Party, consciously and deliberately. Educational policy is shaped with the 'building of a communist society' constantly in mind, and policies which do not appear to be in keeping with this achievement are ruthlessly scrapped. The degree to which the system is consciously guided is heightened by the very high degree of centralization and the degree of uniformity which is enforced throughout the whole of the U.S.S.R. 'From ministerial level command is passed on to provincial or city departments of education, then to district departments, and finally to school directors and teachers. The farther down the chain one goes, the greater the amount of detail laid down for the conduct of the schools. By the time it comes to the teacher, the area of personal discretion is very small. Not only basic policy, but the content of the curriculum, schemes of work, teaching methods, and the like are prescribed for the teacher in considerable detail.'[2]

As part of the drive for economic development the educational system is geared very deliberately to the needs of the economy. The first of the aims of higher education as set out in the Statute of 21 March 1961 is 'the training of highly qualified specialists brought up in the spirit of Marxism-Leninism to be well skilled in the developments of recent science and technology, both in the U.S.S.R. and abroad and in practical matters of production, who should be able to make use of

---

[1] The Minister of Higher Education in the U.S.S.R. in 1959, quoted in Grant, N. *Soviet Education*, Penguin Books, 1964, p. 23.
[2] *Ibid.*, p. 34. See also Bereday, G. *et al. The Changing Soviet School*, London: Constable, 1960.

modern technical knowledge to the utmost and be capable of themselves creating the technology of the future.'[1] Accordingly a greater emphasis is placed on science and technology in higher education, even than in the United States, and this bias towards scientific and practical subjects extends back into the secondary schools.[2] In addition there is an attempt to direct labour for the first three years after graduation, in order to ensure that trained personnel go where they are most needed. This attempt is not always successful and there are plenty of cases of evasion and wire-pulling,[3] but it demonstrates the extent to which individual preferences are subordinated to economic needs.

It is no part of the argument in this chapter to deny that the development of the economy is a crucial factor in the expansion of secondary and higher education. On the other hand, it is clear from a comparison of these three very different educational systems that the economic factors do not explain all the variation that we have found. Where there has been a hierarchic conception of society, as in Britain and in Europe generally, there will be strong pressures to retain the elitist elements in secondary and particularly higher education. Moreover, such pressures may operate not only against the expansion of higher education, but against its extension to include non-traditional and non-academic elements. Only where an equalitarian ideology is dominant are there likely to be drastic changes in the scope and content of secondary and higher education. Clearly, therefore, any attempt to assess the relationship between the educational system and the economy must take into account many aspects of a society. Educational changes may reflect its political ideology and its system of social stratification as well as the level of economic and technical development, which may be hindered by adherence to traditional values. It would seem, indeed, that the technical and economic level of a society sets limits on the variations in educational provision but does not operate as a strictly determinist factor. We shall return to this issue again in the discussion in the final chapter on education and social change.

[1] King, E. J. (ed.) *Communist Education*, London: Methuen, 1963, p. 177.
[2] This is accentuated by recent attempts to introduce the so-called polytechnic principle into education. See, for example, *ibid.*, ch. 7.
[3] Grant, N. *op. cit.*, pp. 124–6.

3 Education and social mobility

1 *Education and occupation*

One of the main features of a modern industrial society is the extent to which the educational system is the means by which individuals are not merely trained for but allocated to their occupational roles. This allocative or selective function is a direct consequence of the demands made by an advanced industrial economy for highly trained manpower; demands, moreover, not for traditional, family-based skills, but for new and continually evolving expertize based in large part on a formal educational training. In consequence, entry to these new occupations is increasingly dependent on the acquisition of the necessary educational qualifications. It is not surprising, then, to find that status is increasingly achieved, rather than simply acquired; and achieved, moreover, by means of educational success. It is true that there are many limitations on this development, some of which we shall be discussing in detail in a later chapter. Nevertheless the movement from status ascribed by birth, to status achieved through education, remains accurate as a very general description of the tendencies within modern industrial economies.

The use of the educational system as a means of social and economic ascent is not of course new. The system of scholarships for poor and able boys has a long history and is by no means confined to Western Europe. Nevertheless opportunities for such ascent were rare, and could not be other than rare when the occupations open to the educated man, whatever his social origin, were limited to the learned professions and their ancillaries. Only with the unprecedented expansion in the professions and quasi-professions and in technical and commercial employment does the opportunity arise on any but the smallest scale for social and economic ascent through educational achievement.

One of the effects of the increased demand for scientific and professional skills has been the rise in the importance of formal educational qualifications and the decline in opportunity for the 'self-made' man. As a result there is, in any advanced industrial economy, a close link between educational qualifications and occupational level. Consequently it can be shown that those at or near the top of the occupational structure have more education than those at the bottom. For example, Brunner and Wayland show, for the United States, that professional and similar workers have more than twice as many years of schooling as farm labourers, and nearly twice as many as factory operatives. Using data from the 1950 census they show that, ranking in terms of the median years of school completed by the employed labour force for each major occupational grouping, professional and kindred workers lead, followed by sales workers and managers, and clerical workers. Table Two indicates the relative position of the major groups.

Table Two

Median years of school completed by males by major occupational grouping, U.S.A., 1950[1]

Occupational grouping	U.S. *total*
Professional, technical and kindred workers	16 plus
Sales workers	12·3
Managers, officials and proprietors, except farm	12·2
Clerical and kindred workers	12·2
Craftsmen, foremen and kindred workers	9·3
Operatives and kindred workers	8·7
Farmers and farm managers	8·3
Labourers, except farm and mine	8·0
Farm labourers except unpaid and farm foremen	7·1

Although not presented in the same form, and using slightly different occupational categories, Table Three shows that the same pattern, although with some important variations, also applies in Great Britain.

It will be seen that not only is there a general relationship between education and occupation in both countries, but that the pattern of the

[1] Taken from Brunner, Edmund de S. and Wayland, Sloan. 'Occupation, Labour Force Status and Education', *Journal of Educational Sociology*, vol. XXXII, 1958, no. 1, reprinted in Halsey, Floud, Anderson, *op. cit.*, pp. 55–67.

occupational hierarchy, with the exception of farmers and agricultural workers, is also very similar. The main difference lies in the greater range in the United States. The column in Table Three giving the median years of schooling shows that the differences between the socio-economic groups are smaller in Great Britain.

Table Three

Age of leaving school of male population by socio-economic grouping, Great Britain, 1961[1]

Socio-economic group	Percentage leaving school			Median years of schooling
	15 and under	16, 17, 18	20 and over	
Professional	22·1	40·6	37·2	12
Employers and managers	60·2	32·2	7·2	10
Intermediate and junior non-manual	60·3	32·8	6·9	10
Farmers	76·7	19·8	3·5	9
Agricultural workers	92·0	7·4	0·6	9
Foremen and supervisors	92·1	7·3	0·5	9
Skilled manual	92·1	7·7	0·5	9
Semi-skilled manual	94·2	5·3	0·5	9
Unskilled manual	96·4	3·2	0·3	9

A close relationship between formal education and occupation is bound to have important consequences for occupation and hence social mobility. Under such conditions, educational achievement might well become the most important way to reach a high-status occupation, whether this involves social mobility upwards or the prevention of social mobility downwards. It is customary to use a model of this kind in describing modern industrial societies, and to suggest not only that there has been a movement in this direction in the past, but that it will continue in an accelerated form in the future. Havighurst, for example, suggests that in this type of society 'there is likely to be increased opportunity for people with talent and ambition to get the education they need for "better" positions and to achieve these positions, while those with less talent and ambition will tend to be downwardly mobile. The industrial and democratic society of the year 2000 will be even

[1] Taken from 1961 Census, England and Wales, *Education Tables*, London: H.M.S.O., 1966, pp. 17–20.

more open and fluid than the most highly industrialized societies today, so that education will be the main instrument for upwards mobility, and lack of education or failure to do well in one's education will be the principal cause of downward mobility.'[1]

Studies of social mobility have also demonstrated the important part played by education. For example, Glass's study in Britain[2] showed quite clearly the advantages of a grammar school education for those of working-class or lower-middle-class origin. They were much more likely to be socially mobile than those who had received no more than an elementary education. Similar findings have been reported for the United States.[3] In both these studies, although the detail varies, the pattern is substantially the same; within lower status groups a child is more likely to be socially mobile if he has a superior education, and at the same time a superior education lessens the possibility of downward mobility for those in the higher status group.

To demonstrate that education is a factor in social mobility is not, however, to say that it is the only or the most important factor. Anderson for example argues that 'while education certainly influences a man's chances to move upward or downward, only a relatively modest part of all mobility is linked to education'.[4] Using data from Glass's social mobility study as well as other similar studies, he shows that there is far more mobility than can be explained in terms of education, both in terms of mobility upwards on the part of those with a low level of education, and in a downward movement of those with a high educational level. In none of the three countries for which data exist does lack of education necessarily prevent mobility any more than a good education necessarily prevents a fall in status. He does suggest, however, that education is more closely linked to social mobility in the United States than in Sweden or Great Britain.

The strength of association between education and social mobility will depend upon the extent to which formal educational qualifications

[1] Havighurst, Robert J. 'Education and Social Mobility in Four Societies', in Halsey, Floud, Anderson, *op. cit.* See also Lipset, S. M. and Bendix, R. *Social Mobility in Industrial Society*, London: Heinemann, 1959, p. 91.

[2] Glass, D. V. (ed.) *Social Mobility in Britain*, London: Routledge & Kegan Paul, 1954, ch. x, pp. 291–307.

[3] Centers, R. 'Education and Occupational Mobility', *American Sociological Review*, vol. xiv, February 1949, pp. 143–4.

[4] Anderson, Arnold C. 'A Skeptical Note on Education and Mobility', in Halsey, Floud, Anderson, *op. cit.*, pp. 164–79.

are a necessary requirement for positions of high status. In so far as status can be achieved in other ways, whether by training 'on the job' or by the possession of special talents, as in the world of sport or entertainment, the importance of education as a factor in mobility is reduced. An advanced industrial economy increases the importance of formal educational qualifications but it has by no means succeeded in imposing them universally.

Another vitally important factor is to be found in the distribution of schooling in relation to the occupational structure. One of the consequences of industrialization is, as we have seen, an increase in the proportion of middle- and upper-level jobs. Where this is combined, as it frequently has been, with a low fertility rate in the middle and upper classes so that they fail to reproduce themselves, there is plenty of room at the top and conditions are favourable for considerable social mobility. If at the same time the educational system, as in pre-war Britain, provides few opportunities for the children of working-class families to receive more than a basic elementary education, then we are faced with the kind of situation Anderson describes, in which a great deal of upward mobility occurs irrespective of education.

Industrial management in Britain today provides us with an extremely clear example of precisely this type of situation. Unlike professional occupations it has not been closely tied to formal educational qualifications, except for certain specific technical functions. Promotion from the shop floor has in the past been an important avenue of recruitment. At the same time it has been a rapidly expanding field of employment, providing frequent opportunities for social mobility. Studies of the educational background of managers reflect this general situation quite clearly. The Acton Society Trust,[1] for example, showed that even in the large firms which they examined, 53 per cent of managers had been to an elementary or an ordinary, i.e. non-grammar, secondary school. This is not to suggest that education at a grammar or public school is not an asset in reaching management status. Forty-seven per cent of the managers had been to public or grammar schools, and the authors of the report estimated that, comparing these figures with the general population, grammar school boys have had twice the average chance of becoming a manager, and public schools boys about 10 times the average. Nevertheless we are still left

---

[1] The Acton Society Trust, *Management Succession*, 1956.

with a very large proportion of managers who have almost certainly been upwardly mobile and for other reasons than formal educational achievement.[1]

It is almost certain however that the picture of management qualifications given us by this and other studies is fast becoming out of date. There is a growing tendency to recruit managers with professional and scientific qualifications, rather than to promote from the lower ranks in the firm. Recent years have seen an expansion in the requirement of graduates, and a proliferation of student apprenticeships and other training schemes designed to attract the more highly educated entrant. At the same time changes within the educational system itself are providing a considerable increase in the number available to industry with higher qualifications. Such changes include an expansion in higher education generally and in technical education at all levels. Some of these changes are new, others have been operating for some time and have already produced differences of some magnitude between older and younger managers. For example, younger managers in the Acton Society Trust study are more likely to have a degree or some kind of professional qualification. They are also more likely to have had a grammar or public school education.

At the same time it is also very clear that not all occupations of high status have been equally open to those without educational advantages. Even within industrial management it has been much easier for them to get into junior or middle management than into the levels of top management. Moreover, if we look at occupational groups in which formal educational qualifications have been important the picture is a very different one. There are many professional and semi-professional occupations which require a minimum professional or educational qualification and which may involve a high level of educational achievement. Alternatively, special entrance examinations as in the Civil Service may operate in much the same way. Kelsall's study of the higher Civil Service shows that, even including those who have been promoted from below, only a very small minority have not been educated at either a grammar or, in the majority of cases, a public school.[2] In such types of occupation, social mobility is still possible

---

[1] Although some of them may have acquired technical qualifications by means of part-time education.

[2] Kelsall, R. K. *Higher Civil Servants in Britain*, London: Routledge & Kegan Paul, 1955, p. 125, table 14.

but it will be largely dependent upon educational achievement, and it is this pattern of social mobility which seems to be increasing in importance.

On the other hand, although it has just been argued that an increase in the provision of higher education in Britain is likely to increase the relationship between education and occupation, it is also possible for higher education to become so general in the population that it no longer differentiates sufficiently to act as a criterion for occupational selection. Indeed, it has been suggested that the relationship is already declining in the United States as the proportion with a college education goes on increasing.[1] Under such circumstances it is likely that more subtle distinctions will operate, including the prestige level of the individual college or university, and personality or social status differences.

Yet a further factor of vital importance determining the part education plays in social mobility is the nature of the selective mechanism within the school system. The more efficient this is in predicting school and vocational success, the more closely, that is to say, that educational achievement is related to 'ability', the less likely will it be that ability will operate as a factor independent of schooling, and so serve as a separate factor in social mobility. The study of social mobility is in consequence bound up with the analysis of selective mechanisms and their operation. But before we can begin to consider the question of how efficiently the schools select, we must examine the different mechanisms of selection used in different educational systems.

2 Strategies of selection

Turner's well-known ideal-type analysis of modes of social ascent, with their accompanying strategies of educational selection, would seem to be the most useful framework of analysis for studying education as a selective function.[2] Turner distinguishes two modes of ascent: sponsored mobility and contest mobility, both of which are founded upon quite different ideological positions and also different elite structures.

[1] Folger, J. F. and Nam, C. B. 'Trends in Education in Relation to the Occupational Structure', *Sociology of Education*, vol. XXXVIII (I), 1964.
[2] Turner, R. H. 'Modes of Social Ascent through Education. Sponsored and Contest Mobility', in Halsey, Floud, Anderson, *op. cit.*, pp. 121–39.

EDUCATION AND SOCIAL MOBILITY

For the time being, however, we shall concentrate upon the strategies of selection that accompany them, although it must be borne in mind that the characteristics of these selective mechanisms derive from the differences in ideology.

Sponsored mobility, compared by Turner with sponsorship into a private club, is characterized above all by early selection, followed by a clear differentiation of those singled out from the rest, usually in quite separate institutions. The process that follows has the nature of a special preparation for elite status, and covers not only special skills, but an indoctrination in the standards of behaviour and the value systems of the elite group.

The English educational system of the late nineteenth and early twentieth century was a very close approximation to the ideal type of sponsored mobility. The system of elementary education for the children of the poor was quite distinct from the system of education for the middle classes. Transfer between the two systems was possible, but it was not likely, and was reserved for the working-class child of exceptional ability who showed promise of successful assimilation to the middle classes. The Education Act of 1902 and the Free Place Regulations of 1907 between them destroyed the exclusive hold of the middle classes over the secondary system. Increasingly, after the First World War, working-class children entered the secondary schools until, in certain areas at least, all places were free,[1] and in some schools the majority of children were from working-class families. Nevertheless certain essential characteristics of sponsored mobility remained, notably the stress on early selection and a considerable degree of segregation. It was customary to select children for free places at the age of 10, and to transfer them to the secondary school at 11, leaving the great majority of children in the elementary system. Those who were transferred went to schools with a higher rate of grant, better-paid and better-qualified teachers, and the chance to acquire the formal educational qualifications which were, as we have seen, a great advantage in the transition to or maintenance of middle-class status.

With the 1944 Education Act the elementary system came to an end, and for the first time secondary education became a stage in the education process, rather than a special type of education appropriate to the middle classes. Even so, however, Turner was still able to

[1] Although after 1933 a Means Test was introduced and Free Places became Special Places.

characterize the English system of education as one of predominantly sponsored mobility because, within the new system of secondary education, there has been a distinction between types of school, with the new secondary grammar schools carrying on almost unchanged the secondary school tradition. The old scholarship examination has been replaced by the 11-plus, which is undoubtedly more efficient but performs precisely the same function. The new secondary modern schools are, certainly, an improvement on the old senior elementary schools, but the fact of selection and segregation remains. It is true, also, that all secondary education is free, and that success in the 11-plus is the only way to get into the grammar schools, but this is to emphasize the significance of the selection process rather than to diminish its importance. Moreover, even if it is no longer possible to buy a place in the secondary grammar school, there are still opportunities, for those who can afford it, to enter the flourishing independent sector, which still remains as a segregated middle- and upper-class system. Indeed, in so far as the Direct Grant grammar schools and some of the so-called public schools offer scholarships to a small minority of children from the maintained schools, they repeat precisely the pattern of sponsored mobility as it existed in the late nineteenth century.[1]

The alternative system of selection is based on the ideology of contest mobility, likened by Turner to a race or other sporting event, in which all compete on equal terms for a limited number of prizes. The chief characteristic of contest mobility is a fear of premature judgement and not only is early selection avoided, but any open selection is, as far as possible, avoided altogether. The competitors may drop out of the game of their own accord, but they will not be barred from the competition, as occurs under sponsored mobility. Moreover, in order to allow everyone an equal chance, segregation is avoided or postponed or in some way minimized to avoid giving anyone or any group an unfair advantage.

Turner used the United States system of education as an example of contest mobility, although he is careful to point out that existing systems are only an approximation to the ideal type. There are few overt mechanisms of selection in the United States and certainly nothing corresponding to the 11-plus. Although there are specialized high schools, corresponding to the English grammar schools, the

---

[1] For a description of the post-1944 educational system in Britain from this point of view see Banks, O. *op. cit.*

common or comprehensive school is the normal pattern in the United States. Moreover, although there is increasing opportunity for students of different ability to take different courses, there is no sharp separation between students of different ability levels.

Entry to higher education in the United States also runs true to the principles of contest mobility. Although private colleges can be, and often are, highly selective in their choice of students, those colleges which are supported by public funds often encourage relatively unlimited entry, at least by British standards, and it has been estimated that 'high school graduates of all levels of ability can gain admission to some institution without going very far from home'.[1] Inevitably, large numbers of students of low academic ability fail to meet the standards of performance expected of them, and those American colleges which practice 'open door' admission policies protect their standards by means of a heavy failure rate which may be as high as one in eight in the first term and continues at a high level throughout the course. It has been estimated indeed that in State universities above 40 per cent withdraw in the first two years.[2] Some of these drop-outs will, however, return later, or will transfer to another college, so that failure need never be seen as absolutely final.[3]

Another approach is that of the two-year junior or community college. Unselective, and tuition free, the junior college takes those students wanting to go to college who are not judged to have sufficient academic ability to manage the four-year senior college course. Such students are channelled into the junior college, which provides not only a one- or two-year programme of vocational or semi-professional training for those students who do not aspire any higher, but the possibility of transfer to the senior college for those who can reach the required standard. By this means the 'open door' policy is maintained and college standards are protected without the wastage of a high failure rate.[4]

Higher education in England follows the general pattern of sponsored mobility. All forms of full-time higher education have high admission

[1] McConnell, T. R. and Heist, P. 'The Diverse College Student Population', in Sanford, N. (ed.) *The American College*, New York: Wiley, 1962, p. 232.

[2] Effert, R. E. *Retention and Withdrawal of College Students*, Washington D.C.: Department of Health, Education and Welfare, 1958, pp. 15–20.

[3] Eckland, B. K. 'A Source of Error in College Attrition Studies', *Sociology of Education*, vol. XXXVIII (1), 1964.

[4] Clark, Burton R. *The Open Door College: a Case Study*, New York: McGraw-Hill, 1960.

standards, and this is particularly true of the universities.[1] This is coupled with an extremely low average wastage rate of only 14 per cent for the universities and seven per cent for Training Colleges or Colleges of Education.[2] Only in the field of further education, with its tradition of part-time study, do we find wastage comparable to the American pattern, and here too we find 'open-door' admission policies which allow entrance to all students who meet the minimum entrance requirements. The Crowther Report survey of wastage in part-time technical courses makes plain that the forces operating here are those of contest rather than sponsored ability. The full National Certificate Course, for example, comprises five stages leading to a Higher National Certificate but of those who start on the course only 10 per cent reach this level unless they are already exempted from the earlier stages. Indeed, as in the American context, the drop-out starts very early on, and the Crowther Report showed that only 68 per cent successfully completed stage one.[3] However, the difficulties inherent in this alternative route to the top only serve to point up the importance of sponsorship in full-time higher education.

In general the European tradition is in line with sponsored rather than contest mobility. The U.S.S.R. is, however, a major exception in that it approaches the pattern of contest mobility to a much greater extent than has been customary in Europe. Soviet schools are, with few exceptions, completely comprehensive. Indeed, not only do the Russians refuse the early selection of an elite, but they reject the whole theory of innate abilities upon which so much elite thinking is based, and argue that, within certain limitations, abilities are learned rather than inborn. Mental testing is 'not merely characterized as theoretically unsound but also, and as a consequence practically misleading',[4] and it is generally held that if children are slow to learn it is the teaching which is at fault. Accordingly educational psychologists in the U.S.S.R. are concerned not with devising tests for the measurement of ability but rather with the 'study of human learning, and, particularly, learning under the conditions of organized teaching in schools, under planned educational influences'.[5]

[1] *Report on Higher Education* (Robbins Report), *op. cit.*, vol. I, pp. 38–9.
[2] *Ibid.*, pp. 190–2. There are, however, large variations both between universities and, within universities, between faculties.
[3] *Report of the Central Advisory Council for Education* (Crowther Report), pp. 354–60.
[4] Simon, B. and Joan (eds.) *Educational Psychology in the U.S.S.R.*, London: Routledge & Kegan Paul, 1963, p. 15.
[5] *Ibid.*, p. 18.

Within the schools, comprehensive principles are carried to much greater extents than are commonly found even in the United States. Not only is there a complete avoidance of streaming and setting, but there is an emphasis on all children covering the same course at the same level.[1] This contrasts with the American system, which allows for considerable individual variation within the comprehensive framework. A great deal of emphasis is laid on bringing up the weaker members of the class, and the brighter members of the class are encouraged to help those who are slower with their work, rather than to push ahead with their own studies. Those children who fail to meet the required standards have to repeat the grade. There is some evidence that a fairly high proportion each year do in fact have to repeat the work, although the proportion will vary from place to place. Nigel Grant reports that 'according to the Assistant Director of Education in Leningrad, 16,000 out of a total of 450,000 school children in the city were repeating the year's work during the school year 1962–3'. Since Leningrad is better off than most places for teachers and school buildings, the national proportion is probably a good deal higher. In addition, some of the obviously mentally backward children will be placed in special schools and there are various unofficial ways of getting rid of very unresponsive children, including sending them to a school with lower standards or allowing them to leave school before they reach the statutory leaving age. On the other hand, and in spite of a very formal approach and a highly academic content, Nigel Grant concludes that 'more children make the grade than would be thought possible by those conditioned to the values of a selective system'.[2]

The comprehensive principle does not, however, extend right through secondary education. At the age of 15 there is differentiation into three quite distinct types of school, which correspond quite closely to the three sides of the English tripartite system, except of course that the selection takes place at a much later age. The Russian version of the grammar school is the three-year 'general education secondary school' leading to the school-leaving diploma, which entitles its owner to apply for admission to higher education. Some 20 to 25 per cent of the age-group are in schools of this kind. Secondly there is the technicum, which also takes up to 25 per cent of the age-group. Although it is possible to stay on at the technicum and obtain a school-leaving

[1] Bereday, G. *et al. The Changing Soviet School*, London: Constable, 1960, pp. 362–3.
[2] Grant, N. *Soviet Education*, Penguin Books, 1964, p. 44.

diploma, most of its students do not go on to higher education, at least for the time being. The remaining 50 per cent do not continue in full-time education at all. They are, however, required to attend at afternoon or evening classes of approximately 15 to 18 hours a week, for one, two, or usually three years. The ablest of these pupils are encouraged to go on to the technicum, so that the door is never completely closed, but this part-time route does not by itself lead to the school-leaving diploma.[1] It can be argued, therefore, that there is considerably more selection in the Russian system than in the United States.

Although in theory all who complete the school-leaving diploma are eligible for higher education, in practice the competition is so keen that all kinds of higher education can be highly selective. The institutions themselves have their own entrance examinations, and there are variations in standards, in spite of the theoretical equality of status. Thus it is harder to get into a university than into a pedagogic institute for teacher training. The proportion of applicants accepted also varies according to the popularity of the universities concerned, but nowhere is there room for more than a fraction of those who apply. On the other hand, it is fair to say that this selective entry is a matter of expediency, and results only from an inability to provide sufficient places to keep pace with the demand. At the same time great pains are taken to try to ensure that the most highly educated do not become an exclusive elite. For example, the principle of polytechnic training, which attempts to ensure that the majority of students in higher education have had some first-hand practical experience of the basic processes of production, is designed to prevent the emergence of a narrow academic elite. Moreover, preference is given in higher education to those who have done some practical work in industry or agriculture. Indeed, 'so much attention is now paid to this qualification, that increasing numbers of school leavers go into industry straight away without bothering to apply for a year or two. At the present time, only about 20 per cent of each intake has come into the institutions straight from school with no other hurdle than the entrance examination to pass; these are mostly mathematicians or physicists.'[2]

[1] Figueroa, J. J. 'Selection and Differentiation in Soviet Schools', in King, E. J. (ed.) *Communist Education*, London: Methuen, 1963.
[2] Grant, N. *op. cit.*, p. 119.

Although, with the exception of Russia and other communist countries, it has been argued that the European tradition is one of sponsored mobility and that a modified form of sponsored mobility occurs generally at the present time, it is probably true to say that even in Europe the modern trend is away from a differentiated secondary system and towards the comprehensive school. In Sweden, for example, a large-scale reorganization of the school system has been in process since the early 1950s, and by the early 1970s it is hoped that all those in the public sector of education will be in comprehensive schools.[1] In Britain experiments in comprehensive schools have existed since the 1940s and, after a slow start, have increasingly come to challenge the dominant tripartite system. Although at first only a very small part of the secondary system, their numbers are growing year by year. Moreover the Government, in 1966, pledged itself to a policy of complete, if gradual, changeover to a fully comprehensive system of secondary education.

This is not to suggest that the process has been a smooth one. Indeed it has been marked by a political and ideological battle of some considerable bitterness, in which the arguments of the two sides have reflected with surprising exactness the ideals of contest and sponsored mobility.[2] It does not follow, however, that by the adoption of comprehensive schools the English system will necessarily reflect the principles of contest mobility to the same extent as in the United States. There is some evidence already that many of the English comprehensive schools show much more differentiation between types of pupils than do the American schools. Pedley, for example, has stated that 'it is the almost universal practice to group incoming pupils on the basis of general ability so that the cleverest children learn together, and so on down the scale'.[3] This emphasis on streaming and the general avoidance of mixed-ability groupings, is an attempt to retain the chief characteristic of sponsorship, notably early selection, within the framework of a common school. Moreover it is at least possible that the private and so-called 'public schools' will increase the part they play in sponsored mobility, especially if the small number

[1] Tomasson, R. F. 'From Elitism to Egalitarianism in Swedish Education', *Sociology of Education*, vol. XXXVIII (3), 1965.

[2] For a discussion of these arguments see Miller, T. W. G. *Values in the Comprehensive School*, Edinburgh: Oliver & Boyd, 1961, pp. 1–32.

[3] Pedley, R. *The Comprehensive School*, Penguin Books, 1963, p. 87.

of scholarships they now offer were to be augmented. When this is taken in conjunction with the restricted entry into higher education which is likely to continue to a large extent, it seems probable that strong elements of sponsored mobility will remain characteristic of English education for some time to come.

On the other hand, it should not be assumed that under a system of contest mobility selection is less important. What distinguishes such systems is not the fact of selection but the manner in which it is carried out. Contest mobility is characterized by a selection strategy which relies on the 'drop-out' rather than an overt mechanism of early selection, but in the last analysis the prize of elite status, whether in the United States, Britain or anywhere else, can only be for the few. It is legitimate to ask, however, whether these different types or modes of selection differ at all in their consequences. Do they, for example, select for different characteristics, or do the same kinds of people reach the top whatever the system of selection? In general, when sociologists have asked this kind of question they have phrased it more specifically in the context of equality of educational opportunity. Above all they have wanted to know how efficient selection strategies have been in matching opportunities to ability. A great deal of work has been done in this area in recent years, and since it is easily accessible only a brief review will be attempted here.

3 Equality of educational opportunity : myth or reality

The usual approach to this problem is to attempt to measure specific inequalities in educational opportunity as they apply to different sections of society, and the most fruitful area so far has been the study of social-class and educational differences. Social class is not a particularly straightforward concept, and there are in fact many differences in the precise definition or classification employed in different studies. This makes comparison difficult especially when international differences are involved. On the other hand, there are sufficient common factors to allow rough comparisons to be made, provided it is remembered that the basis of classification is often not identical. It is usual, for example, to take father's occupation as the main basis of classification and to group the manual occupations as 'working class' and the non-manual occupations as 'middle class'. Most classifications are sufficiently close to this pattern to make it workable, provided all the limitations are kept in mind.

On this basis a few general patterns emerge clearly from a number of national studies and international comparisons. It can be shown, for example, that children of manual workers are less likely to enter and to graduate from higher education, not only in Europe but also in the United States, even with its ideology of contest mobility, and its mass provision of higher education. Thus, it has been shown that children of professional and semi-professional parents have five-and-a-half times as great a chance of graduating from college as children of manual workers, and the chances of children of managerial parents, although smaller, are still two-and-a-half times as great as those of manual workers. Such inequalities, however, are much greater in Britain, where children from professional and managerial parents have 17 times as great a chance of entering university as children of even skilled workers, and 30 times as great a chance as children of semi- and unskilled workers. Moreover, the chances of working-class children relative to middle-class children appear to be even lower in France and Germany than in Britain. In the U.S.S.R. in 1958, between 30 and 40 per cent of university students came from worker and peasant backgrounds. This is about the same proportion as in the United States. On the other hand, workers and peasants account for a much higher proportion of the population in the U.S.S.R. and the chances of a working-class child obtaining a higher education there appear to be closer to chances in Britain than in the United States.[1]

When secondary education is of different types, working-class children can be shown to be less likely to enter the more academic schools and, once there, to be more likely to leave early. Table Four, which is adapted from an article by Little and Westergaard,[2] shows clearly the class differential at entry to the school, and the increase in the differential as a result of early leaving, as they occur in England and Wales.

Class differences are however much less important within the sixth form itself. As Little and Westergaard point out, among sixth-formers

[1] Ben-David, J. 'Professions in the Class System of Present-day Societies', *Current Sociology*, vol. XII (3), 1963-4, pp. 284-6.
[2] Little, A. and Westergaard, J. 'The Trend of Class Differentials in Educational Opportunity in England and Wales', *British Journal of Sociology*, vol. XV, 1964, Table 1, p. 304.

leaving school at 17 years or over in 1960–1 the proportion of boys who left with at least two 'A' level passes varies very slightly in terms of social class. Only the sons of semi-skilled and unskilled workers fall

Table Four
Proportions obtaining education of a grammar-school type among children of different classes born in the late 1930s

Father's occupation	At ages 11-13	At age 17
Professional and managerial	62	41½
Other non-manual	34	16
Skilled manual	17	5
Semi-skilled manual	12	3
Unskilled	7	1½
All children	23	10½

below the average level of achievement. For girls the social class differences are larger but they do not begin to approach the earlier differential.[1] There is also evidence that at university level social-class differences are eliminated altogether.[2] This suggests that those who are seriously handicapped by their working-class background have already dropped out.

If we consider the so-called 'alternative route' of part-time education we find the same social-class differences repeated as for the more orthodox full-time route. The Crowther Committee, for example, in their Survey of National Service Recruits found that not only are middle-class boys more likely than working-class boys to go on to full-time further education, but they are *also more likely* to go on to vocational part-time courses. This is illustrated in Table Five.

At the same time there is a relationship between social-class origin and the level of course. The Crowther Report draws attention to the small number of higher-grade trainees deriving from the semi-skilled and the unskilled manual homes and how many come from homes of non-manual workers. Even the skilled manual group provides for

[1] *Ibid.*, p. 305.
[2] Newfield, J. G. H. 'The Academic Performance of British University Students', *Sociological Review Special Monograph No. 7*, October 1963.

Table Five[1]

Proportions of recruits in relation to parental occupation who took a vocational part-time course at any time during the first three years after leaving school

Parental occupation	Took course	Did not take course
	%	%
Professional and managerial	65	35
Clerical and other non-manual	55	45
Skilled manual	52	48
Semi-skilled manual	41	59
Unskilled manual	27	73
Other groups	33	67
	—	—
All occupational groups	46	54
	—	—

fewer at the higher levels of training than its numerical predominance would warrant.

Indeed, although part-time vocational education can serve as an alternative route for the working-class child who has attended the secondary modern school, it is more likely to operate in this way for the grammar school boy who is unable or unwilling to follow the normal full-time route, and the evidence in the Crowther Report indicates that the secondary modern school leaver is at a serious disadvantage in part-time education. Table Six illustrates this point clearly, showing as it does that not only do modern school boys preponderate in the lower-level craft courses but that they are more likely than boys from grammar or technical schools to drop a course without completing it. They are also less likely to have started a course at all.

It is clear that the part-time route does not operate in such a way as materially to lessen the class differentials in educational opportunity. Nevertheless Cotgrove has argued[2] that it has in fact been important in the past in providing access to the middle ranges of the occupational hierarchy, for those in the two lowest status groups. Using data from David Glass's social mobility study he has shown that, taking only those of semi-skilled and unskilled social origin, 74 per cent of those with

[1] Crowther Report, *op. cit.*, vol. II, p. 140, Table 21.
[2] Cotgrove, S. *Technical Education and Social Change*, London: Routledge & Kegan Paul, 1958, p. 108.

Table Six[1]
School background of men in different types of training

Training before National Service	Type of School					
	Independent (efficient)	Grammar	Technical	Modern and all-age	Other types	Total
Craft apprenticeship	% trace	% 12	% 11	% 76	% 1	2,770
Learnership	2	22	7	66	3	1,241
Graduate and student apprenticeship	6	60	15	17	4	217
Articled clerk, etc.	16	63	10	7	4	195
Other training	14	50	7	26	3	122
Abandoned training	1	10	8	79	2	299
No training	5	19	3	70	3	3,147
Percentage total	4	19	7	68	2	7,991

some part-time education achieved social mobility compared with 45 per cent of those who had no further education at all. On the other hand, recent trends away from part-time courses, coupled with increases since 1944 in grammar and technical schools, may well diminish even further the effect of the part-time route in the future.

In other Western European countries the general pattern would appear to be of a very similar kind. Working-class children are less likely than middle-class children to enter the more academic types of secondary education and even if they do so they are less likely to complete the course. Indeed the evidence that we have indicates that on the whole differences between social classes are even greater than in England and Wales. Ben-David, for example, quotes evidence from Germany which suggests that working-class entry to academic secondary education has been considerably more restricted than in England and Wales.[2] Recent studies in Switzerland and Belgium also illustrate the same order of class differences.[3]

---

[1] Crowther Report, *op. cit.*, vol. II, p. 150, Table 31.
[2] Ben-David, J. *op. cit.*, pp. 288–91.
[3] Quoted in Lipset, S. M. and Bendix, R. *Social Mobility in Industrial Society*, London: Heinemann, 1959, footnote 25, pp. 94–5.

In the United States, too, the pattern of class differences is much the same as in Europe. It 'has been demonstrated many times that the socio-economic background of the child is related to school retardation, academic grades, age of leaving school, and percentage of youngsters who remain in school to any designated level.'[1] Nevertheless, although class is an important factor in completing high school its main influence is felt at the point of entrance to college. This is because the biggest drop-out in the whole of the United States educational system occurs at this stage and not, as in the European system, at the statutory leaving age. Accordingly there are in the United States large class differences amongst high-school graduates who go on to college. However, once in college, as in Britain, class differences are much less important. This point is well illustrated in Table Seven, adapted from Wolfle.

Table Seven[2]

The relation between father's occupation and probability that a high-school graduate will enter college and that a college entrant will graduate

Father's occupation

	High-school graduates who enter college	College entrants who graduate from college
	%	%
Professional and semi-professional	67	60
Managerial	50	55
White-collar	48	57
Farmer	24	44
Factory, craftsmen, unskilled, etc.	26	58

This brief review of the main findings on class differentials in educational opportunity has indicated that in spite of national differences the children of the working class are always at a considerable disadvantage, compared with middle-class children. It remains to consider how far this is because working-class children are of lower potential ability than middle-class children, or how far it is genuine

[1] Wolfle, D. in Halsey, Floud, Anderson, *op. cit.*, p. 230. For a brief summary of some of the evidence he refers to see Brookover, W. B. and Gottlieb, D. *A Sociology of Education*, 2nd ed., New York: American Book Co., 1964, pp. 160-70.
[2] *Ibid.*, p. 230.

waste of talent. In attempting to assess the efficiency of education systems as selection processes, it is usual to define ability in terms of intelligence as measured by tests. This is a useful approach to the problem, in so far as it provides us with an efficient and standardized measuring instrument that can be used for a wide variety of comparative studies. Ability so defined is not, however, the same as potentiality, although it may well be the nearest we can get to it at present. A child's score on an intelligence test is to some extent influenced by environmental factors, including his or her own educational experience. To this extent inequalities are built into the measure of ability. Nevertheless intelligence tests can be a most useful way of answering the extent to which wastage can be said to occur, always provided it is remembered that this method will always tend to underestimate the amount of wastage that exists.

A number of methods have been used to assess the 'wastage' of ability in this sense but probably the most useful is the method adopted by the Crowther Committee in their Survey of National Service Recruits. By comparing the educational experience of the main social classes at various ability levels, they were able to show wide class differences even at the highest level of ability. Table Eight indicates the extent of such differences as they apply to the age of leaving school.

Table Eight[1]

School-leaving age for (a) all men in ability groups 1 and 2 and (b) sons of manual workers (except in agriculture)

	Number	School-leaving age			
	= 100%	15 or earlier	16	17	18 or earlier
		%	%	%	%
All men in ability group 1	681	9	33	17	41
Manual workers' sons in ability group 1	295	19	44	13	24
All men in ability group 2	1,824	65	22	6	7
Manual workers' sons in ability group 2	1,286	75	20	3	2

[1] Crowther Report, *op. cit.*, vol. I, p. 9, Table 4.

It is clear from Table Eight that even in the highest ability group, representing the top 11 per cent of the population, there is considerable wastage of working-class ability. Similar findings reported by the Robbins Committee show clearly that 'wastage' can occur at even higher levels of the ability range, and is considerable at slightly lower levels.

Table Nine[1]

Higher education of 'able' children of different classes, born 1940-1

I.Q. at 11	*Father's occupation*	*% obtaining higher education of the following kinds*			
		Full-time degree level	Other full-time	Part-time only	Total
130+	Non-manual	37	4	10	51
	Manual	18	12	10	40
115-129	Non-manual	17	17	4	38
	Manual	8	7	9	24

It will be noted that although the social-class discrepancy is fairly small for those with an I.Q. at the age of 11 of 130-plus, those in the manual group are more likely than the non-manual group to receive their higher education outside the universities.

There is no reason to suppose that this wastage of ability is confined to the British system of education. The pattern of selection in Western Europe leads us to suppose that at least the same order of wastage is repeated there, and that in some cases it will be higher.[2] Moreover it is easy to show that this general pattern is by no means confined to systems of sponsored mobility. Wolfle has made it clear that a similar pattern occurs in the United States.

Even at the top ability level only 69 per cent of high-school graduates graduate from college, and this figure drops steeply as the ability level falls, until of the top 20 per cent, only 34 per cent graduate from

---

[1] Robbins Report on Higher Education, *op. cit.*, Appendix 1, p. 42.
[2] For a discussion of European reserves of ability see Wolfle, P. de, and Harnqvist, K. 'Reserves of Ability; Size and Distribution', in Halsey, A. H. (ed.) *Ability and Educational Opportunity*, O.E.C.D., 1961.

college.[1] It can also be shown that much of this wasted ability follows social-class lines. Using scholastic performance as her criterion Natalie Rogoff shows that, of the top quartile of scholastic ability, measured in each school, 83 per cent of the top socio-economic status quintile plan to attend college, and only 43 per cent of the bottom socio-economic quintile.[2]

On the other hand, it would be wrong to assume that all wastage of ability in the United States or elsewhere is to be explained in terms of social-class inequalities. Some attention has also been paid to regional inequalities, and in particular to the problem of the educational backwardness of many rural areas. Children in such areas have been shown to be at a disadvantage in Europe, including the U.S.S.R., and in the United States. One of the main problems in rural areas would seem to be the difficulty of making adequate educational provision in sparsely populated districts, but this basic limitation common to all such areas can be strongly influenced by administrative arrangement, and cultural and educational traditions.[3] Nor are these the only kind of regional differences. In the United States, for example, it has been found 'that the college-going propensities of youngsters attending high school in the very largest cities is almost as low as that of youngsters residing in the smallest towns and villages.'[4] A similar distinction between the suburbs and the inner areas of big cities is also found in Great Britain. In addition, wherever there is an element of decentralization in educational policy-making, differences in ideology will be reflected on the regional as well as on the national level. In England, for example, local education authorities have pursued widely different policies with respect to the provision of selective secondary education, so that it is much easier to enter a grammar school in some areas than in others.[5] In the United States, because of the relative autonomy granted not only at the State level, but even down to the local school board, regional differences are also very great, both in terms of the proportion of the age-group entering college, and the financial support given to the schools.[6]

[1] Wolfle, *op. cit.*, p. 230.
[2] Rogoff, N. 'Local Social Structure and Educational Selection', in Halsey, Floud, Anderson, *op. cit.*, p. 246.
[3] Halsey, A. H. *Ability and Educational Opportunity*, *op. cit.*, pp. 30–2.
[4] Rogoff, N. *op. cit.*, p. 247.
[5] Douglas, J. W. B. *The Home and the School*, London: MacGibbon & Kee, 1964, ch. IV.
[6] Wolfle, *op. cit.*, pp. 234–5.

Yet another source of educational inequality is found wherever there are distinctive minority groups. The most striking example of such a minority is the American Negro, who is disadvantaged not only by actual discrimination on the grounds of colour but in many cases by the presence of all the other disadvantages which affect white lower-class communities.[1] Moreover not only Negroes, but also 'the French Canadian of parts of New England, Orientals, and the Spanish-speaking immigrants of the southwest all illustrate the better utilization of high intellectual potential of minority group members.'[2] On the other hand, there are times when membership of a minority group has the reverse effect. Wolfle, for example, points out that 'the great esteem which Jewish culture gives to higher education has overcome quota barriers and other forms of discrimination with the result that a Jewish boy is more likely to graduate from college than is a Gentile of equal ability.'[3] In the same way the Welsh and the Scottish working classes have traditionally been more interested in education than their English counterparts.

The final area of inequality to be discussed is that between the sexes. The Robbins Committee on Higher Education was very much aware of the wastage of girls' ability that occurs at the level of higher education and in the senior forms of the secondary schools. Girls were less likely to get 'O' levels than boys and less likely to go on to higher education. Only 7·3 per cent of the age group entered full-time higher education in 1962 as compared with 9·8 per cent of the men. Moreover with higher education girls were less likely to enter the universities. Indeed only 28 per cent of all university students in Britain in 1962–3 were women. If we include all forms of full-time higher education, however, the figure is 40 per cent. On the other hand women take only a very small share in all part-time forms of higher education.[4]

In the United States girls are more likely than boys to graduate from high school but less likely to go on to college. The percentage of men in higher education is 40 per cent, which is the same as in Britain, if we include those in Colleges of Education. America would

[1] For a discussion of this problem see Kerber, A. and Bommarito, B. *The Schools and the Urban Crisis*, New York: Holt, Rinehart, 1965.
[2] Wolfle, *op. cit.*, p. 236.
[3] *Ibid.*, p. 236.
[4] Robbins Report on Higher Education, *op. cit.*, pp. 1,743.

seem therefore to waste as much female ability as Britain, in spite of its different educational system.[1]

In the U.S.S.R. there is strong belief in equality between the sexes, and women play a very active role in the occupational system. There also seems to be less discrimination against them in employment than in either Western Europe or the United States. The proportion of women to men in all forms of higher education is 45 per cent and, in full-time higher education only, 42 per cent.[2] The situation is, therefore, one of near rather than complete equality and does not differ radically from the United States or Britain.

We are now in a better position to discuss the extent to which contest mobility as a mode of selection succeeds in achieving its goal of equality of opportunity. Clearly even the United States has not eliminated class and other differences from its educational system, and the data from Wolfle indicates that at the point of entry to college there is considerable wastage of ability. In the U.S.S.R., too, in spite of its opposition to streaming and to early selection, there are considerable class and regional differences at the entry to higher education. On the other hand, it would appear that the United States has succeeded in providing opportunities for secondary and higher education for a higher proportion of working-class children than has Europe, both in absolute and relative terms. What features of the American system can be said to have contributed to this measure of success? The ideology of contest mobility lays great stress on the postponement of selection, and this is, undoubtedly, an important feature in the situation. Husen, for example, has drawn attention to the loss of ability which can follow from mistakes in selection.[3]

At the same time the postponement of selection does not necessarily lead to greater opportunity, as we can see from the example of the U.S.S.R. It has been argued that what is chiefly distinctive about the United States system is not its postponement of selection alone, but its combination with a highly flexible system of both secondary and higher education. Ben-David, for example, points out that the 'much wider scope of studies creates a more flexible standard of achievement and, as a result, a greater variety of attitudes and motivations can be

[1] Wolfle, *op. cit.*, pp. 232–3.
[2] Robbins Report, p. 43.
[3] Husen, T. 'Educational Structure and the Development of Ability', in Halsey, A. H. *Ability and Educational Opportunity, op. cit.*

satisfied within the educational system. This is why secondary and higher education in the United States can cater to a wider range of class differences and to people with a somewhat wider range of motivations and intelligence test scores than elsewhere. Educational mobility and the rapid expansion of higher education were made possible by this flexibility.'[1]

In Europe, on the other hand, secondary education in particular has been relatively inflexible. The curriculum, especially in continental Europe, places considerable emphasis on the acquisition of items of the traditional culture of the upper middle classes. It seems likely that this characteristically narrow and essentially academic curriculum is an important factor in the loss by early leaving of many able working-class children in the academic type of secondary school. Universities in Europe have also been more narrowly based than in the United States and so have been less attractive to working-class children.

The flexibility of the American system is closely related to the ideology of mass rather than elite education. With the prolongation of school life, and the unprecedented expansion of higher education, 'educationalists are compelled to face the fact of different educational needs and have to adopt measures in order to cope with them'.[2] These measures, as we have seen, include flexibility and variety not only within institutions but between them, so that the umbrella concept of higher education covers an enormous range of institutions, catering for a wide range of abilities and interests. A college education in itself is no longer conceived of as limited to an elite either of class or of intellectual ability. On the other hand, within the whole range of higher education there are important status distinctions, which operate as hidden selectors, so that the American system is in fact less open than it appears.

In spite, therefore, of its success in opening higher education to the working classes it still remains true that there are important differences in educational achievement in the United States, and in recent years a great deal of research has been undertaken to explain why they occur. In Britain, too, research has focused on this same problem as it was realized that the changes in the organization of secondary education that followed the Education Act of 1944 did not in fact do a great deal

[1] Ben-David, J. *op. cit.*, p. 294.
[2] *Ibid.*, p. 294.

to remove educational inequalities. Most of these enquiries have been concerned with class differences in what has come to be called educability and, so far at least, most attention has been paid to their source in the family and the neighbourhood. It is to this aspect of educational sociology that we must now turn.

4 Family background, values and achievement

1 *The family, social class, and educational achievement*

The advance of industrialization has had, as one of its most important consequences, the progressive removal from the family of its educational function. Formal educational institutions have taken over from the family not only the teaching of specific skills, but much normative training as well. The school, that is to say, has become the focal socializing agency,[1] at least for those years during which the child is full-time within the educational system. Yet, even in the most advanced industrial economy the school cannot and does not take over completely from the family. The first five or six years of life are crucial foundation years, and even after starting at school the child normally continues to live with his parents and to be deeply influenced by their behaviour and attitudes. Moreover it is not only that the family shares in the socialization process alongside the school and, indeed, other agencies as well. It is also true to say that the family exerts a profound influence on the response of the child to the school. For this reason educational sociologists have turned increasingly to a consideration of this influence, and in particular to attempt to describe the family environment which is most likely to encourage a favourable response to school, and a good academic performance.

At the same time, the increasing weight of the evidence pointing to the persistence of social-class inequalities in educational performance, in spite of the democratization of educational provision, has made it inevitable that studies of family background should be closely related to considerations of social class. The consistent tendency of working-

[1] Parsons, T. 'The School Class as a Social System', in Halsey, Floud, Anderson, *op. cit.*, p. 435.

class or manual workers' children to perform less well in school, and to leave school sooner than the children of non-manual workers, even when they are of similar ability, calls for explanation, and it has seemed reasonable to look for that explanation in the experiences and attitudes of the working-class family. In addition, the general acceptance that there is some environmental influence on intelligence test performance, even if the amount is in dispute,[1] has also made possible the inference that part at least of social-class differences in test scores may be attributed to factors in the home environment.

It would, however, be far from the truth to conclude that the attention paid by sociologists in recent years to this problem has taken us very far towards a solution. We have many studies into the relationship between social-class background and educational achievement, and many different aspects of that background have been suggested as causal factors in the link between home and school, but up to now we have very little knowledge of the precise way in which these different factors interrelate to depress intellectual performance. It is necessary therefore, to preface an account of the present state of research in this field with a brief indication of why this particular research topic should have proved so difficult to handle.

Perhaps the most important of the several reasons that underly all the problems in this area of study is the enormous complexity of the concept of home environment or home background. Not only are there many different aspects of family life which appear to be important, but these are themselves frequently hard to pin down into suitably operational terms. This is particularly true where, as is often the case, the researchers are attempting to include such factors as child-rearing practices, speech and thought patterns, and fundamental value orientations. In addition, it can be shown that these factors do not operate independently but are closely related to each other. Under such conditions it is almost impossible to discover the precise way in which a particular family background operates to produce under- or over-achievement. Nor, of course, are there such things as working-class or middle-class families in any absolute sense. The households defined as working-class in terms of fathers' occupation contain very many heterogeneous elements, and so do those similarly defined as middle-class.

[1] See, for example, Wiseman, S. *Education and Environment*, Manchester University Press, 1964, pp. 71-2 and 154.

In addition to problems of this kind, similar difficulties surround the attempt to relate the concept of achievement to a particular educational context. Although the tendency of the working classes to under-achieve is a very consistent one, it cannot be assumed that it is always produced by the same combination of factors. Parental interest, for example, may be more important in one kind of school system than in another, and achievement motivation may count for more in one kind of teaching situation than in another. It follows that we cannot infer from one educational system to another, or indeed, even from one school to another, without prior study.

The concept of under-achievement itself presents us with a considerable range of problems, since there is no way of measuring potential as distinct from actual ability. Studies of environmental factors in school achievement usually operate on the basis of the discrepancy, which can be shown to exist, between attainment and ability as measured by intelligence test scores; and indeed this method has been adopted in the discussion of this issue in the previous chapter. There is no doubt that such tests are the best means we have of estimating potentiality, but in so far as they are not themselves free from the effects of environment they cannot be said to be a true measure of potentiality. Moreover the various attempts to measure the extent to which such tests are 'environment free' has been the subject of considerable and bitter controversy.[1]

Finally, the general relationship between social class and educational achievement is one that allows for many exceptions. Although the working-class child is everywhere less likely to enter higher education than the middle-class child, many working-class children do in fact reach this level, particularly in the United States where in 1960 25 per cent of upper-lower-class males and 10 per cent of lower-lower-class males were estimated to have entered college.[2] We need to know the factors responsible for the successful working-class child as well as those making for working-class under-achievement.

2 The material environment

'Until 1945, roughly speaking, the problem of social class in education was seen, by social investigators and policy-makers alike, primarily as

---

[1] For an account of the controversy see Wiseman, S. op. cit., pp. 31–7.
[2] Brookover, W. B. and Gottlieb, D. A Sociology of Education, New York: American Book Co., 1964, p. 167.

a *barrier to opportunity*. The problem was an institutional one; how to secure equality of access for children of comparable ability, regardless of their social origins, to institutions of secondary and higher education designed for, and still used in the main by, the offspring of the superior social classes.'[1] Indeed, one of the most interesting features of an educational system organized on elitist principles is the belief that the working classes do not need more than a minimum of education, and would not, in any case, be capable of making use of it. Once it is accepted that there should be a greater measure of educational equality, and once the major institutional barriers have started to give way, attention can be focused upon the more subtle ways in which inequalities in educational opportunity are preserved.

There is, however, one environmental factor of considerable importance which has been seen for many years as a serious handicap to some working-class children; that is, the effect on school performance of extreme poverty, whether this is due to low wages, unemployment, a large family or the loss of a breadwinner. There are several ways in which extreme poverty might be expected to exert an influence on school performances. Malnutrition and poor living conditions are bound to have an influence on the health of the child, and so directly or indirectly on his ability to learn. Indeed, the early realization that this was so was a factor in the development of such school welfare provisions as free meals and free milk to children in need, and the development of the school medical services. Poverty can also have an influence indirectly, by limiting the family's ability to forgo adolescent earnings. Under such circumstances scholarships and free places will be refused unless there is a generous provision for maintenance. Poor housing and overcrowding can not only seriously impede the child's homework but even his opportunity for reading or constructive play.

There is little doubt that before the Second World War the economic circumstances of working-class life gave little incentive to look elsewhere for reasons for their under-achievement. Since 1945, however, the general improvements in the economic standard of working-class life, and the maintenance of full or nearly full employment, have led researchers to doubt whether it is any longer possible to think of poverty as the only, or indeed as the major factor, in working-class under-achievement. Instead attention has focused on poverty as only

---

[1] Floud, J. 'Social Class Factors in Educational Achievement', in Halsey, A. H. *Ability and Educational Opportunity*, *op. cit.*, p. 94.

one influence amongst many others, and one which may be relatively unimportant. Wolfle, for example, while admitting that 'ability to pay is undoubtedly one of the important determiners of who goes to college' lays far more emphasis upon motivational factors. He draws upon several American studies to show that economic barriers are by no means the most important reason preventing high-school graduates from going on to college.[1]

Similarly, a recent study of the growing up of a whole age-group in a Mid-Western city in the United States found that only five per cent of the school drop-outs gave clear evidence of having to leave school for financial reasons. Seventy-five per cent of them stated quite clearly that there was no financial necessity for leaving school. Furthermore, it was possible to compare the drop-outs with their socio-economic controls who were still in school, on the extent to which they contributed to their own support through jobs, payment for board and room, clothing purchases and the like. When the two groups were compared on these items, it was found that 70 per cent of the controls were mainly self-supporting, whereas only 55 per cent of the drop-outs were mainly self-supporting.[2]

In Britain one of the most influential post-war studies on the effect of the material environment has been the research by Floud, Halsey and Martin into the 11-plus examination in south-west Hertfordshire and Middlesbrough. They showed that in south-west Hertfordshire, where 'virtually everyone enjoys an adequate basic income and good housing', the material environment of the home was of less importance in differentiating between the successful and the unsuccessful child than differences in the size of the family and in the education, attitudes and ambitions of the parents. In Middlesbrough, on the other hand, where incomes were lower and housing conditions less favourable, 'the successful children at each social level were distinguished by the relative material prosperity of their homes'.[3]

The study by Douglas also attempts to distinguish the effect of the material environment, in his case measured by housing conditions only, from the overlapping effect of other aspects of the home and school

[1] Wolfle, D. 'Educational Opportunity, Measured Intelligence, and Social Background', in Halsey, Floud, Anderson, op. cit., pp. 226–9.

[2] Havighurst, R. J. et al. Growing up in River City, New York: Wiley, 1962, pp. 60–1, 104.

[3] Floud, J., Halsey, A. H. and Martin, F. M. Social Class and Educational Opportunity, London: Heinemann, 1956, pp. 89, 145.

environment unfavourable to school achievement. He concludes that unsatisfactory housing conditions depress the test performance of children at the age of eight, irrespective of their social class, but 'whereas the middle-class children, as they get older, reduce this handicap, the manual working-class children from unsatisfactory homes fall even further behind'.[1]

The Crowther Report attempted to discover the part played by financial circumstances in early leaving from grammar and technical schools. They showed that such early leaving 'was negligible if father's income exceeded £16 a week'.[2] At the same time the proportion of young people mentioning the desire to earn money as a reason for leaving school declined as the father's income increased. However, we have no means of knowing how far poverty was the causal factor at work here, or how far parental and children's attitudes were the decisive factor. Since the same study showed that 'even in the lowest income group approximately 30 per cent of children had stayed at school beyond the age of 16',[3] it is clear that poverty is not necessarily a handicap if other circumstances are favourable.

More recently the Plowden Report has made an ambitious attempt to differentiate the effect of what it calls home circumstances from parental attitudes and from the effect of the school. Its definition of home circumstances was very much wider than the definition employed by Floud, Halsey and Martin since it included not only the physical amenities of the home but number of dependent children, father's occupational group and, very surprisingly, parents' education. Nevertheless, even with this very wide and indeed heterogeneous set of variables, it was able to conclude that 'more of the variation in the children's school achievement is specifically accounted for by the variation in parental attitudes than by either the variation in the material circumstances of parents or by the variation in schools. Secondly, the relative importance of the parental attitudes increases as the children grow older.'[4]

A special survey of children in the Manchester area directed by Stephen Wiseman for the Plowden Committee also came to

[1] Douglas, J. W. B. *The Home and the School*, London: MacGibbon & Kee, 1964, pp. 31–8
[2] Report of the Central Advisory Council for Education (England), *15 to 18*, London: H.M.S.O., vol. II, p. 19 *et seq.*
[3] *Ibid.*, p. 20.
[4] Report of the Central Advisory Council for Education (England), *Children and their Primary Schools*, London: H.M.S.O., vol. II, Appendix 4, p. 184.

substantially the same conclusion: 'When we think of the problem of material and cultural deprivation, we see it as a problem affecting the "submerged tenth", the slum dwellers, the poverty-stricken. We tend to assume that it affects only the tail-end of the ability-range as well as the tail-end of the income-range. Both of these views are wrong, and the second is even more radically wrong than the first. Educational deprivation is *not* mainly the effect of poverty; parental attitude and maternal care are more important than the level of material needs.'[1]

Nevertheless, both in Britain and the United States there has been considerable interest in and concern for the children in slum neighbourhoods and slum schools, where material deprivation is only one factor amongst many in producing educational under-achievement. Mays, for example, in describing the schools in down-town Liverpool draws attention to the special problems they have to face. 'This was the area of racial mixing, where there were many people living in rented rooms and flatlets, where, by comparison with other wards, a smaller proportion of the inhabitants had resided for more than a decade, where there were more shared dwellings, less wage-earners per household than for the survey district as a whole, and where the incidence of delinquency as measured by the number of children on probation, and of mental illness and child neglect were the highest for the whole conurbation. It also appeared to have the least favourable educational attainments record. School D which is located in the heart of this area not only occupied the oldest building, but recorded the smallest number of successes in the General Entrance Examination (the 11-plus) of any of the survey schools. During a seven-year period it obtained only eight selective school places.'[2]

Since then two Reports of the Central Advisory Council for Education, the Newsom Report on pupils of average and less than average ability, and the Plowden Report on primary schools, have both paid special attention to the problems of children living in the slums. The Newsom Report found that the average reading age of fourth-year pupils in schools in slum areas was 17 months worse than the average for modern schools generally. Moreover, among third-year pupils half as many again as in modern schools generally missed more than half a term's work.[3]

[1] *Ibid.*, Appendix 9, p. 369.
[2] Mays, J. B. *Education and the Urban Child*, Liverpool University Press, 1962, p. 59.
[3] Report of the Central Advisory Council for Education (England), *Half Our Future*, H.M.S.O., 1963, pp. 24-5.

The Plowden report, too, in drawing attention to what it termed educational priority areas, pointed out that 'in our cities there are whole districts which have been scarcely touched by the advances made in more fortunate places'.[1] They recommended that the schools in these areas should be given priority. 'The first step must be to raise schools with low standards to the national average; the second, quite deliberately to make them better.'[2]

In the United States the problem of the slum child and the slum school have been described in the same terms. Conant, for example, draws attention to the disparities in school achievement between city schools in different kinds of neighbourhood, and paints a disturbing picture of the city slum, and its effect on the schools and on the morale of the teachers.[3] Sexton's recent study also provides us with a very clear picture of the extent to which poverty still acts as a major factor in school achievement in the United States. She showed that not only were children from poor homes handicapped by poor attendance and higher rates of sickness but even when in school were likely to be worse off than other children in terms of average class size, the number of unqualified teachers and the condition and equipment of the school building. It is not surprising therefore to find that the drop-out rate was three times greater for children whose family income was below $7,000 than for those whose income was above that figure.[4]

The relative paucity of grants to attend college is also likely to be a factor in the wastage that occurs in the United States between high-school graduation and entrance to college. Moreover, although the current tendency is to increase financial aid, especially for the able student, there is evidence that the benefit has been greatest for the larger wealthier schools in suburban and urban settings, who are better able to take advantage of the opportunities.[5]

Yet, even in studies on the slum child, we find an emphasis on factors other than material deprivation. Most of the work on educational under-achievement in recent years has been into those more subtle

[1] *Children and their Primary Schools*, *op. cit.*, vol. I, p. 52.
[2] *Ibid.*, p. 57.
[3] Conant, J. *Slums and Suburbs*, New York: McGraw-Hill, 1961, pp. 7–32. See also Kerber, A. and Bommarito, B. *The School and the Urban Crisis*, New York: Holt, Rinehart, 1965.
[4] Sexton, Patricia. *Education and Income*, New York: Viking Press, 1961.
[5] Campbell, R. E. and Bunnell, R. A. 'Differential Impact of National Programs on Secondary Schools', *School Review*, vol. LXXI, 1963.

areas which touch upon the role of values and motivation. This is particularly true of those studies which have attempted to understand the underlying causes of under-achievement, or which have tried to develop a theoretical framework. Indeed one of the basic weaknesses of all the studies of material deprivation has been the lack of any theoretical scheme which attempts to explain the manner in which the material environment handicaps a child. We have already noticed the disparate and heterogeneous indices which characterize many of the studies in this field, and which betray at once the lack of any systematic attempt to develop theory. Yet if we are to understand the part played by material factors in school achievement we need to know how they operate. This is particularly important in this area because obviously they do not in themselves influence school performance directly. In consequence the true indices of material deprivation are not poverty and housing as such but school absence through illness, neglected homework and the inability to pay fees or take up a scholarship.

At the same time there is obviously a close relationship between material deprivation and the whole way of life of the family. Poverty can make a parent less willing to keep a child at school; can make it difficult for him to afford books and toys, or expeditions which help a child to learn; can enforce housing conditions which make the whole family strained and unhappy or make it almost impossible for parents and child to talk or play together. Moreover, even when these conditions are no longer present, the fact that they have existed in the recent past, or were a feature of the parents' own childhood, may exert an influence on attitudes, values and aspirations for a generation or even more. It is for this reason that it is sometimes suggested that school achievement should be related not to isolated factors in the environment but to family life as a whole. We shall consider this point more fully after a consideration of the other aspects of the home environment which have occupied the attention of sociologists in recent years.

3 *The achievement syndrome*

Sociologists have long been interested in the existence of differing value systems and value orientations which can be used to explain differences in behaviour as between different groups in society. Moreover, studies of social class differences in beliefs and values can be shown to have considerable relevance for the explanation of class differences in educational performance. These differences centre upon the emphasis each social class characteristically places upon achievement. Hyman, for example, has drawn attention to the extent to which the beliefs and values of the lower classes actually reduce 'the very *voluntary* actions which would ameliorate their low position'. Using American data Hyman showed that working-class parents tended to place less value on formal education; they were, for example, less anxious for their children to stay on at school, or to go on to some form of higher education. They were also less likely to be ambitious either for themselves or their children.[1] Children of working-class parents also tended to have lower aspirations than the children of middle-class parents even when I.Q. was controlled.[2]

Several studies have also drawn the same conclusions from English data. The greater interest shown by middle-class parents in the education of their children was exemplified, for example, by Floud, Halsey and Martin in their study of Middlesbrough and south-west Hertfordshire.[3] Douglas also found comparable results in his national sample. 'The middle-class parents take more interest in their children's progress at school than the manual working-class parents do, and they become relatively more interested as their children grow older. They visit the schools more frequently to find out how their children are getting on with their work, and when they do so are more likely to ask to see the Head as well as the class teacher, whereas the manual working-class parents are usually content to see the class teacher only. But the most striking difference is that many middle-class fathers visit the schools to discuss their children's progress whereas manual working-class fathers seldom do.'[4] More recently the Plowden Committee found similar social-class differences amongst the parents of a national sample of primary-school children. Middle-class parents were more likely to want their children to stay at school longer and more likely to prefer a grammar school, and, as in the Douglas study, middle-class fathers were more likely than working-class fathers to take an interest in their children's education.[5]

[1] Hyman, H. H. 'The Value-System of Different Classes', in Bendix, R. and Lipset, S. (eds.) *Class Status and Power*, London: Routledge & Kegan Paul, 1954.

[2] Sewell, W. H., Haller, A. O. and Straus, M. A. 'Social Status and Educational and Occupational Aspirations', *American Sociological Review*, vol. XXII, 1957.

[3] Floud, Halsey, Martin, *op. cit.*, p. 82.

[4] Douglas, J. W. B. *op. cit.*, p. 52.

[5] *Children and their Primary Schools*, *op. cit.*, vol. II, pp. 118–23.

The aspirations of English children, while related to social class, have also been shown to be related to the kind of secondary school attended. Those at grammar school have higher aspirations than those at modern school, the secondary modern school quite clearly having a depressing effect on aspirational level.[1] Indeed there is some evidence that school is more important than social-class background. Himmelweit, for example, found than 'many of the middle-class boys in the modern school expect to go in for jobs of lower social prestige than those listed by lower working-class boys in the grammar school'.[2] Within grammar schools, however, this same study found that middle-class children are more anxious to succeed at school and wish to stay on at school longer.[3]

The conclusion, that the working-classes are less ambitious for their children, and that the children are less ambitious for themselves, has not however gone unchallenged, and some studies have stressed the importance of relative rather than absolute measures of ambition, or what Turner has called the ladder model of mobility. According to this model, mobility is measured by the number of 'rungs' an individual moves up the ladder. 'Each individual starts from a given rung, and the unskilled labourer has as far to climb in moving up two rungs to the skilled labour category as the small business owner has in moving up to a managerial position in large business. On the other hand, the son of a large business owner or official has nothing more to do than to "stay put" in order to remain in the same category, and requires no more ambition to do so than the semi-skilled labourer's son who becomes a semi-skilled labourer himself.'[4]

In a study of high-school seniors Empey found that although lower-class boys had lower occupational aspirations than those from a higher class their ambitions were by no means limited to their fathers' status, and in relative terms they were as ambitious if not more so than boys of higher status.[5] Turner similarly found that although the boys of higher social background had the higher aspirations, they were in fact

[1] Elder, G. H. Jnr. 'Life Opportunity and Personality. Some Consequences of Stratified Secondary Education in Great Britain', *Sociology of Education*, vol. XXXVIII, 1965.

[2] Himmelweit, H. T., Halsey, A. H. and Oppenheim, A. N. 'The Views of Adolescents on Some Aspects of the Social Class Structure', *British Journal of Sociology*, vol. III, 1952.

[3] Halsey, A. H. and Gardner, L. 'Selection for Secondary Education and Achievement in Four Grammar Schools', *British Journal of Sociology*, vol. IV, 1953.

[4] Turner, R. *The Social Context of Ambition*, San Francisco: Chandler, 1964, p. 47.

[5] Empey, L. T. 'Social Class and Occupational Aspirations', *American Sociological Review*, vol. XXI, 1956.

ess ambitious in relative terms. It should be pointed out, however, that both studies by focusing on senior high-school classes excluded those pupils who had already dropped out from school. Both, therefore, almost certainly over-estimate the level of ambition of working-class pupils.

Turner concludes from his findings that neither the ladder model of mobility nor the race model, in which everyone starts equal, can be taken as adequate representations of mobility in modern society, largely because of the impact of the educational system itself which has to some extent blunted the influence of family background but has not obliterated it completely.

Other writers have suggested that there is no genuine differentiation in the values attached to success, and that the working classes put less emphasis upon it only because they perceive the obstacles in the way of its achievement. Several studies in recent years have found that there is little difference between the social classes in the importance they attach to 'getting ahead', and that if anything it is the working class to whom occupational success is the most important. They are also, however, much more likely to see the path to occupational success closed to them.[1] Moreover, a number of studies comparing aspirations and expectations have shown that the discrepancy between the two is higher for the working class. Stephenson, for example, in a comparison of British and American studies found that in both countries it is the working-class pupils 'who lower most their aspirations when it comes to considering plans or expectations'.[2] More recently Caro and Pihlblad reached the same conclusion in a study of male high-school seniors in the United States.[3] Turner's study, already referred to, found no relationship between confidence in occupational choice and social-class background, but this may be because of his particular sample of working-class boys. The findings of Caro and Pihlblad are of particular interest because they show that the size of the aspiration–expectation disparity was related not only to social class but also to academic

[1] Scanzoni, J. 'Socialization, Achievement, and Achievement Values', *American Sociological Review*, vol. XXXII, 1967. This article summarizes a number of recent studies. See also Weiner, M. and Murray, W. 'Another Look at the Culturally Deprived and their Levels of Aspiration', *Journal of Educational Sociology*, 1963.
[2] Stephenson, R. M. 'Stratification, Education and Occupational Orientation', *British Journal of Sociology*, vol. ix, 1958.
[3] Caro, F. G. and Pihlblad, C. T. 'Aspirations and Expectations', *Sociology and Social Research*, vol. XLIX, 1965.

aptitude. This suggests strongly that one of the many obstacles to opportunity perceived by working-class boys is their lack of achievement at school.

A more recent study by Caro, also of male high-school students, found that although both working-class and middle-class groups preferred the higher-status occupations, the middle classes rated them higher, and the medium-status occupations lower, than did the working classes. They had also more confidence of their ability to succeed both in college and in a career. Caro sees the acceptance by the working class of a lesser degree of success as a process of adjustment to his circumstances.[1]

It has also been suggested that the goals of success may vary according to social-class background. Katz, for example, has argued that the middle class emphasize 'status achievement and a procedure emphasizing personal effort and personal worthiness', whereas the working classes, and particularly the unskilled, define success 'in terms of possessions which are procured by personal exertion'.[2] This, of course, is the same point as that made by Chinoy, in another context, in his now classic study of automobile workers, who as hopes of promotion recede, turn for satisfaction to the house in the suburb, and the new car.[3]

Accordingly attention has tended to move away from educational and occupational aspirations as such and towards a conception of ambition as a complex set of values which aid in the achievement of occupational and indeed educational success. Most of the work in this field, moreover, depends to a considerable extent on the concept of value orientation as it has been developed by Florence Kluckholn in association with Strodtbeck. Value-orientations are 'complex but definitely patterned . . . principles . . . which give order and direction to the ever-flowing stream of human acts and thoughts, as these relate to the solution of common human problems.'[4] Fundamentally there are five such problems, which are universal in the sense that they face everyone, everywhere, and which are also essentially philosophical in

[1] Caro, F. G. 'Social Class and Attitudes of Youth relevant for the Realization of Adult Goals', *Social Forces*, vol. XLIV, 1966.

[2] Katz, F. M. 'The Meaning of Success', *Journal of Social Psychology*, vol. 62, 1964.

[3] Chinoy, E. *Automobile Workers and the American Dream*, New York: Random House, 1955.

[4] Kluckholn, F. R. and Strodtbeck, F. L. *Variations in Value Orientations*, Chicago: Row, Peterson, 1961, p. 4.

that they are all concerned with meaning. Moreover each problem has a limited number of possible solutions. Accordingly, societies and individuals can be classified in terms of the kind of answer they give to each of these problems. Since there are five problems, and a number of possible solutions to each problem, the varied combinations of answers can give rise to considerable variety, although in practice it appears that there is a certain amount of clustering amongst solutions so that a preference for one answer to a problem will also to a large extent imply the answer to several of the others. Table Ten outlines the five 'problems' and the postulated 'solutions'.

Table Ten

Problem	Possible solution		
1 Human nature	evil	a mixture of good and evil	good
2 The relationships between man and nature	subjugation to nature	harmony with nature	mastery over nature
3 An evaluation of the past, the present, and the future time	an emphasis on time past	an emphasis on time present	an emphasis on time future
4 An evaluation of the meaning of activity	an emphasis on being	an emphasis on being in becoming or development	an emphasis on doing
5 Significant relationships	individuality	collectivity	

The preferred choices, and so the whole pattern of value orientations, will vary not only between whole societies but within societies, both between sub-groups and classes and between individual persons. Moreover, it is anticipated that value orientations will operate on both a manifest and a latent level, since the degree of consciousness individuals have of the value orientations which influence their behaviour, will vary from the completely implicit to the completely explicit.

As developed by Kluckhohn this concept is, of course, intended as part of a general theory of social action but it is clear that it has great relevance for our understanding of differences in the level of achievement orientation. Kluckhohn herself has pictured the dominant American value orientation as held by the middle classes as emphasizing human nature as a mixture of good and evil; the relationship between man and nature as one of mastery; the time orientation as future-directed; the activity orientation as doing; and the relational orientation as individualistic. Thus belief in man's mastery over nature encourages a perception of the world as something to be used or manipulated which contrasts strikingly with the belief that man's fate is determined. It provides a world-view, that is to say, which sees human achievement as possible. The doing-orientation, which Kluckholn sees as characteristically American, is important because it emphasizes what the individual can do rather than what he is. It is, therefore, close to the concept of achieved rather than ascribed status. Kluckholn defines it as 'a demand for the kind of activity which results in accomplishments that are measurable by standards conceived to be external to the acting individual'.[1] The relational orientation is also important for achievement, in so far as the dominant American preference is for lineal or individualistic rather than collateral or collectivist relationships. The consequent freeing of the individual from kinship ties is seen as an important ingredient in social mobility. It is, however, in the concept of future-time orientation that we have the most striking of the Kluckholn orientations. Its chief characteristic is a high evaluation of the future, rather than the past or the present. The concept of future orientation, therefore, overlaps with the concept of deferred gratification developed by Schneider and Lysgaard.[2]

Although Kluckholn's value orientations are frequently used in discussions of educational achievement, we do not have many attempts to measure the actual extent of class differences in the value orientations she has described. Most of the attempts to do so were summarized by Kahl in 1965. He concluded: 'Each of the field studies reported here had its own purpose, and accordingly devised its own measurements. Samples included high-school boys, adult men, and adult women. Yet the studies all came from the same theoretical stance, and their results proved to be comparable and parallel. Simple attitude items were devised to measure abstract values about certain social relationships and behaviour connected with achievement orientation, and they produced scales that "worked" in two senses; the same items clung together to define given scales, despite the distances of time, geography

[1] Kluckholn, F. R. *op. cit.*, p. 17.
[2] Schneider, L. and Lysgaard, S. 'The Deferred Gratification Pattern: a Preliminary Study', *American Sociological Review*, vol. XVIII, 1953, pp. 142-9.

and language that divided the field studies; and the correlations of the scales with an outside variable, socio-economic status, were stable.'[1]

The concept of deferred gratification has also been studied in relationship to social class, and many of the findings have been summarized by Murray Straus.[2] He is critical of most of the work in this field, chiefly owing to its methodological limitations. As he points out, 'most of the literature is at the theoretical and case study levels of empiricism, and relatively few studies report quantitative data'. There is also a certain amount of confusion between the adolescent's deferment of gratification and the parent's demands for deferment on the part of the child. On the basis of his own study of adolescents he suggests that in fact there seem to be two deferred gratification patterns rather than one, willingness to defer material needs, and willingness to defer interpersonal interaction needs such as sex, aggression and affiliation. Although he found that the willingness to defer material needs was related to socio-economic status, this was not so for interpersonal interaction needs. However, since his sample virtually eliminated the 'lower-lower' class, this finding does not necessarily apply to the working class generally.

More recently Turner has also sounded a note of warning with respect to the findings on class differences in value orientations. He points out that the relationships found have often been quite modest, and often 'indices composed of several items conceal the fact that some of the items are not themselves related to stratification'.[3] His own study of Los Angeles high-school seniors found no relationship between willingness to defer gratification and social-class background and few differences with respect to other value-orientations, although the absence of the school 'drop-outs' is likely to have influenced his findings. Turner also introduces the interesting concept of *value-relevancy*. There is, he points out, 'a difference between accepting a value and translating it into a goal in one's own behaviour'. He hypothesized, accordingly, that social strata 'would differ more in the values they accepted as goals for their own behaviour than in the values they would endorse in less personal contexts'. Moreover his data

---

[1] Kahl, J. A. 'Some Measurements of Achievement Orientation', *American Journal of Sociology*, vol. LXX, 1965.
[2] Straus, M. A. 'Deferred Gratification, Social Class and the Achievement Syndrome', *American Sociological Review*, vol. XXVII, 1962.
[3] Turner, R. *The Social Context of Ambition*, San Francisco: Chandler, 1964, p. 213.

provided 'impressive support for this view', at least in the case of his male pupils.[1] The implications of this argument are of great interest, and suggest that the expectations and perceptions both of themselves and of others, held by working-class parents and their children, have perhaps been neglected as a subject of study.

The attempt to find class differences in value orientations is clearly an interesting and promising approach to the problem of under-achievement, even if, as this brief review has indicated, much more needs to be done in the way of empirical testing. On the other hand, we need to know not only whether there are differences in the patterns of basic value orientations between social classes, but how these different patterns of values actually relate to achievement. Consequently, the most useful studies are those which hold social class constant, and attempt to relate measures of value orientations directly to achievement.

An example of this kind of study is the Harvard Mobility Project. This study, using a questionnaire distributed to boys in public high schools in eight towns in the Boston metropolitan area, found that 'the I.Q. scores of the boys and the occupations of their fathers turned out to be of practically equal utility as predictors of the boys' educational ambitions. Most boys with high intelligence or from high status homes planned a college career, whereas most boys with low intelligence or from low status homes did not aspire to higher education.'[2] Within the middle and most populous part of the status hierarchy however it was much more difficult to predict college aspirations. 'Thus a boy from the top quintile of intelligence whose father was a minor white collar worker or a skilled labourer had almost a 50–50 chance of aiming at a college career.' A later follow-up study also showed that most of the boys planning a college career actually did go on to college.

In order to discover more about the aspirations of boys in the lower middle range of the status hierarchy, 24 boys were chosen for interview. 'They fell into two groups; 12 boys were in the college preparatory course, had marks in the top half of their class, and definitely planned to go to a regular academic college after high school. The other 12 were not in the college preparatory course and did not plan to go to college.' The boys all had I.Q. scores in the top three deciles of their school, and all came from petty white-collar, skilled or semi-skilled

[1] *Ibid.*, p. 214.
[2] Kahl, J., A "Common-Man" Boys', in Halsey, Floud, Anderson, *op. cit.*, p. 349 *et seq.*

workers. Both the boys and their parents were interviewed at length, and from the interviews emerged a picture of two very different basic value orientations which appeared to be related to the different aspirations of the boys. Eight of the 12 boys with college aspirations and only one of the 12 boys without them came from families who believed in what Kahl in his description of the interviews describes as 'getting ahead'. Such parents 'used the middle class as a reference group that was close enough to have meaning, though far enough away to be different'. They were aware of their own failure to get on and felt themselves, in part at least, to be failures. Consequently they did everything they could to get their sons to take school seriously and to aim to get to college.

The other parents 'accepted the scheme of things and their own place within it'. Living for the present rather than the past or the future, the children were encouraged to enjoy themselves while they were young. The value of 'doing what you like' was applied to school work, to part-time jobs and to career aspirations.

These parental attitudes were matched very closely by those of the boys who had learned to look at the occupational structure, the school, and college, from their parents' points of view. Only a few boys differed from their parents. Kahl concluded that only boys who had internalized what he describes as the 'getting ahead' values were sufficiently motivated to overcome the obstacles which, as lower-middle- and working-class boys, they had to face in school.

Kahl's study does not refer specifically to Kluckholn's scheme, but it is clearly related to it, and indeed Kluckholn was one of those involved in the direction of the research. Moreover, although not intended as anything other than exploratory, it does at least suggest that parental value orientations may well be a most important factor in the boy's own attitude to school. A later study by Rosen, however, has attempted to relate various measures of value orientation to the school achievement of high-school boys in a more systematic way. Items were constructed to cover three of Kluckholn's orientations, active-passive, present-future and familistic-individualistic. Those responses which indicated an activistic, future-orientated, individualistic point of view were classified as reflecting achievement values and a score was derived for each boy by giving a point for each achievement-orientated response. Achievement value, using this measure, was related both to social class and to educational aspirations, but not actual achievement as measured by school grades. Of particular interest, however, is his finding that over-aspirers, i.e. those with higher aspirations than the norm of their social class, tend also to have higher-value scores, while under-aspirers tend to have lower-value scores than the norm of their social class.[1]

Rosen's findings, however, conflict to some extent with those of Straus in his study, already referred to, of the deferred gratification pattern. Straus found that his measures were related both to achievement, as measured by school grades, and to occupational aspirations, although they were not, except for material deprivation, related to social class. It is not clear whether this difference in the findings is due to the nature of the two samples, or the use of a different instrument.

In Britain a number of studies have been made, using Kluckholn's general theoretical framework, and here too the results suggest that this particular approach is worth-while. Swift, for example found that, in the lower-middle classes, the mobility-pessimism of the father was associated closely with 11-plus success.[2] This may be compared with Kahl's findings with respect to his 'common-man' boys and their parents. There have also been studies using a modified form of the instruments devised by Rosen. Jayasuriya, for example, has related the value orientations of secondary-school boys to their father's occupation, and found a class difference not only for the instrument but for its three separate elements, active-passive, present-future, and familistic-individualistic. However, as soon as he holds I.Q. and school constant, the social-class differences disappear.[3] There is, that is to say, an approximation to middle-class norms by working-class boys in grammar schools. More recently Sugarman, using similar questions in four secondary schools, has found that over- and under-achievement relative to I.Q. was associated with high and low scores respectively on all three of the value orientations *except for* the one grammar school in the study, in which only the active-passive orientation related to over- and under-achievement.[4]

[1] Rosen, B. C. 'The Achievement Syndrome: a Psycho-cultural Dimension of Social Stratification', *American Sociological Review*, April 1956, pp. 203–11.
[2] Swift, D. F. 'Social Class and Achievement Motivation', *Educational Research*, vol. VIII (2), 1966, p. 93.
[3] Jayasuriya, D. L., from an unpublished Ph.D. thesis, University of London, 1960, reported in Sugarman, B. H. 'Social Class and Values as Related to Achievement and Conduct in School', *Sociological Review*, vol. XIV, 1966, p. 290.
[4] Sugarman, B. H. *ibid.*

Before leaving the 'achievement syndrome' as Rosen calls it, it is necessary to say something about a rather different concept with quite distinct theoretical antecedents. This is the need for achievement, or achievement motivation, a psychological concept developed by Mc-Clelland and his associates. 'The behaviour of people highly motivated for achievement is persistent striving activity, aimed at attaining a high goal in some area involving competition with a standard of excellence. In relation to these standards of excellence the achievement orientated person directs his efforts towards obtaining the pleasure of success and avoiding the pain of failure.'[1] In order to measure achievement, or n. Ach. as it is called, projective tests have been devised. The subject is presented with a set of rather ambiguous pictures and asked to make up a story about them. These stories are then scored for evidence of achievement motivation using an elaborate scoring system.

Further work has shown that those who have high scores on achievement motivation also tend to do better in a number of other tests. For example, they tend to solve more arithmetic problems in a given time, they tend to use a greater number of abstract nouns and more future tenses. They also tend to set themselves higher standards of aspiration. In a work situation where they can set their own goals they will choose challenging but achievable tasks for themselves. Moreover, in choosing a working partner they will tend to select an expert rather than a friend.

In McClelland's writing on achievement motivation it is presented as a very generalized drive which appears to influence behaviour in any competitive situation. Moreover, he believes that it is related both to individual occupational success and to the economic growth and decline of whole societies.[2] On the other hand, there is no reason to suppose that it will necessarily be directed towards economic goals. It could conceivably be satisfied by artistic, religious or other types of success which may be irrelevant or even opposed to occupational success.[3] Indeed, the relationship between achievement *motivation* as measured by projective techniques, and achievement *values* as measured by questionnaire are unrelated.[4] There is, on the other hand, some evidence that it is related both to social class, the middle classes

[1] Rosen, B. C. *op. cit.*, pp. 204-5.
[2] McClelland, D. C. *The Achieving Society*, Glencoe, Illinois: Free Press, 1961.
[3] See, for example, Scanzoni, J. *op. cit.*
[4] Strodtbeck, F. L. 'Family Integration, Values and Achievement', in Halsey, Floud, Anderson, *op. cit.*

tending to score higher in achievement imagery, and to over-achievement, when performance is related to measured ability. Rosen has concluded that achievement motivation and achievement values represent 'genuinely different components of the achievement syndrome',[1] and Strodtbeck suggests that 'the joint use of these measures would provide a more efficient predictor of over-achievement'.[2]

It is obvious, therefore, that all the studies of the achievement syndrome, whether in Britain or in the United States, are far from conclusive. There is, in the case of both achievement value and achievement motivation, a fairly elaborate theoretical structure, but the measures are by no means entirely satisfactory. In the case of achievement value in particular, the measures employed are still largely exploratory and different studies will frequently use quite different sets of questions. Moreover, in so far as these studies try to relate the achievement syndrome to some form of achieving behaviour, they have to face the problem of defining achievement. This may be done in a variety of ways and there is considerable variation in the methods used. For example it may be measured in terms of task performance in an experimental situation, or in terms of school grades. Alternatively the attempt may be made to assess over- and under-achievement by a comparison between ability as measured by test performance and school performance. All of these ways of assessing achievement have some value but all have disadvantages. Moreover they cannot be used interchangeably. In short, a good deal of work needs to be done on the measures themselves, before we can be confident that the theory has been adequately put to the test.

A further problem which affects particularly the concept of value orientations is the need to fill the theoretical and empirical gap between parental values and the school performance of the child. We need to know, that is to say, not only how far parents actually succeed in transmitting their values to their children, but by what means this transmission is carried out. Increasingly, therefore, sociologists operating in this research field are turning their attention to studies of child-rearing, in an effort to provide a fuller picture of the influence of different child-rearing patterns on the child's own behaviour. In particular, in this context, attempts have been made to discover what forms of parental attitude and parental behaviour are likely to influence

[1] Rosen, B. C. *op. cit.*
[2] Strodtbeck, F. L. *op. cit.*

the presence or absence of the achievement syndrome in the child. At the same time, attention has been directed to those aspects of a child's family environment which may affect not only his motivation but even his cognitive development. Stimulated particularly by the work of Bernstein, this approach has led not only to a great deal of interest on the part of sociologists in child-rearing studies, but also to a renewed interest in interdisciplinary research. Developments in this area are relatively new in the sociology of education but they are vitally necessary if we are to show, not simply in what ways family background can influence educational performance, but the actual process by which this takes place.

5 The family, the socialization process, and achievement

1 *Child-rearing studies and the achievement syndrome*

The aspect of the achievement syndrome which has been most thoroughly explored in relation to parental influence is achievement motivation. Several empirical studies have suggested that achievement motivation is likely to be high when the child is urged to obtain and rewarded for achieving independence and mastery. Winterbottom's questionnaire study of mothers, for example, showed that mothers of children with high achievement motivation made more demands on their children at an early age, and gave more intense and frequent rewards when these demands were met, than did the mothers of children with low achievement motivation.[1]

Rosen has also carried out an interesting observational study of parent–child relationships in an experimental situation. Although only 40 boys and their parents were studied they were carefully selected and I.Q. was held constant. The boys were given five tasks involving both mental and intellectual skills, and an attempt was made to involve the parents in their sons' performance. Rosen concluded that the parents of boys with high achievement motivation tended to have higher aspirations for them to do well at the tasks. 'They set up standards of excellence for the boy even when none is given, or if a standard is given will expect him to do better than average. As he progresses they tend to react to his performance with warmth and approval or, in the case of the mother especially, with disapproval if he performs poorly.' The mothers of boys with high achievement motivation tended to become emotionally involved in the boys' performance,

[1] Winterbottom, M. 'The Relation of Need for Achievement to Learning Experiences in Independence and Mastery', in Atkinson (ed.), *Motives in Fantasy, Action and Society*, Princeton, N. J.: Van Nostrand, 1958.

whereas the fathers were willing to take a back seat. Rejecting dominating fathers were associated with low achievement motivation in
their sons.[1]

A further study by Rosen compares socialization patterns and
achievement motivation using samples of boys from the United States
and from Brazil. There were considerable differences in the scores
for achievement imagery, the mean score for the American boys in
the sample being more than twice as large as the Brazilian score. At
the same time Brazilian mothers were less likely to train their sons in
self-reliance, autonomy and achievement. This is associated with a
characteristic family structure in which authoritarian fathers were
combined with protective and indulgent mothers.[2] These cross-
national comparative findings are, therefore, very much in line with
the conclusions drawn from the previous studies. Moreover, there is
fairly widespread agreement that approving, but at the same time
demanding, mothers are an important determinant of a high need for
achievement. Bronfenbrenner has summed up the work of several
investigators as follows: 'High achievement motivation appears to
flourish in a family atmosphere of "cold democracy" in which initial
high levels of maternal involvement are followed by pressures for
independence and accomplishment.[3]

Studies of school achievement have also emphasized the same
features of parental control. For example, a study of high scorers in
reading amongst Grade One school children described this same
mixture of 'emotionally positive interaction' and 'controlling, preventing and prohibiting disciplinary techniques'. Low scorers, on the
other hand, 'seem to be liberally treated to direct physical punishment'.
The study concludes that the high scorers 'perceive their parents as
having a controlling and limiting role', but that 'this circumstance is
counterbalanced by concrete evidence that these controlling persons
love them'.[4] A more recent study by Drews and Teahan investigated
the attitudes of mothers of over- and under-achievers, of both high

[1] Rosen, B. C. and d'Andrade, R. 'The Psychosocial Origin of Achievement Motivation',
Sociometry, vol. XXII, 1959.
[2] Rosen, B. C. 'Socialization and Achievement Motivation in Brazil', *American Sociological Review*, vol. XXVII, 1962.
[3] Bronfenbrenner, U. 'The Changing American Child', *Journal of Social Issues*,
vol. XVII (1).
[4] Milner, E. 'A Study of the Relationship between Reading Readiness in Grade
One School Children and Patterns of Parent-Child Interaction', *Child Development*,
1951.

and average intelligence. The two groups were matched with respect to father's occupational status. The authors found that the mothers of high achievers were more authoritarian and more restrictive than the mothers of low achievers.[1]

On the other hand, the findings of other studies are to some extent contradictory. Morrow and Wilson, for example, studied the family relations of bright over-achieving and under-achieving high-school boys as they were perceived by the boys themselves. The groups studied were relatively homogeneous in intelligence and socio-economic status. The authors found that over-achievers were more likely to describe their families as sharing recreation, ideas and confidences, and 'as approving and trusting, affectionate, encouraging (but not pressuring) with regard to achievement, and relatively non-restrictive and non-severe'.[2] It is not clear, however, how far the contrast in the two sets of findings is due to the differences in method between the two studies. Morrow and Wilson studied the boys' reports of their families, whereas Drews and Teahan studied the responses of the mothers to a questionnaire. This difference may be quite an important one in that several studies have suggested that the successful high-school student is conforming, orderly, docile and conventional.[3] If this is so, then it is possible that such conforming and docile boys do not perceive their parents as controlling even when they are making considerable demands upon them.

Another important difference between the two studies is that, whereas Drews and Teahan were concerned only with mothers, Morrow and Wilson asked the boys about their parents. Yet the work by Rosen and others on the achievement motive has indicated that the roles of mother and father may be very different in the development of a high need for achievement. Indeed, in the study of *boys* it is the mothers who play the dominant role in 'achievement training', and the fathers must be prepared to stand aside. Authoritarian fathers are associated with low achievement motivation. Studies which mix boys and girls and which ask simply about parental attitudes and behaviour may therefore be misleading.

[1] Drews, E. M. and Teahan, J. E. 'Parental Attitudes and Academic Achievement', *Journal of Clinical Psychology*, 1957.

[2] Morrow, W. R. and Wilson, R. C. 'Family Relations of Bright High-Achieving and Under-Achieving High School Boys', *Child Development*, 1961.

[3] See, for example, the studies quoted in Drews and Teahan, *op. cit.*

The other aspect of the achievement syndrome is achievement value, and there are some, although not many, studies which attempt to relate child-rearing methods to level of achievement values. Douvan, for example, investigated the occupational aspirations of 1,000 high-school boys from white-collar and skilled-manual families. On the basis of these aspirations she separated those whose aspirations were above those of their fathers' occupations, that is those whose aspirations were upward, from those whose aspirations were downward. Using the boys' own perception of their parents, she found that the upward-aspiring boys reported their parents as likely to employ 'mild and essentially verbal discipline and use physical punishment infrequently'. At the same time these boys reported a congenial relationship with their parents. They shared leisure activities, and projective measures revealed little covert hostility towards parental figures.[1] This study has a number of weaknesses. The boys' own perceptions were the basis rather than the parents' attitudes and behaviour, and no attempt was made to differentiate between mothers and fathers. Nevertheless it points up two features which have received considerable attention in child-development studies, the emotional involvement of parents and child and the use of verbal rather than physical methods of discipline.

A number of writers have drawn attention to the significance of love-orientated techniques of discipline, which focus on using the love relationship with the child to shape his behaviour. These techniques 'are more likely to be correlated with internalized reactions to transgressions (feelings of guilt, self-responsibility, confession) and with non-aggressive or co-operative social relations. On the other hand, power-asserting techniques in controlling the child are more likely to correlate with externalized reactions to transgression (fear of punishment, projected hostility) and with non-co-operative, aggressive behaviour.'[2] Reasoning along similar lines, Rosen has suggested that the employment of love-orientated methods of control are likely to lead to the internalization of parental values. Using questionnaires based on Kluckholn's value orientations he compared 122 mother–son

---

[1] Douvan, E. and Adelson, J. 'The Psychodynamics of Social Mobility in Adolescent Boys', *Journal of Abnormal and Social Psychology*, vol. LVI, 1958.
[2] Becker, W. C. 'Consequences of Different Kinds of Parental Discipline' in Hoffman, M. and Hoffman, L. W. (eds.) *Review of Child Development Research*, New York: Russell Sage Foundation, 1964, vol. I, p. 177.

pairs, the boys varying in age from 8 to 14. Mothers whose values were similar to those of their sons were found to resort to love-orientated techniques, such as displays of affection, reasoning and appeals to standards, rather more frequently than mothers whose sons tended not to share their values. They were also more likely to resort to early independence training as measured by Winterbottom's questionnaire items. On the other hand, mothers with a strong achievement orientation were no more likely to have a son sharing their values than mothers with low achievement values.[1]

The most interesting attempt both theoretically and methodologically to investigate the relationship between child-rearing techniques and value orientation is undoubtedly Strodtbeck's study of family power, need for achievement and achievement values.[2] Family power was measured in terms of the amount of participation in family discussion by family members, using Bales' interaction process categories to analyse a tape-recording of the discussion. Strodtbeck found a very complex relationship in which the crucial factor appeared to be the balance of power between the father and mother in relation to the power of the son. Where the mother's power was high, so were her achievement value scores, and those of her son. Strodtbeck suggests as a possible interpretation of these findings that low decision-making power in the family results in a generalization of this inadequacy to matters outside the family. However, as Strodtbeck himself points out, it is 'unwise to generalize too much on the basis of one specially selected set of families', and he offers his hypothesis as 'highly tentative until confirmed by further research'.

More recently, Katkovsky, Crandall and Good have found a relationship between children's beliefs in their own control and responsibility for events and parental behaviour. Using both interviews with parents and questionnaires, they found that where parents were rated as protective, nurturant, approving and non-rejecting, children were more likely to believe that they, rather than someone or something else, were responsible for their intellectual achievement.[3] Elder, in

[1] Rosen, B. C. 'Family Structure and Value Transmission', *Merrill-Palmer Quarterly*, vol. x, 1964.

[2] Strodtbeck, F. L. 'Family Integration, Values and Achievement', in Halsey, Floud, Anderson, *op. cit.*, pp. 315–47.

[3] Katkovsky, W., Crandall, V. C. and Good, S. 'Parental Antecedents of Children's Beliefs in Internal–External Control of Reinforcements in Intellectual Achievement Situations', *Child Development*, 1967.

another recent study, has laid emphasis on power legitimation or the frequency of parental explanation. He found, in a study of adolescents, that the strongest commitment to high-school graduation and to obtaining a college education occurred under reported conditions of frequent explanations and moderate or low parental power.[1]

Although there is enough agreement in these studies to provide encouragement for further research it is obvious that the field is an extremely complex one, and the work undertaken so far is no more than a very small beginning. In particular we need to know very much more about the process by which values are learned by the child, before we can expect to understand the mechanism for the transmission or acquisition of particular values. Moreover the study by Strodtbeck suggests that the process may be a very complicated one indeed.

On the whole, however, research has neglected the admittedly complex task of relating parental behaviour to measures of achievement value, to an even greater extent than was true of achievement motivation, and instead there has been a tendency for studies to look simply at class differences in child-rearing behaviour, or attitudes to child-rearing. Obviously the assumption, which is frequently made, that class differences in child-rearing will be found to relate also to the various measures of achievement and the achievement syndrome, needs empirical verification. The studies that we have which merely relate child upbringing to social class are not therefore in themselves adequate for the establishment of causal relationships in this field. Nevertheless they can be useful in providing hypotheses for further study, and can be used in conjunction, for example, with the studies already described to indicate the areas of working-class family life which may relate to working-class under-achievement.

There have been numerous studies which attempt to relate child-training to social class, but many of them have been summarized conveniently by Bronfenbrenner, and consequently no attempt will be made to review them here. Bronfenbrenner concluded that 'though more tolerant of expressed impulses and desires the middle-class parent has higher expectations for the child.' Moreover, in matters of discipline, working-class parents are more likely to employ physical

---

[1] Elder, G. 'Parental Power Legitimation and its Effect on the Adolescent', *Sociometry*, 1963.

punishment, while middle-class families rely more on reasoning, isolation, appeals to guilt, etc. At least two independent lines of evidence suggest that the techniques preferred by middle-class parents are more likely to bring about the development of internalized values and controls. At the same time, studies report the middle classes as 'more acceptant and equalitarian while those in the working class are orientated toward maintaining order and obedience'.[1] Rosen's study, described earlier, is in agreement with these conclusions but also found a greater mother–son similarity in values in the middle classes.[2]

Kohn has attempted to relate working-class techniques of child-rearing to working-class values. He argues that 'the conditions under which middle- and working-class parents punish their pre-adolescent children physically, or refrain from doing so, appear to be quite different. Working-class parents are more likely to respond in terms of the immediate consequences of the child's actions, middle-class parents in terms of their interpretation of the child's intent in acting as he does. This reflects differences in parental values. Working-class parents value for their children qualities that ensure respectability; desirable behaviour consists essentially of not violating prescriptions. Middle-class parents value the child's development of internalized standards of conduct; desirable behaviour consists essentially of acting according to the dictates of one's own principles.'[3] The inter-class differences are, however, quite small.

In a later paper with Carroll, Kohn considered class differences in the allocation of parental responsibilities. He found that middle-class mothers tended to emphasize the father's obligation to be as supportive as the mother herself, whereas working-class mothers saw the father's responsibilities as lying more in the imposition of constraints. Middle-class fathers tended to agree with the mothers' conception of their role, especially as it applied to sons, but working-class fathers seemed to see child-rearing as their wives' responsibility and rejected not only the supportive but also the constraining or disciplinary role.[4]

[1] Bronfenbrenner, U. 'Socialization and Social Class Through Time and Space', in Maccoby, Newcombe and Hartley, *Readings in Social Psychology*, 3rd ed.

[2] Rosen, B. C. 'Family Structure and Value Transmission', *Merrill-Palmer Quarterly*, vol. x, 1964.

[3] Kohn, M. L. 'Social Class and the Exercise of Parental Authority', *American Sociological Review*, vol. xxiv, 1959.

[4] Kohn, M. L. and Carroll, E. E. 'Social Class and the Allocation of Parental Responsibilities', *Sociometry*, 1960.

The research described so far has been entirely American, and it is interesting to speculate how far national differences in child-rearing affect this picture. Cross-national studies made at the Department of Child Development and Family Relationships at Cornell University have found, for example, considerable differences in child-rearing methods between England, Germany and the United States, including such aspects as parental warmth, parental control, and parent–child contact. On the whole, parents in the United States are higher in parental warmth and parental contact and lower in parental control than are English parents.[1]

It seems likely, however, that within countries class differences will elsewhere follow similar patterns to those reported for the United States. In England, for example, the study by the Newsons of social-class differences in infant care, suggested that working-class families used more physical punishment. Working-class fathers were also less likely to participate in the care of the child.[2]

There appears, then, to be greater consistency in the research findings on class values and behaviour than in studies which attempt to relate parental behaviour to its effects on the child. On the other hand the differences between social classes are often quite small, and there is evidence of considerable intra-class variation not only in values but in child-rearing behaviour. A more promising line of approach would, therefore, appear to be differences within the working classes, rather than simple cross-class comparisons. Moreover child-rearing practices need to be related very much more closely to actual achievement measures, including both achievement motivation and achievement values.

In spite therefore of some very interesting and challenging findings it is clear that much more hard thinking and many more research studies are needed before we are sure which methods of child-rearing or child-training are associated with different aspects of achievement. Indeed, recent studies have emphasized the methodological difficulties in the whole field of child-rearing research, and the need for caution in the interpretation of findings. It is not easy in the first place to discover a simple and yet effective technique for studying parental behaviour

---

[1] The final report on this study, which is being carried out by Edward C. Devereux, Jnr., Urie Bronfenbrenner, George Suci and Robert R. Rodgers, is not yet published.

[2] Newson, J. and E. *Patterns of Infant Care in an Urban Community*, London: Allen & Unwin, 1963.

as distinct from attitudes. At the same time child-upbringing is an extremely complex phenomenon that cannot be contained within a simple formula. The 'validity of using maternal behaviour in one area of child-rearing to indicate general maternal orientation' is now seriously questioned, particularly when this involves generalization from infant-care practices to child-rearing generally.[1] The effects of a particular training may also vary with the sex or constitution or age of the child.[2] This is not, in consequence, a field in which we can expect rapid results.

At the same time it would be wrong to dismiss the work that has been done in this field so far. In spite of the inconsistencies in definition, and, to some extent at least, in the findings, a beginning has been made, and there is enough common ground to make possible hypotheses of the kind put forward by Strodtbeck. Moreover, studies of the kind described so far in this chapter do not cover every aspect of the socialization process that might be related to achievement. A great deal of interest has been shown in recent years in the child's linguistic and cognitive development and the way in which this too might be influenced by methods of socialization as they vary between social classes, and it is necessary therefore to consider in some detail the work now going on in this particular field.

2 Linguistic development and social learning

Bernstein's theory of linguistic development is based upon the idea that 'certain forms involve for the speaker a loss or an acquisition of skills—both cognitive and social—which are strategic for educational and occupational success, and these forms of language are culturally not individually determined.'[3] He suggests that the two main social classes, especially at the two extremes, are characterized by two different modes of speech which arise from their grossly different environments. The lower working classes are more or less restricted to what Bernstein

---

[1] Leslie, G. R. and Johnson, K. R. 'Changed Perceptions of the Maternal Role', *American Sociological Review*, vol. XXVIII, 1963.

[2] Argyle, M. and Delin, P. 'Non-universal Laws of Socialization', *Human Relations*, vol. XVIII (1), 1965.

[3] Bernstein, B. 'Social Class and Linguistic Development: a Theory of Social Learning', in Halsey, Floud, Anderson, *op. cit.*, pp. 288–314.

calls a public language, in which individual selection and permutation are severely limited. Sentences are short, grammatically simple, and there is a limited number of adjectives, adverbs and conjunctions. There is a tendency, too, to select from a number of traditional phrases and stereotyped responses, and the stress is on emotive terms employing concrete descriptive, tangible and visual symbolism.

The middle-class child, on the other hand, is brought up in an environment which places great value on verbalization and conceptualization, and this is reflected in the speech mode typical of this class, which Bernstein calls a formal language. This is both complex and subtle. Whereas public language is a language of nouns, formal language makes great use of adjectives and adverbs and, in particular, conjunctions. Formal language is, therefore, a suitable vehicle for logical argument, for the discussion of relationships, and for subtleties of personal analysis and considerations of status.

Within the middle-class family, communication between mother and child will be primarily verbal. The child must, early on, learn to recognize that quite small changes in word position and sentence structure signal important changes in feeling. The necessity to verbalize, which is then forced upon the child, exposes him to a whole range of potential learning which is denied to the lower-working-class child precisely because of the linguistic mode in use within the working-class family.

At an even more fundamental level, because of the different function performed by language for each social class, there is a different perception of the world around them. The middle-class child is aware of his environment in a different way; he is more aware, in particular, of what Bernstein calls the formal ordering of his environment and notions of its extension in time and space. For the working-class and especially the lower-working-class child, there is, on the contrary, an emphasis on the here and now, and an emphasis on the description of objects in the environment rather than on their relationships. At this point in his theory Bernstein is clearly relating aspects of Kluckholn's value orientations explicitly to linguistic development. He argues, for example, that working-class children have a shorter time-span of anticipation; that they are passive rather than active in their response to the environment; and have a greater sensitivity to the demands of the group.

Moreover, like some of the theorists working with the concept of the achievement syndrome, Bernstein directs attention to the child-rearing techniques of the parents. The authority structure within the working-class family, he suggests, does not give rise to the well-ordered universe of the middle classes. 'The exercise of authority is not related to a stable system of rewards and punishments but may often appear arbitrary.' At the same time authority is centred upon *persons* rather than *reasons*. A child who challenges that authority is told 'Because I tell you', or 'Because I'm your father.' Within the middle class on the contrary the relationships with authority are more often mediated by the use of reasoned principles. At the same time 'a heightened sensitivity to the motivation of self and others facilitates the development of a low guilt threshold'.

Once at school, the middle-class child is clearly at an advantage, for he 'is predisposed toward the ordering of *symbolic* relationships and, more importantly, *imposing order* and seeing new relationships'. Consequently his level of curiosity will be high. Since he is able to orient towards the future he will be at home in an institution 'where every item in the present is finely linked to a distant future'. In all these ways the social structure of the school creates a framework that he is able to 'accept, respond to, and exploit'. The working-class child, by contrast, is often bewildered and defenceless in the teaching situation, and unable to make the methods and goals of the school personally meaningful.

In using concepts like working class and middle class Bernstein is careful to emphasize that what he has to say applies only at the extremes. Indeed public and formal modes of speech are ideal-type constructs, and all that one would expect to find is that working-class speech tends towards the one, and middle-class speech tends towards the other. Where a working-class family, for whatever reason, employs a large number of the characteristics of formal language it will, Bernstein thinks, provide a favourable environment for educational mobility.

In support of his theory, Bernstein cites studies on the effect of special environments on language skills. The language development of institutional children, for example, can be shown to be grossly retarded.[1] The environment of a large family has also been shown by Nisbet to constitute a handicap to verbal development, and through it

[1] Bernstein, B. *ibid.*, p. 289 and notes 1–7.

to general mental development, a handicap which Nisbet himself explains as a limitation to the amount of verbal communication with adults.[1] Bernstein also cites studies, including two of his own, which indicate that the verbal scores of working-class children are often much below the scores they can achieve on non-verbal tests.[2]

More recently Bernstein has undertaken the direction of a large-scale enquiry designed to test some of his theoretical assumptions, and several papers have been published. One of the most interesting of the findings to date is the variation found in mothers' answers to children's questions. Mothers of five-year-old children were asked to say how they would reply to questions supposedly posed by their children. Middle-class mothers differed from working-class mothers in that they evaded fewer questions, gave more accurate answers, gave more information in their answers, and were more likely to use compound arguments and analogies. They were as likely to give a greater variety of purposive answers and were less likely to repeat the question as an answer.[3]

Other studies have emphasized the richer verbal family environment of middle-class children, and those who are high school-achievers. A study by Esther Milner as long ago as 1951 found that reading readiness in grade one children was associated with high verbal interaction with their parents and other adults. For example, they are read to more frequently by their parents, and they talk more with adults.[4]

The Institute for Development Studies at the New York Medical College, under the direction of Martin Deutsch, has for some time been conducting investigations into the language patterns of deprived children, and their findings, too, are in general agreement with Bernstein, that lower-class and minority groups are associated with poorer language functioning. Deutsch's findings also suggest that this deficiency shows itself 'chiefly in measures which reflect the abstract and categorical use of language as opposed to a denotative and labelling usage'. Moreover, the association between lower-class grouping and

[1] Nisbet, J. 'Family Environment and Intelligence', in Halsey, Floud, Anderson, *op. cit.*, pp. 273–87.
[2] Bernstein, B. *op. cit.*, pp. 290–1.
[3] Robinson, W. P. and Rackstraw, S. J. 'Variations in Mothers' Answers to Children's Questions', *Sociology*, vol. 1, 1967.
[4] Milner, E. 'A Study of the Relationships between Reading Readiness in Grade One School Children and Patterns of Parent–Child Interaction', *Child Development*, 1951.

poorer language functioning is stronger for fifth- than for first-grade children, suggesting what Deutsch calls a 'cumulative deficit pheno-menon'.[1]

Of particular interest is the recent work by Hess and Shipman, which is focused very directly on to Bernstein's theoretical position. In their study, maternal and child behaviour was observed by means of experimental teaching sessions in which negro mothers and their four-year-old children were engaged. Their findings suggested that 'the growth of cognitive processes is fostered in family control systems which offer and permit a wide range of alternatives of action and thought and that such growth is constricted by systems of control which offer predetermined solutions and few alternatives for consideration and choice.'[2]

An interesting study by Schatzman and Strauss also reported differences in modes of communication as revealed in interviews with lower-class and middle-class respondents. These differences included a greater tendency on the part of lower-class respondents to describe events as seen through their own eyes, and less ability to take the listeners' role. Middle-class speech was also less concrete and the middle-class respondents were more likely to use organizing framework and stylistic devices.[3]

The evidence from these sources is, of course, quite inadequate as a full test of Bernstein's theory. Indeed the very nature of his approach, and the many concepts involved, makes it almost certain that it will remain highly speculative for some time to come. The theory, indeed, is not only complicated and subtle but extremely general and com-prehensive. Although primarily a linguistic theory, in that he seeks to explain the cognitive development of the child in terms of the linguistic codes in use in the family, he also believes that the limitations imposed by certain speech forms will influence the child's whole perception of the environment. It is important to notice that this is clearly intended to refer to the child's actual thinking and not simply to his verbal expression. However, not all types of thinking are in-volved, as Bernstein's own data on the non-verbal abilities of working-

[1] Deutsch, M. 'The Role of Social Class in Language Development and Cognition', *American Journal of Orthopsychiatry*, vol. XXXV (1), 1965.

[2] Hess, R. D. and Shipman, V. C. 'Early Experience and the Socialization of Cognitive Modes in Children', *Child Development*, 1965.

[3] Schatzman, L. and Strauss, A. 'Social Class and Modes of Communication', *American Journal of Sociology*, vol. LX, 1955.

class children indicate. Moreover Deutsch has found that deprived children seem to understand more language than they speak, and that they express themselves quite well in spontaneous and unstructured situations.[1] Clearly we need further studies not only of the linguistic pattern of these children but also of their general cognitive functioning.

Since value-orientations, as Kluckholn has described them, involve learned ways of perceiving the environment it is reasonable and indeed plausible to conceive of them, as Bernstein does, as determined by the nature of linguistic forms. The evidence that they are in fact determined in this way has, however, still to be discovered. All that we can safely conclude at the present time is that value-orientations could conceivably be derived in this way. Much the same may be said of Bernstein's most interesting attempt to relate types of parental authority to the child's cognitive as well as his emotional development. Too little is known about the effects of child-rearing techniques on child development to make this more than an attractive hypothesis.

Nevertheless, in spite of its speculative nature, Bernstein's theory of social learning, as he himself calls it, has been of very great importance. In the first place it has provided research in this field with an interesting and plausible theoretical position to replace the crude empiricism which has so frequently prevailed. Even more important, however, is the part it has played in providing a framework which can include within it not only the empirical findings in the field of school achievement but also the various theoretical positions. It could, that is to say, become the starting point for a general theory of achievement. This general theory would need to relate the cognitive, motivational and evaluative factors involved in achievement, not only to each other, but also to the socialization which had influenced them. Only then will the concept of educational achievement be satisfactorily explained. At the same time, we also need to know why the various types of behaviour and attitude associated with achievement should be so often linked to social class. What is it about working-class life experiences that predisposes the working-class family to adopt behaviours and attitudes that influence their children towards low achievement? An explanation of this relationship must also provide reasons for the many exceptions

[1] Reported in Riessman, F. *The Culturally Deprived Child*, New York: Harper & Row, 1962, pp. 76-7.

to the general rule. Why is it, that is to say, that not all working-class children are low achievers? Is it because of high innate ability which either overcomes all obstacles, or masks at least some measure of under-achievement? Alternatively it may be the effect of other socializing agencies outside the immediate family which counteracts its influence. Yet another possibility, and one that is strongly supported by evidence, lies in the variability of behaviour and attitudes within, as well as between, social-class or occupational groupings. It is this last possibility that we shall explore in the rest of this chapter.

3 Social class and family life

The attempt to explain how it is that working-class families hold different values from middle-class families, and behave in different ways towards their children, depends essentially upon the development of a theory to explain how their different life chances and life experiences predispose them towards different views of the world around them and of their place in it. This problem has always interested sociologists, and there is no space here to review all the work, both theoretical and empirical, which has been done in this sphere. All that will be attempted is to draw attention to those aspects of it which appear to be particularly relevant to the problem of achievement. In general, attention has been focused upon three different aspects of working-class life, all of them to some degree interrelated. They may be briefly summarized as material life chances, working conditions, and opportunities for status.

Traditionally, those in working-class or manual jobs have earned less than those in middle-class or non-manual occupations. Moreover this is still largely true, in spite of a rise in the standard of living of the working classes, and some overlap between certain highly paid workers and certain types of non-manual employment. Working-class employment has also been characteristically insecure. Not only has it been more liable to unemployment during periods of depression, but also few manual workers are employed on more than a weekly basis. This contrasts with the typical monthly, quarterly or even permanent tenure of most non-manual jobs. Manual workers also have less chance of advancement in their jobs.

Within the work situation itself there are also important differences which may have implications for working-class attitudes. Manual work is frequently carried out in unpleasant working conditions. It may be dangerous, dirty, or physically strenuous. Frequently it involves long hours, or shift work. Often it is less intrinsically rewarding, and perceived as such, even when it is highly paid. It is also less likely to involve authority, responsibility or power. Finally, many studies have shown that manual work is low in the prestige or status hierarchy of all modern societies.[1]

It is reasonable to expect that these radically different life and work experiences will be reflected in the attitudes of the working classes both to work itself and to other aspects of their lives, and there have been many attempts to show that this does indeed occur. It has been argued, for example, that the working class will value different aspects in their working situation, prizing such qualities as security more than other aspects of the job, and there are a number of studies which show that this is the case. In a widely based international comparison using national sources, Inkeles has shown that those in higher-status occupations report more job satisfaction and are more likely to want a job which is interesting and stimulating. They are also less likely to want security or certainty in a job and are more willing to take risks to get promotion.[2]

The lack of security, combined with lack of opportunity, are also likely to influence the expectations of the manual worker. He may well lower his aspirations to what seems meaningful or reasonable in his circumstances, and this may influence his hopes not only for himself but also for his child. Many studies have in fact shown that the working classes are less ambitious for their children.

The deprivation of the manual worker, both in his working situation and in his material standard of living, is also seen as profoundly influencing his view both of himself and of the world around him. In particular he is less likely to share in the middle-class, achieving orientation described by Kluckholn. His own lack of power to alter his situation, his uncertainty about the future, his sense of insecurity,

---

[1] Routh, G. *Occupation and Pay in Great Britain 1906–1960*, Cambridge University Press, 1965. See also Goldthorpe, J. H. *et al.* 'The Affluent Worker and the Thesis of Embourgeoisement', *Sociology*, vol. I, 1967, pp. 12–31.

[2] Inkeles, A. 'Industrial Man: the Relation of Status to Experience Perception and Value', *American Journal of Sociology*, July 1960. See also Lyman, E. L. 'Occupation Differences in the Value attached to Work', *American Journal of Sociology*, 1961.

will, it is suggested, lead him to see the world as dominated by luck or chance,[1] rather than under his control. He is not likely to spend time planning for a future which is not only unpredictable but largely out of his hands. He will naturally gravitate towards the getting-by attitude described by Kahl, and he will do this because of his own experiences in coming to terms with his own environment. Neither is he likely to share in the individualistic approach of the middle classes. 'Getting ahead' for the manual worker 'must rest in the progressive increase of the rewards which they gain *from their present economic role*'.[2] For this reason he is likely to emphasize collective or group mobility through trade-union representation and trade-union power.

The low status ascribed to manual work, and especially to unskilled work, may also influence the worker's own self-esteem. He may accept the opinion of others as to his lack of ability and may transfer this to his children. High ambition in such circumstances may appear as inappropriate or even absurd. Parents with such an attitude may not only fail to encourage their children to achieve; they may not even recognize the achievement of their children unless it is drawn to their attention.[3] Recent work on the child's self-concept of ability has suggested not only that it is related to achievement but that parents are an important source of the child's self-image.[4]

It has also been suggested that the material, power and status deprivation of the working-class parent will affect his actual handling of the child. Kohn, for example, specifically relates parent–child relationships to differences in the conditions of life, and particularly the occupational conditions of the different social classes. It is, he suggests, the greater degree of self-direction present in middle-class occupations which leads them to value self-direction in their children and so to encourage in their children such qualities as curiosity and self-control. Working-class parents, on the other hand, stress such

---

[1] See, for example, Gouldner, A. W. *Patterns of Industrial Bureaucracy*, London: Routledge & Kegan Paul, 1955, pp. 117–36; and Katz, F. M. 'The Meaning of Success. Some Differences in Value Systems of Social Classes', *Journal of Social Psychology*, vol. LXII, 1964.

[2] Goldthorpe, J. H. *et al.*, *op. cit.*

[3] See, for example, the descriptions of working-class parents in Jackson, B. and Marsden, D. *Education and the Working Class*, London: Routledge & Kegan Paul, 1962, p. 88.

[4] Brookover, W. B. and Gottlieb, D. *A Sociology of Education*, New York: American Book Co., 2nd ed. 1964, pp. 468–77.

qualities as honesty, obedience and neatness, because in their working lives what is mainly required of them is that they should follow explicit rules laid down by someone in authority.[1] A small study by Roy also suggests that the home environment itself may be a factor in working-class disciplinary practices. She found an increase in the permissiveness of child-rearing attitudes as the number of rooms in the house increased.[2]

The most thorough-going attempt to relate the occupational situation of the family to the socialization of the child is the recent study by McKinley, which combines an extensive review of the literature with data of his own, based on a questionnaire given to adolescent boys. As a result of his own work and his interpretation of research findings in this field, McKinley argues that 'the greater punitiveness and the more common rejection of the child by parents in the urban lower classes is a consequence of the parent's greater frustration and stronger feelings of threat. The parent's aggression is displaced from the frustrating system (the power and reward structure of industrial society) to the relatively powerless child.'[3] The frustration of the lower-class father leads him not only to aggressive behaviour but to withdrawal from the family and an attempt to gain status in some alternative behaviour system, such as sexual prowess, masculinity and the adult male peer-group. This in turn has important influences on the pattern of identification with the two parents. The lower-class boy is likely to identify with the mother rather than the father, which may lead to adolescent rebellion in an effort to escape this identification. The inadequacy of the father will also mean that the peer-group is likely to be of particular importance for the lower-class adolescent as he seeks a masculine model. This general picture is in sharp contrast to the family situation of the upwardly mobile, which is characterized by moderate socialization techniques, shared parental authority and identification with the father. McKinley's study, therefore, is an important attempt to relate aspects of occupational status, socialization processes, and achievement behaviour. However, we cannot

---

[1] Kohn, M. K. 'Social Class and Parent–child Relationships: an Interpretation', *American Journal of Sociology*, January 1963.

[2] Roy, K. 'Parents' Attitudes toward their Children', *Journal of Home Economics*, vol. XLII, 1950, quoted in Becker, W. C. 'Consequences of Different Kinds of Parental Discipline', *op. cit.*, p. 171.

[3] McKinley, D. G. *Social Class and Family Life*, Glencoe, Illinois: the Free Press, 1964, p. 54.

fully assess its significance without further research in all these areas.

So far in this discussion we have treated social class as if it were a homogeneous category. In fact, this is very far from the case, and studies in the differences within social classes show them to be both complex and heterogeneous. This serves to emphasize the importance of research into intra-class differences. Although much fewer in number than those concerned with comparison between classes, the researches carried out in this field are sufficient at least to indicate certain important areas to which further attention should be paid.

One of the main ways in which to differentiate between working-class jobs is in terms of skill, and it has been shown several times that the children of skilled workers perform better at school and are more likely to go on to higher education than are the children of the unskilled. This finding holds even when ability is held constant. Within the middle classes there is a similar distinction between the upper and lower strata.[1] There is also evidence, from the same studies, that skilled and semi-skilled workers have higher aspirations for their children than unskilled workers, and the upper-middle than the lower-middle classes. Some studies have also suggested that foremen as a group stand in an intermediate position between the middle and the working classes.[2]

There is, therefore, clear evidence of differences both within the working classes and the middle classes, corresponding to the level of skill demanded in the job. In the absence of sufficient evidence we can unfortunately only speculate as to why these differences occur. The more favourable position of the skilled worker or foreman relative to the unskilled worker, in terms of the status of the job, its chances of promotion and, usually, its material rewards, offers several possible reasons for the working-class differences that have been found. The lower-class family may well have fewer expectations for the future and so lower aspirations for themselves and their children. They may have less self-esteem and be less self-confident. They tend to have larger families, and to be less well-educated, which will increase their chances

[1] See, for example, the Crowther Report, *op. cit.*; Floud, Halsey, Martin, *op. cit.* Similar data for the U.S. is summarized in Brookover and Gottlieb, *op. cit.*, ch. 7. See also Turner, R. *The Social Context of Ambition*, San Francisco: Chandler, 1964.
[2] See, for example, Floud, Halsey, Martin, *op. cit.*; Cohen, E. C. 'Parental Factors in Educational Mobility, *Sociology of Education*, vol. XXXVIII.

of using Bernstein's public language forms. They are also less likely to have acquired achieving values as a consequence of their particular life experiences, either during their own childhood or later. Within the middle classes those in lower-middle-class occupations will be differentiated from the upper-middle classes by their earnings, their status and their education level. This may well reflect upon the horizons they set for their children.

On the other hand, we cannot overlook the possibility that the cause of the difference is of a much more complex and subtle kind, arising not as a consequence of their class position but as one of its causes. The foremen and skilled workers are likely to include far more upwardly mobile individuals than the unskilled workers, and so are those in the upper-middle rather than the lower-middle occupations group. It is at least possible that the personality and value orientations which helped the upwardly mobile families to succeed will also be passed to their children. Smelser, for example, in a study of upwardly mobile, stationary, and downwardly mobile families concluded that 'achievement at the level of the family was influential in the development of such personality factors as strength, power, self-direction and distance from others'.[1]

On the other hand, other workers have emphasized downward mobility, and especially maternal downward mobility as an important factor in school achievement and parental ambition. Cohen, for example, found that mothers who had married downward from a white-collar background had a higher probability of having a son planning to go to college than mothers who came from a manual-worker background. This was also true of mothers holding white-collar rather than manual jobs. Fathers' downward mobility was however unrelated to the sons' plans for entering college.[2] Floud, Halsey and Martin also found that mothers whose occupation before marriage was superior to that of their husbands were more likely to have children who were successful in the 11-plus than other mothers.[3] Kohn, in his study of parental values towards the upbringing of children, found that working-class mothers holding white-collar jobs were closer to the middle class than other working-class mothers, and so were those

[1] Smelser, W. T. 'Adolescent and Adult Occupational Choice as a Function of Socio-economic History', *Sociometry*, vol. XXVI, 1963.

[2] Cohen, E. C. *op. cit.* See also Kraus, I. 'Aspirations among Working Class Youth', *American Sociological Review*, vol. XXIX, 1964, p. 869.

[3] Floud, Halsey, Martin, *op. cit.*, p. 88.

with relatively high educational attainment.[1] Such mothers therefore are not only likely to be motivated by a strong desire to regain status; their close association with the middle classes through their social origin, their job or their educational background, has provided them with the necessary knowledge, and quite possibly values, which will ensure for their children a successful school career. Cohen, for example, concludes that 'we can speculate that the influence of the parents on the probability of mobility takes place at a very early stage when basic attitudes towards school work are being formed. The crucial role of the parents may be to send the child to school with a receptive attitude toward the values and norms advocated by the school personnel.'[2] Such mothers, of course, are also more likely to use Bernstein's formal language.

In discussing fathers, emphasis is more often placed upon blocked mobility, or mobility pessimism. Swift, for example, found that 'with the middle class, the father's dissatisfaction with his job and its prospects related significantly to the likelihood of his child's success in the 11-plus'.[3] Cohen found for her sample that working-class fathers who were similarly dissatisfied were more likely than other fathers to have sons planning to go to college.[4] Kahl found that his 'getting ahead' fathers were unhappy and dissatisfied with their occupational status.[5] This would appear, indeed, to be a factor of some considerable importance, but we still need to know whether it operates simply as a determinant of parental ambition vicariously expressed through the child, or whether, as Kahl's argument would suggest, it operates at a deeper level. The 'mobility pessimism' itself, that is to say, may be the result of strong achievement values or an achievement drive which has for some reason been blocked.

At the same time Harrington has suggested that when blocked mobility leads to frustration, and pressure on the child to succeed *in place of* the parent, the result is likely to be unfavourable for the child's mobility. 'The family in which educational success is too much the price of parental approval to be enjoyed for its own sake', she

---

[1] Kohn, M. L. 'Social Class and Parental Values', *American Journal of Sociology*, vol. LXIV, 1959.

[2] Cohen, E. C. *op. cit.*, p. 422.

[3] Swift, D. F. 'Social Class and Achievement Motivation', *op. cit.*, p. 93.

[4] Cohen, E. C. *op. cit.*

[5] Kahl, J. A. ' "Common Man" Boys', *op. cit.*

argues, 'is unlikely to throw up creative ability, and where the child is treated as an extension of the parental self-image, self-direction cannot be expected.'[1]

This review of working-class family life serves therefore to underline the general conclusions already drawn, that our only hope to understand more about class differences in achievement is by a greater understanding of the general socialization process. We need to know how the child acquires not only the values and skills of his group but, even more significantly in a society where education is a major key to social mobility, the ability and the motivation to learn new skills and new values. This requires, it is hardly necessary to add, more than the sociological approach alone. It is an interdisciplinary concept and requires interdisciplinary methods, and in particular an emphasis on the relationships between personality and social structure. If however sociology is to make its full contribution it is vitally necessary that it should go beyond the descriptive studies of social-class differences with which it has frequently been content in the past, and consider, as it is indeed beginning to do, the actual process of socialization itself.

The family is of course the earliest and the most important area in which socialization occurs. Yet, however important the family is, and has been shown to be, it would be false to assume that it is the only factor in explaining either inter-class or intra-class differences in educational achievement. The school itself is a socializing agency of some considerable importance, in which the teachers and the peer group each play their part, a part which may reinforce or may conflict with the influence of the family.

For this reason the sociology of education has come to pay increasing attention to the school. Jean Floud pointed out in 1961 that although home and school in interaction determine educability, the school has been neglected. 'Little has been done to explore with any thoroughness or in any detail the explicit and implicit demands of life in school to which we find pupils responding selectively in terms of their differing social experience outside its walls.'[2]

Since then a number of sociologists have turned to the study of

---

[1] Harrington, M. 'Parents' Hopes and Children's Success', *New Society*, 26 November 1964, p. 9.
[2] Floud, J. 'Sociology and Education' in *The Teaching of Sociology to Students of Education and Social Work*, Sociological Review Monograph No. 4, 1961, p. 64.

educational institutions, and in particular there has been considerable interest recently in the study of the school as an organization. At the same time work has been undertaken into the peer group and the adolescent culture, and into the teacher's role. A beginning has therefore been made in the creation of a sociology of the school.

6 Who controls our schools?

1 *The influence of the State*

Sociologists working in the field of education have so far shown little interest in the relationship between educational systems and the State. This is almost certainly because there have so far been few attempts to consider educational institutions in a genuinely comparative way. Moreover, when such attempts have been made, as for example in Turner's interesting comparison between Britain and the United States, the main emphasis has been on differences in culture and ideology rather than in terms of different types of control. On the other hand, studies in comparative education rarely include the use of sociological concepts and tend in any case to be descriptive rather than explanatory or analytic. Yet it is essential to consider the means by which State control is exercised and the implications this will have on the functioning of the school. In the absence of sufficient attempts by sociologists to include this area of study in the sociology of the school, the following discussion will however be, of necessity, brief and inadequate, and will attempt to indicate the range of problems to be considered rather than to present definite findings.

In general, discussion of State control of education is couched in terms of the extent to which such control is or is not centralized. For example, comparisons are frequently drawn with France, where the schools are tightly controlled by the central authority, even down to the details of the daily curriculum. The U.S.S.R. is another very highly centralized system where details not only of school policy but of day-to-day administration are laid down by the State. These include fairly strict regulation of curricula, textbooks, educational methods and activities. In the Netherlands, too, State supervision is all embracing. The State provides not only the necessary finances but also decides very largely what will be taught.[1]

The United States, in contrast, has a very decentralized system. Any interference on the part of the Federal Government has been jealously guarded against, and it is only very recently that Federal Aid has come to play more than an insignificant part in the financing of education. For this reason the State is the administrative unit concerned with educational control. Even at the State level, however, there is relatively little central control. Although all States lay down certain minimum standards which cover such general issues as the certification of teachers, the school buildings, and provision for the teaching of certain subjects, these are minima only. Maximum standards, or even the detailed regulation of minimum standards, are considered undesirable. Consequently the local school districts have considerable power and considerable autonomy. 'Generally the people throughout the United States have considered education so basic and so essential to the welfare of the State that they have insisted that the residents of the local school should have opportunity to decide upon the kinds of schools they want and the extent of financial support they desire to provide, without the necessity of referring these matters to local agencies of government that may be concerned with other issues as well.'[2]

England, like the United States, has a tradition of decentralization, which has deeply influenced educational administration for many years. Not only was there a reluctance on the part of the State to enter the field of education, so that even today considerable emphasis is placed upon the private or independent school, but there was also a reluctance on the part of the State to control local enterprise. Not until 1944 did the minister in charge of education have the power to compel backward authorities to raise their standards. At present the State has considerable powers of veto on educational policy if it seeks to use them, and indeed these powers have been used since 1944 to prevent certain experiments in the organization of comprehensive secondary-school systems ardently desired by certain local education authorities. Nevertheless, the initiation of educational plans still remains the prerogative of the local authority, and the control of the curriculum and of activities within the school are still very largely under the control of the school

[1] Reller, T. L. and Morphet, E. L. *Comparative Educational Administration*, Englewood Cliffs, New Jersey: Prentice-Hall, 1962, p. 88.
[2] *Ibid.*, p. 170.

itself. For this reason the English system has been described as a partnership between central control and local initiative.[1] It must be admitted, however, that the State is very much the senior partner.

On the other hand, although this dichotomy between centralized and decentralized control is useful as a first step in the description and analysis of educational systems, it fails to do justice to the very numerous administrative patterns that prevail. The control of higher education may, for example, follow a different pattern from that of the control of schools. In the United States higher education in public as distinct from private institutions is very largely the direct responsibility of the individual State. Founded as they were on State initiative and on public money, such institutions have been traditionally governed by a board of trustees who are appointed or elected to office to represent community interests within the State. Intended as the principal line of defence against political interference, these boards are not always able or willing to stand out against strong pressure, and in practice State universities and especially the smaller State colleges can be subjected to considerable State interference at the level of both educational and administrative issues. States,[2] for example, often demand that certain courses be required, or they may prohibit certain subjects. They may order certain kinds of research to be undertaken and reject others. They can and do exercise considerable control over the admissions of students, and less frequently over the appointment and dismissal of academic and other staff. Under certain circumstances they can exercise very detailed financial control over buildings and equipment. They may even keep a watchful eye on all expenditure so that they vet all purchases, and grant or withdraw permission for visits or conferences attended by the teaching staff. When this has happened it is no longer possible to talk of university autonomy.

By contrast British universities enjoy a climate of freedom 'that is perhaps unequalled in the world today'.[3] University education is subject to State control only through the intervention of the University Grants Committee, a body which is appointed mainly from amongst university teachers, and so may fairly be said to represent university rather than community interests. It is the University Grants Committee

[1] *Ibid.*, pp. 58-65.
[2] For many examples of this kind of interference see Moos, M. and Rourke, F. E. *The Campus and the State*, Baltimore: Johns Hopkins Press, 1959.
[3] *Ibid.*, p. 292.

which determines the needs of the universities and which negotiates for grants direct from the Treasury. The University Grants Committee also has responsibility for allocating the grants and the funds for capital building programmes. The State therefore can determine only the amount of the grant and not the way it is spent.[1]

The relationship between financial support and administrative control is generally a very complex one which permits of no easy generalization. It is true that the granting of public funds will usually be accompanied by some degree of public control, so that private institutions usually have more autonomy than similar bodies receiving public funds. This is true, for example, of public and private secondary schools both in the United States and Britain. On the other hand, as Mushkin has pointed out, there are many ways in which school systems can be given aid from national funds, while still preserving a high degree of local autonomy. 'Grants-in-aid and even tax-sharing schemes are highly flexible tools of inter-governmental finance. They can be shaped in small or large sizes; they can be designed to cover all the costs or only a negligible share. They can be used to equalize variations in local tax resources or make more equal the local tax burdens required for new programme expenditures. They can be used to shape the direction of certain educational programmes, for example more or fewer vocational schools. Supporting grants have been given to finance all or part of educational programmes, and in addition grants have been offered to encourage demonstrations and experiments.'[2]

As we have seen in the case of the British universities, national funds can be given with few if any strings attached. All universities receive the bulk of their income from the State, but the autonomous University Grants Committee is entrusted with the responsibility of safeguarding the public as well as the university interest. The only control exercised by the State is that of giving or withholding money, including university salaries, to the university system as a whole. In this way it can of course encourage or hinder university expansion in general, but there is no attempt to control university policy or university government. Moreover, within the United States system of higher education there are

---

[1] This high level of autonomy is not shared by any other types of higher education in Britain, which are under the control of the local authority. This applies both to Colleges of Education and Colleges of Technology.

[2] Mushkin, S. J. 'Financing Secondary School Expansion in O.E.C.D. Countries', *Sociology of Education*, vol. XXXVIII, 1964-5.

many universities and colleges founded and largely maintained by the State which still retain a high degree of autonomy over the conduct of their affairs. These institutions, like the British universities, have undoubtedly been protected by a powerful belief in the community at large, and in the State government, of the necessity of maintaining academic freedom. This is their main if not indeed their only safeguard.

At the other extreme, as Mushkin points out, grants may be used not to obtain complete control but to secure the furtherance of particular policies. It is fairly frequent, for example, to use grants to encourage particular innovations or experiments in education. The 1907 Free Place Regulations in England were a deliberate attempt to open up secondary schools to able working-class children, and grant-aid was given only on condition that at least 25 per cent of free places were made available to children from the public elementary schools. It is interesting to notice that these grants were conceived, not only as a spur to local authorities, but also to the, then numerous, endowed grammar schools.

Much of the Federal aid available to schools in the United States also comes into this category. There are, for example, national grants available to develop new high-school textbooks in chemistry and mathematics, to retrain high-school teachers; and to provide summer schools for gifted high-school students interested in science and mathematics. The National Defense Education Act of 1958 also provided a new national system of student aid. All of these examples of financial aid involve no attempt to take control of the actual administration of the schools. A high level of financial assistance is therefore quite compatible with local and institutional autonomy, even if the two are by no means always found together. Mushkin has also shown that there is no need for the decentralized system to forego the advantages of government support. The extent to which government grants can be used to initiate experiments or benefit particularly disadvantaged areas has already been noted. Other government agencies have the task of giving information and advice when it is needed. In Britain, for example, the H.M.I.s have long played a significant part in both primary and secondary education.[1]

---

[1] See, for example, Edmonds, E. L. *The School Inspector*, London: Routledge & Kegan Paul, 1962.

Discussions of centralized and decentralized systems of education frequently assume the greater efficiency of centralized forms of control. Brookover, for example, argues that a decentralized system is likely on the whole to be less efficient in meeting the educational goals of a modern industrial society. School districts within a highly decentralized system, he points out, are likely to be parochial in their attitudes, so that they will fail to see or respond to the needs of the wider social unit. They may also be too small or too poor to meet the needs of their own students for qualified teachers or specialized equipment, as is the case in sparsely populated rural areas and in the slum areas of great cities. Faced with these problems the United States has seen the need in the last 10 or 20 years to reorganize school districts so that some of the very small school districts and the very small schools are tending to disappear.[1] At the same time there is a growing tendency to increase the power of the State and even the Federal government. In Britain, too, the same tendencies have been apparent, to increase the size of the local education authority areas, to amalgamate small schools and to increase the power of the State.[2]

On the other hand, if it is easy to demonstrate the weaknesses of the very small school district, it does not follow that equal advantages will follow from each increase in the size of the administrative area. There is considerable danger that the highly centralized system will be out of touch with both the wishes and the needs of the local community. Moreover, if the small school district is in danger of becoming narrowly parochial, the centralized system may equally well become rigid and stereotyped. Indeed one of the advantages of a measure of decentralization is that it makes possible a high degree of innovation and experiment. In Britain, for example, it is possible for schools of all kinds to explore a variety of types of organization, of curriculum, and of teaching methods on the initiative of local educational authorities, or of individual school heads or teachers. Since 1944 some local education authorities have taken the lead in introducing new forms of comprehensive secondary education, some secondary modern schools have developed interesting pre-vocational and vocational courses, and some primary schools have experimented with new teaching methods.

[1] Brookover, W. B. and Gottlieb, D. *op. cit.*, pp. 236–45.
[2] Reller, T. L. and Morphet, E. L. *op. cit.*, pp. 58–65.

2 *The school and the local community*

The distinction between centralized and decentralized administrative control does not, however, do more than begin to touch on the problem of locating the source of control over the educational process. Even within the most decentralized system we still have to discover the precise locus of power, and it by no means follows that this will lie within the individual school or even the local school system itself. Although our knowledge of this area is still extremely limited, it is one in which American sociologists at least have become deeply interested, so that it is possible to come to some general, if still mainly tentative, conclusion.

In the United States the school board is the most powerful agency through which community needs and community wishes are represented. For this reason it is useful to begin with an examination of the role of the school board in the American system. The system of elected school boards responsible for the educational needs of the local community, as distinct from all-purpose local authorities which cover a wide variety of functions, has persisted in the United States from the earliest days of public education. This is in contrast to England where school boards were replaced by all-purpose local authorities as long ago as 1902. Moreover the American school boards are normally responsible for much smaller districts than are the English local authorities, so that it is possible to consider them as community agencies in a way that is no longer possible in England. Nevertheless, it is still possible for the school boards to have little real relationship with community affairs and little actual influence on the schools. Consequently we have to ask both how and under what circumstances the school boards actually represent the community, and also to what extent the school boards are able to exert control over the school system. These two questions are, as we shall see, interrelated but it is convenient to begin by treating them separately. It is also necessary to consider the extent to which a community may impinge upon the school system by other means.

Another source of community pressure which has received considerable attention in the United States is the extent of control over the teacher's private life. He, or more usually she, is expected to take part in a wide range of community activities, such as Sunday-school teaching, youth-club leadership and work for charity. There may be restrictions, too, on where the teacher lives and shops, and how she spends her leisure time. For example, smoking, drinking, dancing and card-playing may all be taboo. According to this view, these restraints reflect the predominant values of the community. Charters, however, has pointed out that these restrictions on the teachers' community role, are only likely to be successful in the 'culturally homogeneous small town or village, relatively untouched by urbanization or industrialization. The city and the suburb were ignored in the educational sociologists' descriptions of the modes of social relations between the teacher and community.'[1] It seems, therefore, that even if such restraints were frequent in the past, they are much less likely to occur in the present, if only because fewer and fewer schools in America are located in this type of community. This is partly because of increasing urbanization, partly because of the massive programmes of school district reorganization since the 1940s. Charters has also drawn attention to the inadequacies of much research in this field, both in terms of its method, the conflicting nature of its findings, and its descriptive rather than analytical approach.[2]

Bidwell has summarized a large number of studies which seem to indicate that the school board is most likely to represent community values when 'the school itself is a community institution, that is the extent to which the schools of a community symbolize its identity and values and provide a focus for the integration of community life.'[3] In such areas there is considerable and active interest in the school and its affairs. The teacher and the principal are likely to be well known in the community, and the school building may be a centre for community activities. Under such circumstances the board is likely to speak for the community rather than the school.

Although school systems as community institutions, in this sense, are more likely to be found in rural areas and small towns where school districts are still small, Bidwell argues that the degree of urbanization alone does not seem to be a critical variable. 'The crucial factors would appear to be the pluralism and segmental quality of community life typical of but not always present in large urban centres.' For

---

[1] Charters, W. W. Jnr. 'The Social Background of Teaching' in Gage, N. L. (ed.) *Handbook of Research on Teaching, op. cit.*, p. 765.

[2] *Ibid.*, pp. 767–71.

[3] Bidwell, C. E. 'The School as a Formal Organisation', in March, J. G. (ed.) *Handbook of Social Organisation*, Chicago: Rand, McNally, 1965, pp. 972–1022.

example Seeley, Sim and Loosley, in their study of Crestwood Heights,[1] show that a suburban community, even in a highly urban area, can make the school system the centre of community interest if the population is sufficiently homogeneous and child-centred. In Crestwood Heights community control was indirect but nonetheless strong. For example, the board of education used adherence to community values as an important criterion in their choice of director of education.

Where the community is heterogeneous or divided there is no longer sufficient social solidarity to maintain community control of the schools. A study by Vidich and Bensman of a small rural community in New York State shows clearly how this can happen even in a small community which continues to take considerable interest in the affairs of its schools. For historical reasons the majority of members of the school board represent rural interests, and the 'rural members have traditionally been "respectable" prosperous farmers who have been residents of the township for all or most of their lives',[2] but the rural interest is by no means the dominant one in the town, which includes the professionals, industrial workers, traditional farmers, shack people and the marginal middle class. Moreover rural dominance has had important consequences for the school. Although farmers represent only one-third of the population, great emphasis in the school curriculum is placed on home economics and agricultural training. Between 1945 and 1951, 21 out of a total of 57 male graduates took the agricultural course, yet only four of the 21 were engaged in farming in 1951. Although the major opportunities for the school graduates lie in industry, business or college, courses preparing them for their career remain at an elementary level. Nor are these the only ways in which rural interest predominate. Jobs in the school bus service, which provides the major political plums that the board has to offer, tend to go to farmers, and teachers from a rural background are favoured in making appointments. Local business interests challenge the school board when school policy affects local business, and these occasions are a major source of controversy over school board affairs, but other interests in the town are represented only through the Parent–Teacher

[1] Seeley, J. R., Sim, R. A. and Loosley, E. W. *Crestwood Heights: a Study of the Culture of Suburban Life*, New York: Basic Books, 1956.
[2] Vidich, A. J. and Bensman, J. *Small Town in Mass Society* (Garden City, New York), New York: Doubleday, 1960, p. 179.

Association. We may say therefore that the school board in this town does not serve the interests of the community as a whole.

In such heterogeneous areas, where common values can hardly be said to exist at all, one of the most important sources of community pressure on both the school boards and the school system itself is the parents, either as individuals or organized through Parent–Teacher Associations. The school superintendents studies by Gross[1] mentioned the P.T.A. as a major promoter of public education more frequently than anything else, and both the school superintendents and the school board members mentioned parents as a source of pressure. Indeed 92 per cent of school superintendents and 74 per cent of school board members cited parents and the P.T.A. in their answers to this question.

On the other hand, Bidwell has argued that the P.T.A. is primarily a school-dominated organization since it is 'a means of channelling parent pressures in organizationally acceptable ways, while maintaining parents' involvement and adequate school parent communication'.[2] Vidich and Bensman show how the high-school principal in a small town can use the P.T.A. for the purpose of gaining acceptance for his educational programmes, 'without, however, making this obvious to the community. For, through the process of committees and agendas, it appears publicly that P.T.A. members themselves, when making their reports, have originated the ideas which have been given them by the principal. Through the complexities of this procedure, the P.T.A. voices the policies of the principal and, in turn, the principal uses the P.T.A. as an informal political instrument against those interests in the village and town which oppose his programme. While doing this, however, he is careful to restrain the P.T.A. if it gets over ambitious.'[3] The success of this particular principal in manipulating the P.T.A. should not however conceal the potential influence of both the P.T.A. and individual parents. We badly need more case studies both of the kinds of pressures that parents exert and the manner in which the schools deal with parental demands.

More recently, moreover, studies in role expectations have revealed that teachers may be misinformed as to the nature of community and parental expectations. A study by Jenkins and Lippitt, for example, suggested that teachers may exaggerate the extent to which parents

[1] Gross, N. *Who Runs Our Schools?*, New York: Wiley, 1958.
[2] Bidwell, C. *op. cit.*, pp. 1010–11.
[3] Vidich, A. J. and Bensman, J. *op. cit.*

want teachers to give special attention to their own child.[1] A recent English study has also found that teachers tended to under-estimate the extent to which parents expected the schools to give moral training, while over-estimating the weight parents placed on instruction and social advancement. In fact, parents' expectations were much closer to those of teachers than the teachers themselves realized.[2] The danger of assuming that respondents can report accurately on the expectations held by other people are also underlined by Biddle and his associates, who found a tendency on the part of respondents to attribute to people in general, expectations of the teacher which they themselves did not hold. Moreover there was a consistent tendency for respondents to report other people as more restrictive than they really are.[3] Consequently, these findings do much to confirm the need for studies of actual situations of the kinds of interaction that go on between parents and the schools.

Other local community influences which are likely to exert pressure either on school board members, or on school superintendents, or on both, include local business and commercial organizations, tax-paying associations, the press, churches and political pressure-groups. At the same time Gross's study indicates the extent to which individuals bring pressure to bear for purely personal reasons. Once again we have far too few studies which analyse these pressures and assess their influence. Vidich and Bensman, however, describe the way in which local businessmen unsuccessfully attempted to coerce the school into supporting local shops rather than patronizing lower-priced firms elsewhere. Business and taxpayer interests have, however, ensured that a low-tax low-expenditure ideology has dominated school board policy.

Baron and Tropp[4] have drawn a very strong contrast between the power of the local community in the United States and in England. 'Whereas in England it is the teacher who represents to the community in which he works "nationally" accepted values, in America it is the community that interprets to the teacher the task he is to perform.'

[1] Jenkins, D. H. and Lippitt, R. *Interpersonal Perceptions of Teachers, Students and Parents*, Washington D.C.: Division of Adult Education Services, National Education Association, 1951.

[2] Musgrove, F. and Taylor, P. 'Teachers' and Parents' Conceptions of the Teachers' Role', *British Journal of Educational Psychology*, vol. XXXV, 1965.

[3] Biddle, B. J., Rosencranz, H. A. and Rankin, E. F. *Studies in the Role of the Public School Teacher*, Social Psychological Laboratory, University of Missouri, 1961, vol. V.

[4] Baron, G. and Tropp, A. 'Teachers in England and America', in Halsey, Floud, Anderson, *op. cit.*, pp. 545–57.

This fundamental difference flows in large part from differences in the administrative structure. In England, as we have seen, the educational system is, in contrast to the United States, highly centralized, and the Department of Education and Science exercises a fairly close supervision over many aspects of school policy. At the local level, moreover, education is in the hands, not of locally elected school boards, but of general-purpose local authorities elected very largely upon national party lines and pursuing national rather than local policies. The effect, Baron and Tropp argue, is to insulate the schools from popular pressure at the local level.

Nor is the English parent so likely to exert pressure on the schools. Parent–Teacher Associations are not only less common but, when they do exist, appear to have more limited functions. Moreover they are often strongly opposed by head teachers, who fear that they will lead to interference by parents in the working of the school. A recent study of West Ham for example concluded 'that the hostility of the Head Teachers towards Parent–Teacher Associations is the decisive factor in their virtual absence from the local sphere of influence'.[1] In Reading, too, Parents' Associations are severely limited to fund raising and social activities. 'In the main when there is interest in the school, heads try to channel it into fields other than the actual courses given in the school. The nearest approach to pressure arose when the Parents' Association of one school which was to have new buildings went to the M.P. when the school was repeatedly expunged from the building programme. This is not to say that there have not been attempts to found more ambitious types of associations, but they have been very definitely discouraged.'[2]

If, however, pressure groups at the local level appear to be less influential in England than in the United States, there is some evidence that pressure groups at the national level are stronger. It is at least arguable, for example, that national political parties exert considerably more influence in England, partly because of their role in local elections, but chiefly because of the greater amount of central control exercised in the English system. The return of a Liberal government in 1906, for example, resulted in the 1907 Free Place Regulations, which were an

---

[1] Peschek, D. and Brand, J. 'Policies and Politics in Secondary Education: Case Studies in West Ham and Reading', *Greater London Papers No. 11*, London School of Economics, 1966, p. 47. See also Mays, J. B. *Education and the Urban Child*, *op. cit.*, pp. 49–55.

[2] Peschek, D. and Brand, J. *op. cit.*, p. 101.

attempt to widen the rather narrow scholarship ladder, and to make the secondary schools accessible to all classes of the community. The first Labour government also set up the Hadow Committee, which reported in favour of secondary education for all.[1] Perhaps the most interesting illustration of the effect of party politics on English education is, however, the controversy since the 1944 Education Act, on the organization of secondary education. The Conservative party, both in office and in opposition, has consistently favoured the continuation of the grammar school, and has approved the setting up of comprehensive schools only where no existing grammar school was thereby endangered. The Labour party, on the other hand, has tended to favour the comprehensive school. Moreover, opinion within the party has gradually hardened against the selective system, in favour of a gradual changeover to a comprehensive system.

It has also been argued very convincingly that the Church in England has operated as a particularly powerful and influential pressure group.[2] In the United States the parochial schools are independent of the public educational system and have little or no support from public funds. Nor is religious teaching allowed within the public system. This is in quite striking contrast to the situation in England, where parochial schools receive very generous financial aid in return for some measure of local authority control. Certain schools, known as controlled schools, have transferred all their financial liabilities to the local education authority while retaining minority representation and a limited amount of denominational teaching. Moreover, apart from the favoured position of parochial schools, all schools within the State system are required to give religious instruction according to an agreed syllabus drawn up by representatives of local religious interests, of teachers, and of the local authority.

One other interesting comparison between the two countries is the much greater extent to which English teachers are able to influence educational policy. Tropp, for example, has drawn attention to the considerable influence of the National Union of Teachers, not only on such professional matters as salaries, pensions and tenure, but also

[1] For an analysis of political-party influences on English secondary education since the 1890s, see Banks, O., *op. cit.*

[2] Cannon, C. 'The Influence of Religion on Educational Policy 1902–1944', *British Journal of Educational Studies*, vol. XII, 1963–4. For a very full discussion of the relationship between Church and State see Bereday, G. and Lauwerys, J. 'Church and State in Education', *The World Year Book of Education, 1966*, London: Evans Bros., 1966.

upon many issues of national policy. It was, for example, in the fore-front of the opposition to the system of 'payment by results', which did so much harm to elementary education in the nineteenth century, and was one of the early supporters of the doctrine of secondary education for all.[1]

Peschek, in his study of secondary education in West Ham, has also illustrated how teachers' organizations can operate as a powerful local pressure group. Indeed, surveying the influence of the West Ham Teachers' Association over a number of years, Peschek concludes that no major changes in local education authority policy have taken place in West Ham without consultation with the Teachers' Association.[2] This is in marked contrast to the United States, where teachers' organizations appear to be weak even in their influence on matters of great professional concern. Lieberman has argued that 'it is safe to assert that teachers' organizations ordinarily have little influence in shaping employer policies or in preventing unwarranted interference in educational matters by other groups'.[3]

3 The role of the administrator

In spite of the informal pressures of community interests, formal control of the school system lies, of course, with the elected repre-sentatives. Bidwell, however, has suggested that in the United States the school boards are in fact relinquishing many of their administrative functions to the school superintendent. The important study by Gross, Mason and McEachern[4] into consensus amongst and between Massa-chusetts school superintendents and their school boards suggests that school superintendents and school board members perceive their roles differently, with each group tending to assign greater responsibility to its own position. The professional ideology of superintendents is one that restricts the role of the school board to a mainly fiscal responsibility, whereas school board members tend to see themselves as having wider

[1] Tropp, A. *The School Teachers*, London: Heinemann, 1956.

[2] Peschek, D. and Brand, J. *op. cit.*, pp. 41–5.

[3] Lieberman, M. 'The Influence of Teachers' Organizations upon American Education', in Henry, N. B. (ed.) *Social Forces Influencing American Education*, National Society for the Study of Education, 1961, pp. 182–202.

[4] Gross, N., Mason, W. and McEachern, A. W. *Explorations in Role Analysis: Studies of the School Superintendency Role*, New York: Wiley, 1958.

powers. This view is supported by a study made by Bowman[1] which indicates that it is the better-trained superintendents who hold the professional ideology. These findings suggest that there is considerable scope for role conflict, and it is unfortunate that we have so few studies of actual board–administrator interaction. At the same time there is evidence that the better-educated board members are themselves more likely to adhere to the professional view of their role. These same studies show that better-educated board members and better-trained superintendents are more likely to be found in the larger school systems. It is not altogether clear why this should be, and Bidwell has suggested that large systems may well recruit 'both school executives and board members whose personal attributes predispose them to the professional ideology'.[1]

If Bidwell is correct, such a selection process would considerably reduce the likelihood of conflict. Alternatively Kerr in a recent study has presented a picture of the school board member as relatively helpless when confronted with the expertise of the administrator. He argues that under some conditions, which may not be uncommon, school boards chiefly perform the function of legitimating the policies of the school system to the community. This is particularly likely to happen where the electorate through apathy fails to watch the behaviour of its representative after the election; under such circumstances the school board member easily becomes alienated from the public he is supposed to serve.[3]

Vidich and Bensman, on the other hand, describe a situation in which the school principal and the school board are in effect jockeying for power. As in the case of his handling of the P.T.A., this particular school principal adopted a strategy for handling the members of his board. On many issues the principal had taken power from the board on the basis of his administrative and manipulative skills, but he had at all times to carry the board with him and, on some matters, as for example the control of his teaching staff, he was forced to defer to the board. In contrast to this situation of disguised conflict, Vidich and Bensman also describe how the school board was able to dismiss a

[1] Bowman, T. R. 'Participation of Superintendents in School Board Decision Making', *Administrator's Notebook*, 1963, quoted in Bidwell, C. *op. cit.*, p. 998.
[2] Bidwell, C. *op. cit.*, p. 999.
[3] Kerr, N. D. 'The School Board as an Agency of Legitimation', *Sociology of Education*, vol. XXXVIII, 1964.

previous principal, without giving a reason, and in the teeth of opposition from the local community. It is clear that many more studies of this kind are badly needed.

English studies of the relationship between the local education committee and the chief education officer and his staff are few in number but are generally agreed that the elected representatives have a very limited part to play. J. M. Lee in his study of Cheshire has strongly emphasized the importance of the permanent officials in the administration of local government at the county level. This is a direct consequence of the scope and complexity of the tasks facing a local authority. Only those councillors who had educated themselves in the processes of a department's work were able to share in the taking of decisions. 'It is', he concludes, 'misleading to think of the County Council primarily as a body of elected representatives who make decisions of policy and then order officials to execute them. Although such a view constitutes the theory the reality is vastly different. It is better to regard the system of county government as a body of professional people, placed together in a large office at County Hall, who can call upon the services of representatives from all places throughout the area which they administer. Some of these representatives by sheer ability and drive make themselves indispensible to the successful working of the machine; others merely represent points of view which come into conflict with it.'[1]

Peschek, in his study of West Ham, also draws attention to the power of the officials, and in particular the Chief Education Officer. The education committee as such has little power and it is the members of certain key sub-committees such as the Schools Sub-committee who share power with the officials. In Reading the Director of Education has been a particularly powerful figure. 'Percy Taylor, who died suddenly in 1962, was looked up to as one of the best education officers Reading had ever known. He was an efficient administrator and had a great gift for getting people to like him and accept his way of looking at things. During his period of office there were few things on which the Education Committee did not take his advice. The whole of the Development Plan was his. . . . No question came up without leadership from Taylor. No building programme would be proposed but by Taylor. When some pressure group wanted something it was to Taylor

---

[1] Lee, J. M. *Social Leaders and Public Persons*, Oxford University Press, 1963, p. 214.

that they came and the Committee would largely take Taylor's judgement on whether or not to grant their request.'

If, however, the chief education officer appears as a powerful figure in English education, it must be noted that there are some ways in which he has less influence than his American counterpart. Not only is there a greater degree of State control in England, but the power of the administrator over the schools in his care is very strictly defined so as not to usurp the authority of the head of the school. Traditionally the headmaster or headmistress of an English school is expected to function as a leader rather than as a part of an administrative bureaucracy. All the teaching methods and procedures, all matters relating to curricula, the relationships with parents and the control of teachers and their duties are recognized as matters for the head to decide and education committees will rarely try to interfere. Moreover this view of the head is supported and encouraged by the central government and by the H.M.I.s, so that it is not easy for a local authority to take control, even if it wished to do so. This is in sharp contrast to the American school principal. 'By and large, the American school superintendent is responsible to his school board for all aspects of the education given in the schools of a city or district; school principals are his subordinates and he is expected to give leadership, whether autocratic or democratic in nature, in purely educational topics, such as curriculum-building and the evolution of appropriate teaching methods.'[1]

The balance of power between the 'politicians' and the 'bureaucrats' must also be taken into account at the State as well as at the local level, but on the whole the weight of the evidence would appear to favour the civil service.[2] This is illustrated above all by the career of the great Permanent Secretary, Robert Morant, whose influence, although it has been much misunderstood,[3] was nevertheless of far greater importance than any of the politicians under whom he served.[4] Although of course power ultimately lies with the political head of the government, and the influence of party decisions can be discerned within educational policy, there is no doubt that the general impression is one of continuity, and that changes, when they occur, are usually gradual rather than

[1] Baron, G. and Tropp, A. op. cit., p. 550.
[2] Brittan, S. The Treasury under the Tories, 1951–1964, Penguin Books, 1964.
[3] Kazamias, A. M. Politics, Society and Secondary Education in England, University of Pennsylvania Press, 1966, ch. 5.
[4] Eaglesham, E. J. R. The Foundation of Twentieth-Century Education in England, London: Routledge & Kegan Paul, 1967, pp. 90–2.

127

abrupt. The 20 years after 1944, for example, showed few variations in government educational policy according to either individual ministers or the party in power, even on such controversial party issues as comprehensive reorganization or the reform of the independent schools. In fact, of course, this is due to the superior expertise of the permanent civil servant, but it is undoubtedly exacerbated by the frequent changes in political appointments in many government departments.

It is very clear, therefore, that the question of who controls our schools is of considerable complexity. To locate the area of formal authority, whether it is at the local level as in the United States, or whether it is a 'partnership' as in England, is only the beginning of the search for the real seat of power. Groups, organizations and even individuals may operate at both the local and the State level as powerful pressure groups, and can at times exert a profound influence upon educational development. Moreover although the elected representatives may have the legal responsibility, in practice this power frequently passes into the hands of the administrator. The conditions under which this is likely to occur are not really known, but the scale of the administrative unit and the complexity of the task appear to be the crucial variables. Indeed any circumstances which lead to apathy on the part of the electorate and ignorance on the part of the elected representatives favour the bureaucracy, as of course Max Weber pointed out many years ago.

Nor does a highly centralized system such as that of France or the U.S.S.R. necessarily mean that all decisions are made by the formal authority. Not only is there likely to be a struggle for power between the various interests involved at the central as distinct from the local level, but there will also be the possibility of conflict between the central authority and the schools. At the same time the relative autonomy of the classroom situation itself makes it likely that the teacher will enjoy a certain amount of freedom even in a highly centralized system. What is needed therefore is more research into the decision-making process in education at all levels down to, and including, that of the school itself.

7 The teaching profession

1 Development of the profession

In any attempt to construct a sociology of the school, a study of the teacher must at all times have a central place. The crucial position of the teacher in the educational process has indeed been widely recognized, and studies of teachers as a group have been fairly widespread, so that we now have a fair amount of knowledge of the characteristics of teachers in Britain and, to some extent, elsewhere. First, however, it is necessary to look briefly at the structure of teaching as an occupation, since, although it is customary nowadays to think of teaching as a unified profession, in reality teachers form a very diversified group. As Brookover and Gottlieb have pointed out, 'The range of teachers is very great. They teach in everything from kindergarten to graduate school; in schools supported by churches, by private corporations, by foundations, by taxpayers; on assignments ranging all the way from the entire first eight grades in one to private sessions with a student in need of individual attention. A roll call would include those engaged in such diverse activities as driver education, training prison inmates, rehabilitation of veterans, and work with the physically and emotionally handicapped, in addition to the countless specialities usually identified with the traditional teacher role.'[1] Brookover and Gottlieb are writing about the U.S.A. but the point they make is equally valid in Europe. Moreover these different types of teacher not only perform different roles: there are also frequently differences in remuneration, status, qualifications, sex, social-class background, and many other characteristics.

One of the most usual ways to categorize teachers is in terms of the

[1] Brookover, W. B. and Gottlieb, D. *A Sociology of Education*, *op. cit.*, pp. 299–300.

age-range of the pupils. Those teaching younger pupils in primary or elementary schools are distinguished in this way from those who teach in secondary schools, while those working in higher education form another and quite distinct category. An alternative system of classification is in terms of the subjects taught. The broad differentiation here is between academic and practical subjects. When this is combined with the age-level of the pupils, it gives us important subdivisions between teachers in different types of secondary school, or between various kinds of higher education. Yet a further distinction which has been of great importance historically is made in terms of the social origin of the pupils. This is particularly important where middle- or upper-class children are educated in separate schools. In addition, wherever State education has been provided, mainly for the children of the poor, there may be important distinctions between teachers in State and in independent schools.

Tropp has described the development in Britain during the nineteenth century of the new profession of elementary school teacher. Faced with the need to give the rudiments of education to the children of the poor, the demand was for a whole new army of teachers who could be provided at little cost. As Tropp puts it, 'in the 1830s and 1840s the great question was whether education could mitigate the dangers inherent in an ignorant industrial population or whether it would, by teaching the poor to read and write, make them a still greater danger to society. An important but secondary question was—who was to provide the education and what should be its nature? Once it was conceded that education should be extended to the poor through the medium of voluntary religious societies and that this education should be suffused with morality and religion, it became obvious that the main need was for a supply of efficient, religious and humble teachers.'[1]

The answer was found in the pupil-teacher system, a method of teacher training already practised on the continent. Under the pupil-teacher system the most intelligent and moral pupils of the elementary schools were apprenticed as pupil-teachers to the headmaster at the age of 13. During their five years' apprenticeship they received one and a half hours a day teaching from the headmaster and for the rest of their time acted as a teacher in the school. After five years of satis-

[1] Tropp, A. *The School Teachers*, London: Heinemann, 1957, p. 8.

factory service, those who were successful in a competitive examination were given scholarships for a further period of education in a Training College. A teacher's certificate, which carried the right to an augmented salary and a pension, was granted either on the successful completion of the Training College course or to those passing an external examination for practising teachers. The certificated teachers were, however, the elite of the profession. In 1855, for example, almost all certificated teachers had headships, and even at the end of the century a shortage of Training College places, especially for women, meant that not only were many teachers uncertificated, but that many of the certificated teachers were untrained.

The effect of the pupil-teacher system was to produce several generations of teachers who had been educated within an almost completely closed system. Only the period at Training College was, for those who achieved it, a break from the elementary school, and even this was an enclosed world within the elementary tradition. Moreover the educational background, even for the teacher who had been to Training College, was inevitable limited. For the rest, 'it was impossible to expect a high proportion of "cultured" teachers from pupil-teacherdom with its one and a half hours of instruction a day, after a hard day's work, and with a tired teacher and tired pupil-teachers',[1] especially when we remember that full-time education for these young people had ended at the age of 13. As befitted their social origin and limited educational background, teachers were expected to be humble, to show gratitude for the 'charity' to which they owed their education and training, and to refrain from any excessive ambition to improve their lot.[2] Indeed, during the middle years of the century in particular teachers were constantly under fire for their conceit and ambition. A particular cause of complaint was the teacher who after training used his education to move into a better-paid job.

At the other extreme from the elementary school teachers were the masters at the major public schools. 'The task of a master in a public school was to teach the classics to the sons of the upper class and to those who were being educated with them. He had to be acceptable both to the parents and to the headmaster on academic and personal

---

[1] *Ibid.*, pp. 24–5.
[2] The Newcastle Commission Report, for example, pointed out that 'boys who would otherwise go out to work at mechanical trades at twelve or thirteen years of age, are carefully educated at the public expense'. Reported in Tropp, A. *op. cit.*, p. 72.

grounds, and his background was a matter of some importance.'[1] Not only was an Oxford or Cambridge degree almost essential but there was a tendency on the part of public schools to recruit from amongst their own boys, which reached an extreme form at Eton. According to Bamford, 74 per cent of those appointed to Eton between 1801 and 1862 were old Eton boys. In the main the masters at the major public schools were of middle-class professional origin, and the headmasters often came from eminent families.

The high status of the public school master was maintained not only by means of his educational background but also by his connection with the Church. Until the second half of the nineteenth century it was customary for the masters as well as the head to be clergymen. 'The first significant number of lay appointments for Eton, Harrow and Rugby occurred in the 1850s but not till 1870 for Shrewsbury.'[2]

The position of the headmaster was particularly important. Not only was he in complete control of his school and its staff, but he enjoyed great prestige outside the school. Moreover, even after the introduction of laymen as masters, the headmaster remained a clergyman. Frequently, too, the headship of a major public school was only a 'stepping stone to higher things'.[3] Promotions to deaneries and bishoprics were common, and even an archbishopric was by no means out of the question.

It was customary too for the headship to command a high income even where the assistant masters were poorly paid. Indeed, in spite of their qualifications, assistant masters in all but the top public schools were frequently not only very badly paid but had little hope of promotion. In such schools the turnover of staff was often high. Moreover, below the ranks of the public schools, in the endowed grammar schools and preparatory schools, salaries were so poor that frequently the master looked jealously at 'the rapid improvements which were being made in the training and education of the masters of schools of a lower grade'.[4] Nevertheless, even if poorly paid, the grammar school teachers shared in the public school rather than the elementary school tradition and enjoyed a higher status than elementary school teachers.

The completely separate elementary tradition did not, however,

[1] Bamford, T. W. *The Rise of the Public Schools*, London: Nelson, 1967, p. 120.
[2] *Ibid.*, p. 55.
[3] *Ibid.*, p. 150.
[4] Tropp, A. *op. cit.*, p. 40.

outlast the nineteenth century. Modifications to the system had started in the 1880s with the development of pupil-teacher centres in the large towns, where pupil-teachers were taught in central classes. At the same time attempts were made to improve the teaching in the Training Colleges and to bring them into closer contact with the universities. Gradually, however, educational opinion was moving away from the view that elementary education needed to be narrow or rudimentary, and with this change in attitude towards the nature of the education to be provided came severe criticism of the systems of teacher-training and the teachers it had trained. Instead of the pupil-teacher centres, *The Report of the Departmental Committee on the Pupil Teacher System* of 1898 'looked forward with confidence to the use of secondary schools as the best means of overcoming that narrowness of intellectual and professional outlook which had long been felt to be one of the weakest points of the profession and which, it can hardly be doubted, was largely due to the inhuman and deadening influences under which generations of pupil-teachers had been educated.'[1] With the reorganization of secondary education that followed the 1902 Act normal entrance to the elementary teaching profession was only through the secondary school.

The immediate effect of this change of policy was tragic for the existing teachers. Branded as 'uncultured and imperfectly educated—creatures of tradition and routine',[2] they were considered as no longer fit even for those posts in the inspectorate and the training colleges that they had previously held. At the same time the higher-grade work which had been developed in the elementary schools in the 1880s and 90s was transferred to the new secondary system, which tended to be staffed by teachers from secondary or public schools. Even in the long term the ending of the pupil-teacher system did not remove the cleavage within the profession. In practice the elementary school teacher continued to be recruited from the training colleges and the secondary school teacher from the universities. 'Until the 1940s', asserts Tropp, 'only unemployment could drive the graduate into the elementary school.'[3] The abolition of the elementary system in 1944 was a further and indeed a major step in the unification of the profession, but the elementary tradition is still perpetuated, partly by the distinctions

[1] Quoted *ibid.*, pp. 165–6.
[2] Quoted *ibid.*, p. 271.
[3] *Ibid.*, p. 194.

operating within secondary education, and partly by the continuation of the college training. These differences, which will be examined in more detail later in this chapter, perpetuate many aspects of the dual system even within the framework of a unified profession.

The development of teacher training in Britain has been described at length because it is paralleled in general terms, if not in detail, in all the European countries and in other parts of the world. The education of the poor, that is to say, has developed separately from the education of the elite. Whereas secondary education has always had close ties with the universities in its outlook and its subject-matter and has had as its function the transmission of 'culture', elementary education in its origin at least was simply intended to 'gentle the masses'. Consequently whereas the teacher in the secondary school needed to be educated in the full sense of the word, the elementary school teacher had only to be trained. Primarily, it was the limited conception of the education of the masses which entailed the narrowness of the education and training of their teachers, and only as the standards expected of elementary education have risen do we find any major changes in the pattern of teacher training. Thus the normal schools of continental Europe were designed as institutions parallel to the academic secondary school, giving some limited general education and some practical training for teaching. For example, in the normal schools set up in France by a decree of 1833, the sons of small farmers and manual labourers were trained as elementary teachers. 'They received a moral and religious education, lessons in reading, grammar and practical geometry. They were given some notions of the everyday applications of science, of French history and geography. They were shown how to draw up certificates of births, deaths and marriages, and how to graft and prune trees. They were initiated into teaching method by attending the primary schools attached to the *Écoles Normales*.'[1]

Gradually the level of education in the normal schools was improved and entrance standards were raised, but frequently they have remained a separate system, recruiting from elementary rather than secondary schools. In France the *école normale* has remained as a parallel to the academic secondary school although, since the war, the rigid separation between elementary and secondary education has ended. It is, for

[1] Thabault, R. 'The Professional Training of Teachers in France', *Year Book of Education*, 1963, London: Evans Bros., 1963, pp. 244–5.

example, possible now for a student at normal school to prepare for the *baccalauréat* and pass on to a university, or for a pupil from the *lycée* to enter elementary school teaching after a shortened course at the normal school. In Germany the situation prevailing at the present time is much nearer to the English system. The *Pedagogische Hochschule*, which prepares for elementary school teaching, demands as an entry qualification the leaving certificate of the academic secondary school or its equivalent but, like the English training colleges, it is not yet a full part of the university structure.

In the United States the progress towards a unified system of teacher-training has gone much further than anywhere in Europe, even though standards initially were just as low, and improvements during the nineteenth century were no faster than in Britain. Normal schools were founded from the 1830s onwards, but the growth in their numbers was very slow. Moreover, like their European counterparts, entry requirements were so low that one of their main functions was to complete the pupils' secondary education. Many went straight into teaching on leaving school. Improvements in teacher-training in the United States have occurred chiefly in the present century, and it is in this period too that the system has moved away from the European pattern. In 1910 two-year normal schools were common, following after two years or less at a high school. By 1930 the normal schools were being supplanted by teachers' colleges organized to provide a three- or four-year programme and asking for four years of high-school preparation. Today a bachelor's degree representing four years of preparation beyond high school is almost universally required, and the teachers' colleges are themselves undergoing transformation into multi-purpose institutions.[1] An even more important development is that elementary and secondary teachers are frequently trained in the same institutions, although secondary school teachers are usually expected to have higher qualifications.

In attempting to understand the reasons for the direction taken by teachers' education in the United States, the absence of a distinctive elementary and secondary tradition must take pride of place. The early appearance of the comprehensive high school, and its dominance in the field of secondary education, has meant that all prospective teachers pass together through the high school. At the same time the

---

[1] Stiles, L. J. *et al. Teacher Education in the United States*, New York: Ronald Press, 1960.

meaning of secondary education has been altered. It is no longer a selective education, preparing a minority for elite status, but must cater for the needs of all children. Moreover, the frequent absence of streaming and setting in the schools, and the existence of many small schools, means that the specialist subject-teacher is rare in the American context. Consequently, not only has much greater attention been paid to teaching methods in the training of secondary school teachers, but their education is much less subject-centred than is customary in Europe. Bachelors' degrees held by both elementary and secondary teachers are normally degrees in Education. Indeed critics of the American teacher-training system frequently argue that American teachers are inadequately prepared for academic teaching.[1]

The scope and flexibility of American higher education also makes it easier to integrate it with teachers' education than is likely to be possible in most of Europe, where university teachers often show resistance to a closer relationship with teacher-training institutions. This is partly because of the greater willingness in the United States to accept practical and vocational subjects as part of higher education. At the same time, the existence of what Riesman calls the academic procession allows an aspiring teachers' college to turn itself into a multi-purpose college or university. Consequently, even if the education of teachers frequently has less prestige than other kinds of higher education, this is not a distinction which creates a rigid barrier within the profession.

Teachers in universities in Britain are not normally regarded as members of the same professional group as school teachers, although they share with the public school teachers the same origin within the Church. Changes in Oxford and Cambridge and the growth of the newer universities has ended the relationship with the Church, but university teachers are still recruited on the basis of their ability as scholars, even if notions of scholarship have now widened to include science and technology. Recruits to the profession are not trained in teaching methods, nor is ability in teaching a criterion, and achievement in scholarship or research is the most important ingredient in professional success. In this sense the image of the scholar or, increasingly, the scientist, is dominant over that of the teacher.

---

[1] See, for example, Conant, J. B. *The Education of American Teachers*, New York McGraw-Hill, 1963.

At the same time there have been quite rigid distinctions between teachers in universities and teachers in other forms of higher education in terms of qualification and pattern of recruitment. The teaching staff in colleges of education, for example, have been recruited principally from the ranks of practising teachers,[1] and have for this reason tended to represent the higher reaches of the teaching profession, rather than to link up with the university teachers either in interests and attitudes or in their sense of identity. The technical college teacher has also been quite sharply differentiated, in part by the tradition of part-time teachers, in part by the emphasis on industrial experience. Technical colleges also seem to attract recruits from school teaching, although not of course to the same extent as the colleges of education. At the same time the range of work carried out in technical colleges means that the qualifications of the staff vary accordingly, and nowadays, although many, especially of those doing advanced work, hold degrees or degree equivalents, others hold lower qualifications such as the H.N.C. or craft qualification.[2] In no sense, therefore, can we talk of teachers of higher education as a single group.

In the United States, in contrast, the structure of higher education does not allow for differentiation of quite this kind, although, as we have seen, there is a distinct tendency for status distinctions to occur between departments and also between institutions, according to their position in what Riesman has called the academic procession. Nevertheless, teachers of higher education can be and are viewed as a single group in a way that is at present impossible in Britain.

However, the pattern of recruitment to college teaching in the United States still has much in common with the more elitist European tradition from which it sprang, and entry to the profession is still governed entirely by academic qualifications. This emphasis is supported by the pattern of doctorate training which is now the major pathway for entry into the profession, for very few PH.D. programmes include any provision for teacher training and they can be viewed essentially as apprenticeships in research.[3] At the same time the main promotion opportunities arise as a result of publication and research.[4] Indeed it could be argued that there is even less emphasis on the teaching

---

[1] *Report of the Committee on Higher Education* (Robbins Report), 1963, Appendix 3, p. 92.
[2] *Ibid.*, pp. 117–9.
[3] Berelson, B. *Graduate Education in the United States,* New York: McGraw-Hill, 1960.
[4] Caplow, T. and McGee, R. J. *The Academic Marketplace,* New York: Basic Books, 1958.

function in the United States than in Britain. The effect of this is not only to differentiate college teachers from school teachers, but to emphasize loyalty to the discipline rather than to the profession as such, with implications that will be discussed in a later section.

At the same time the very rapid development of college education in the United States since 1900 has meant an enormously rapid expansion in the number of college teachers, so that they now represent a vast and historically unique professional class in American society.[1] The consequences of this enormous expansion are likely to be very far-reaching both for the standards of the profession and for its status in the community. Some of these implications will be taken up later in the chapter.

2 The social-class background of teachers

The social origin of the teaching profession is closely related to the method of recruitment, and the availability of training. As we have seen already the pupil-teacher system in nineteenth-century England was an important avenue of social mobility for the clever and ambitious working-class child. At the same time the lowly social origins of the elementary school teachers was a factor in the low status given to the teaching profession. Consequently it is of interest to examine the few studies which give us accurate information on the social origin of teachers. Fortunately, the study by Floud and Scott[2] based on a sample survey of teachers in England and Wales in 1955 provides us with a very detailed picture of the social origins of the profession, which confirms the impression received from earlier and smaller studies. Their results show clearly that although teachers are recruited from all levels of the status hierarchy they come predominantly from the lower middle and the skilled working classes. These overall figures however are less interesting than the differences which the study shows to exist within the profession. The following table,[3] sets out these differences as they occur not only between various types of school, but between men and women teachers.

[1] Knapp, R. H. 'Changing Functions of the College Professor', in Sanford, N. (ed.) *The American College*, *op. cit.*, p. 290.
[2] Floud, J. and Scott, W. 'Recruitment to Teaching in England and Wales', in Halsey, Floud, Anderson, *op. cit.*, pp. 527–44.
[3] *Ibid.*, Table 11 (adapted), p. 54.

Table Eleven

**Social origin of teachers in grant-earning schools,
England and Wales, 1955**

(A) MEN

Father's occupation when teacher left school	*Type of School*			
	Primary	Modern	Maintained grammar	Direct-grant grammar
	%	%	%	%
Professional and administrative	6·0	7·5	12·5	19·8
Intermediate	48·3	45·9	55·1	61·9
Manual, skilled	32·5	36·5	25·3	14·6
Manual, semi-and unskilled	13·2	10·1	7·1	4·0
All	100·0	100·0	100·0	100·0
(N)	1,251	1,178	1,209	544

(B) WOMEN

Professional and administrative	8·8	11·4	17·8	30·4
Intermediate	52·2	54·8	63·1	57·4
Manual, skilled	29·6	28·1	16·4	10·4
Manual, semi- and unskilled	9·3	5·7	2·7	1·8
All	100·0	100·0	100·0	100·0
(N)	1,449	1,083	1,100	733

It will be noticed that women teachers in all types of school, but particularly in grammar schools, have a higher social origin than men teachers. This undoubtedly reflects the greater alternatives open to men, and particularly to male graduates. Teaching still offers more opportunities to the educated girl than most other careers open to her. The other important distinction is between those schools inheriting the elementary tradition and those still influenced by the secondary tradition. The social origin of the teachers is quite considerably higher in the grammar schools than in either the primary or secondary modern schools. The difference between the maintained grammar and direct-grant grammar is an interesting reflection of the relationships generally found between the social class of the pupils and of their teachers. Nevertheless, although teachers of working-class origin are rare in the direct-grant grammar schools, it is true for these schools, as for the rest, that the largest group of teachers are from the lower middle classes.

Floud and Scott have also tried to trace changes in the recruitment of teachers by means of a comparison between cohorts of teachers entering the profession at different periods. Such a comparison shows remarkably little change in the proportion of elementary school teachers from working-class families entering the profession before 1920 and of those entering since 1945. On the other hand, there has been a fairly steady decline in the social-class origin of grammar school teachers. In the case of men teachers this has mainly taken the form of a decline in those entering from the professional and administrative classes, but for women teachers there has been in addition an increase in those entering from manual-worker families.

It is more difficult to get comparable information from the United States. According to Brookover and Gottlieb, 'most studies of the social class background of teachers do not provide us with a foundation for generalizations about teachers across the nation'.[1] The studies available to us, however, suggest that the social background of teachers in the United States does not differ very profoundly from that of Britain, and that, although a sizeable minority are from working-class families, the largest group are those from the lower middle classes. There is also evidence that women teachers have a higher social origin than men teachers. On the other hand, although secondary school teachers are frequently expected to have higher qualifications than elementary school teachers, there is no evidence that they are of a higher social origin. Indeed a study by Carlson[2] suggests that the reverse is true. He found that female elementary school teachers had the highest social origins, and male secondary school teachers the lowest. As many as 48 per cent of male secondary teachers, according to his study, are from the working or lower classes as compared with 23 per cent of female elementary school teachers. While these findings may not be typical of the United States as a whole, and while they may conceal important differences within secondary education, they do lend

---

[1] Brookover, W. B. and Gottlieb, D., *op. cit.*, p. 309.
[2] Carlson, R. O. 'Variations and Myth in the Social Status of Teachers', *Journal of Educational Sociology*, vol. XXXV, November 1951, pp. 104–18.

support to the impression that the United States system has avoided the stigma of the elementary tradition.

This is not to assert, of course, that differentiation is absent from the American teaching profession, any more than it is absent from the American school system. Rather it is less institutionalized than in Europe with its sponsored mobility and selective secondary school. It may well be, for example, that there are differences in social origin within schools between teachers trained in different ways or teaching different subjects. There also seems to be differentiation between schools of the same type according to the social characteristics of the pupils. There is some evidence, for example, of 'a tendency for Negro teachers to be placed in schools where there are strong concentrations of Negro youth',[1] and it may well be that teachers of working-class origin are to be found predominantly in working-class schools. Becker, for example, in his study of the Chicago public school teacher found that one major career pattern consists in moving from the lower-class school, in which teaching begins, to a school with a higher proportion of middle-class pupils.[2]

Becker's findings are reinforced to some extent by the recent study by Herriott and St. John. They report that teachers in schools where the pupils are in the lowest socio-economic status come from a background 'which can be characterized as more urban, more "blue collar", with less formal education and lower incomes than those of the teachers from schools of highest socio-economic status.'[3] Of these differences, however, only those relating to the type of community and father's occupation were statistically significant. Moreover, nowhere are the differences extreme. In the case of father's occupation, for example, 30 per cent of teachers in schools of high socio-economic status, and 43 per cent of teachers in schools of low socio-economic status had fathers in 'blue collar' occupations. Thus, even in schools where the majority of pupils were from low-status families, the majority of teachers had come from 'white collar' homes.

The social origin of college and university teachers is to some extent governed by the social background of the college and university student and, as we have seen, this is likely to be predominantly middle class in

[1] Brookover, W. B. and Gottlieb, D. *op. cit.*, p. 310.
[2] Becker, H. S. 'The Career of the Chicago Public School Teacher', *American Journal of Sociology*, vol. LVII, p. 952.
[3] Herriott, R. E. and St. John, W. H. *Social Class and the Urban School*, New York: Wiley, 1966, pp. 70-4.

character even in countries like the United States. There is, however, some evidence that American college teachers are of lower social origin than other comparable professional groupings.[1] This is probably because of the emphasis placed upon academic distinction rather than social and financial considerations in recruitment to the profession. It is likely, however, that as in the case of school teachers there are considerable differences in social origin of college teachers both nationally and between different types of institution. Wilson, for example, writing in 1942, compared the American college teacher 'with the new quasi-proletarian intelligentsia of the U.S.S.R.' rather than with the 'aristocratically inclined university staff of pre-Nazi Germany'.[2] It is very likely, too, that in Britain university teachers have a higher social origin than those teaching in other forms of higher education. We should also expect to find that the differences in student composition between Oxford and Cambridge and the provincial universities are also reflected in the social origin of their teaching staffs.

3 The status of the teacher

The social origin of any occupational group both reflects and is a reflection of the status of the group; and undoubtedly the social origin of the teachers is a reflection above all of the ambiguity of their status, which needs to contain the two traditions: the teacher of the rich and the teacher of the poor. Undoubtedly the status of the grammar school teacher, in Britain as in Europe generally is higher than that of the elementary school teacher, yet in judging the profession as a whole it is the influence of the elementary tradition which seems to be the stronger. The Registrar General, for example, places school teachers in Class II, the Intermediate class, and not in the category of higher administrative or professional employees in Class I. Similarly, the London School of Economics, in its study of social mobility, found that the elementary school teacher was ranked by members of the general public alongside the news reporter, the commercial traveller and the jobbing master builder, but below a non-conformist minister, and certainly below the traditional professions.[3]

[1] Knapp, R. H., op. cit., p. 297.
[2] Wilson, L. The Academic Man, London University Press, 1942, p. 19.
[3] Glass, D. V. (ed.) Social Mobility in Britain, op. cit., p. 34.

In the United States, too, the status of the teacher is an intermediate one. In 1947, in a study of the status of various occupations, the National Opinion Research Centre found that the school teacher was ranked in public opinion surveys only slightly above the average. Indeed, Lieberman in a critical survey of the teaching profession in the United States concludes that 'teachers are finding it more difficult than ever before to maintain their present intermediate status, let alone raise it to the level of such occupational groups as doctors and lawyers'.[1] Moreover, even though teacher-training is now carried out more and more frequently in multi-purpose institutions, Conant, amongst others, has pointed to the low esteem in which degrees in education are generally held.[2] It is therefore worth looking closely at some of the factors influencing the present status of teaching as an occupation.

One of the major problems facing the teaching profession is its very rapid rate of expansion. At first this affected only the elementary school teacher, and we have already examined some of the effects of this expansion on recruitment and training. During the twentieth century, however, secondary and, later, higher education have experienced rapid development and, although the United States was affected earlier and more profoundly, since the last war there have been rapid increases in both secondary and further education in most European countries. Both the scale and the rapidity of the expansion have meant that there has been an almost continuous shortage of qualified personnel to staff the schools, and at all times, but particularly during periods of rapid expansion, the profession has included large numbers of un-qualified teachers. In the nineteenth century the proportion of un-qualified women teachers was as high or higher than those who were qualified, and even in 1900 as many as 40 per cent of teachers in elementary schools were not qualified.[3] During the twentieth century, however, standards in elementary school teaching have risen con-siderably, and a survey in 1962 by the National Union of Teachers found that only six per cent of teachers in primary schools were unqualified. However, this figure appears to be rising.[4] On the other hand teaching, even secondary school teaching, is a long way from

[1] Lieberman, M. *Education as a Profession*, Englewood Cliffs, N.J.: Prentice-Hall, 1956, p. 480.
[2] Conant, J. B., *op. cit.*, ch. 1.
[3] Tropp, A. *op.c it.*, p. 262.
[4] *Children and their Primary Schools*, Report of the Central Advisory Council for Educa-tion (England), 1967, vol. I, p. 315.

being a graduate profession. Although the majority of teachers in grammar schools are graduates, this is true of only a minority in the secondary modern schools, who are still recruited in large part from the training colleges. The N.U.T. survey found 20·2 per cent of graduates amongst men teachers in secondary modern schools and 13·0 per cent of graduates amongst the women. In maintained grammar schools they were 81·5 per cent and 72·7 per cent, respectively. Primary schools are staffed almost entirely by non-graduates.[1]

In the United States the teacher shortage is more serious and the problem of unqualified staff more acute. We have already noticed the low level of education of elementary school teachers, which lasted into the early years of the present century. Even as late as 1908 a study of 735 high-school graduates in the State of New York showed 117 of them directly entering teaching, as compared with 122 going to the normal schools.[2] The very rapid increase in the number of high schools at the end of the nineteenth century also produced a similar problem in the secondary schools. Indeed it has been estimated that the development of high schools had outrun the available supply of college-trained teachers as early as the 1870s and 80s, and the situation was to worsen later. Moreover, there were substantial variations even among neighbouring states.[3]

From the 1920s the level of education of school teachers gradually improved, but so did the standards expected of the profession, so that the number of unqualified teachers continued to be high. Moreover, since the 1940s there has been a serious shortage of teachers, which has accentuated the problem. Consequently although the great majority of teachers in elementary as well as secondary schools by the 1950s had a bachelor's or higher degree, in 1955 'there was not a single state in which every elementary teacher possessed at least four years of college training'.[4]

Consequently, as Lieberman points out, although the higher requirements now expected of teachers 'may eventually help to raise the status of education as a profession, the present status of education as a

[1] Blyth, W. A. L. *English Primary Education*, London: Routledge & Kegan Paul, 1965, vol. I, pp. 158–9.
[2] Quoted in Krug, E. A. *The Shaping of the American High School*, New York: Harper & Row, 1964, p. 289n.
[3] *Ibid.*, p. 187.
[4] Lieberman, M. *op. cit.*, p. 134.

profession is based chiefly upon the much lower requirements in force during the past four decades.'[1]

Another problem for the teachers is that although their educational level is rising, so is that, not only of other professional occupations, but of the population in general. Consequently the improvements in the last 50 years have enabled teachers to maintain their status but not necessarily to improve it. This is particularly true in the United States, where the meaning of a bachelor's degree has changed radically, due to the rapid expansion in higher education. In Britain, however, as in Europe generally, expansion in higher education has been at a much slower rate, and it seems likely that the improvements in the educational background of the school teachers has done more to improve their status than have the even greater improvements in teacher education in the United States.

A further characteristic of the teaching profession which is closely related to its status is the balance within it of male and female teachers. The proportions of women in elementary school teaching in the United States is so high that it can be reasonably described as a woman's occupation. A survey made by the National Education Association in 1956 found only 14 per cent of elementary school teachers to be men. Teachers in secondary education are, however, fairly evenly balanced between men and women.[2] Altogether about 75 per cent of all school teachers in the United States are women.[3] This preponderance of women has characterized the profession since the end of the nineteenth century. Men, however, predominate in educational administration, including the post of school principal.

The proportion of women in education in the United States is probably greater than anywhere else in the world. In Britain, for example, although the proportion of women teachers is higher than in many European countries including France and Germany,[4] it is less than in the United States. About three-quarters of teachers in primary schools are women and roughly half of those in secondary schools. This is another reason to believe that the status of teachers in Britain and in Europe generally, is higher than in the United States.

---

[1] *Ibid.*, p. 130.
[2] Reported in Brookover, W. B. and Gottlieb, D. *op. cit.*, p. 313.
[3] Lieberman, M. *op. cit.*, p. 242, Table 14.
[4] Hans, N. 'Status of Women Teachers', *Year Book of Education, 1953*, quoted in Lieberman, M. *op. cit.*, p. 244, Table 15.

One of the main reasons why teaching can still attract women into the profession when it is hard to recruit men, lies in the lack of alternatives open to the educated woman, even when there are many such alternatives available for a man with similar qualifications. Not only is the salary scale favourable in comparison with what she could earn elsewhere, but working conditions, hours and holidays are often not only reasonable in themselves but fit in well with the responsibilities of a family. The profession is, therefore, particularly attractive to the girl who is looking for a job she can return to after she is married.

The fact that many women in the profession see it as a temporary job rather than as a permanent career also has a profound effect on their expectations. The initial salary, the length of training, the possibility of re-joining the profession after a break of several years: all of these considerations are of more importance than ultimate salary or promotion possibilities. Consequently, the aspects of jobs which deter potential male recruits may not appear as disadvantages at all to many of the women entering the profession.

At the same time, the very appeal of the profession to women may diminish its attractiveness to men; for once any occupation becomes accepted as a woman's job, the idea grows that it is unsuitable for a man. According to Brookover and Gottlieb, 'teaching is associated with motherhood, with the training and socialization of the young, and with the protection of the needy. So firmly entrenched is this popular image in our society that it becomes difficult for a man who wants to enter the field to withstand the social pressures against doing so. The authors have talked with numerous college girls who are majoring in elementary education and find that few of them would be willing to consider as a husband a man who makes teaching his life's work.'[1]

The size of the teaching profession is also an important factor in the status it is awarded and, particularly, in the extent to which it can expect high rewards for its services. The cost of maintaining a well-qualified and highly-paid teaching profession in the context of mass secondary education and an expanding system of higher education requires the backing of a community which is not only wealthy, but highly committed to education and willing to spend generously on the public services. The United States, with its tradition of private affluence

[1] Brookover, W. B. and Gottlieb, D. *op. cit.*, pp. 312-3.

and public squalor, is not likely to be willing to reward the large number of school teachers on the same level as the doctors. Lieberman has calculated that in the year 1954–5 equalizing teachers' salaries with the incomes of doctors would have required a sum larger than the total amount spent upon public education in that school year.

The rapid expansion in the number of teachers also makes it difficult to maintain the standards of entrants not only, as we have seen, in the short run but, as the size of the profession goes on increasing, equally in the long term. Indeed Lieberman has suggested that *already* in the United States within the limits of the country's resources of skilled manpower it is doubtful if additional teachers can be secured without lowering the qualifications for teaching. It is true that the present shortage of skilled manpower must be seen within the context of a considerable waste of ability, but in the absence of any immediate expectation of solving this problem it is difficult to see how the current teacher shortage is going to be met. Lieberman's own solution is essentially a more efficient use of teachers, both by the development of a more advanced educational technology, and by changes in the organization of the teaching role. In particular, he advocates the utilization of semi-professional assistants on the model of the medical profession. Pointing out the routine nature of many of the teachers' activities, he suggests that the use of assistants by teachers to carry out routine tasks would permit larger salaries to be paid to the professionals.

On the other hand, the teaching profession also suffers, as Bryan Wilson[1] has pointed out, from the high level of diffuseness of the teaching role. The roles of the doctor or the lawyer, for example, are easier to define; there is a definable expertise involving an objective body of knowledge which is almost completely lacking in the case of teaching. It is true that teachers sometimes attempt to claim such a body of knowledge, and in the United States in particular there has been a widespread development of courses in 'education', but such courses have not yet met with general acceptance as either desirable or even necessary for the intending teacher. Conant,[2] for example, points out that 'many academic professors believe that the courses given by professors of education are worthless'. In Britain, teachers in grammar schools frequently have had no training for teaching at all.

---

[1] Wilson, B. 'The Teacher's Role—a Sociological Analysis', *British Journal of Sociology*, vol. XIII (1) 1962, pp. 15–32.
[2] Conant, J. B. *op. cit.*, p. 7.

Consequently there is a tendency for teachers to fall back on the subjects they are qualified to teach, and where this is a highly esoteric body of knowledge in its own right, teachers can often command high prestige. Yet such a ranking system, by confusing the difficulty of a subject with the difficulty of teaching it, does less than justice to the role of the primary school teachers and, indeed, to the whole primary stage of the education process as well as to the education of the less able child. The development of teaching skills is therefore vitally necessary for the education process itself as well as for the status of the teacher. Although prejudice is an important factor in the attitude to courses in 'education' as a part of teacher-training, there is no doubt that some of the criticisms of educational courses are valid[1] and that on the whole this aspect of teacher-education has serious weaknesses, many of which spring from the relatively underdeveloped state of the 'education sciences'. Since research in this field is now increasing, it is likely that our knowledge of the educational process will increase in future with results of value to the practising teacher. It is unlikely, however, that teacher skills will ever command the mystique that surrounds the skills of the medical profession.

One of the main characteristics of a profession is the high degree of self-determination allowed to and practised by its members; but as we saw in the previous chapter, teachers, particularly in the United States, have very little control over many aspects of educational policy which would come within their expert competence if they were truly a profession. Lieberman has argued that if a decision requires expert skill and knowledge it should be reserved to the proper expert authority, and he lists amongst the decisions that should be made by educators, but which are frequently in the hands of laymen, the choice of textbooks and teaching materials and the choice of subjects and courses of study. Control over entry to the profession is also, Lieberman believes, essential to full professional autonomy, and this is denied to teachers both in Britain and the United States.

The status of the college teacher, although it would appear to be invariably higher than that of the school teacher, is also subject to considerable ambiguities, of which the most important is the discrepancy between the economic rewards of the profession and its educational level. This seems to be particularly acute in the United

[1] See the detailed critique of these courses in Conant, *ibid.*, ch. 6, and Lieberman, *op. cit.*, ch. 7.

States, where academic salaries, especially at the lower end of the professional hierarchy, are not only strikingly low but have declined in relative terms since the pre-war period. Thus 'by 1957, physicians had gained 93 per cent over their 1939 real incomes—and over 400 per cent in dollar income; dentists had gained 54 per cent; lawyers about 45 per cent. During the same period the real income of the academic man actually *declined* 8·5 per cent—from an income already inadequate in 1939.'[1]

Because their earnings are so much less than others of similar educational background, it has been argued that 'there is a strong tendency for academics to withdraw from the general middle class population and establish a distinctive and relatively isolated subculture'.[2] There is also evidence that some college teachers, at least in the United States, experience a high level of status anxiety. For example, Lazarsfeld and Thielens in a study of social-science professors found that a large proportion of their sample felt themselves held in low esteem by other occupational groups and particularly by businessmen.[3]

We can only speculate on the reasons for the relatively low socioeconomic status of college teaching in the United States. It is likely, however, that the rate of expansion has reduced the elite nature of the profession, especially when it has meant the inclusion under the general higher-education umbrella of colleges offering courses and subjects at different academic levels. To this we may add the low prestige of intellectuals in the United States.

In Britain, too, there is a discrepancy between economic reward and educational qualifications, although it seems likely that this is less acute than in the United States. There is also less insecurity in the lower levels of the profession as tenure is customarily obtained at an earlier age. The small size of the profession in comparison with the United States is also an important factor in maintaining its elite status, while distinctions within higher education maintain a fairly clear status differential between university teachers and those in colleges of education and technical colleges. It is likely, too, that the Oxbridge don, with

[1] Ostroff, A. 'Economic Pressure and the Professor', in Sanford, N. (ed.) *The American College, op. cit.*, p. 448.
[2] Knapp, R. H. *ibid.*, p. 308.
[3] Lazarsfeld, P. P. and Thielens, W. Jnr. *The Academic Mind*, Glencoe, Illinois: Free Press, 1958, p. 28.

his distinctly upper-middle-class associations, still dominates the popular image of the university teacher.

One way in which college teachers are undoubtedly closer to professional status than are school teachers is in the much higher degree of self-determination which is generally accorded them, and which has its roots in the historical development of the profession. In the medieval university, teacher and student guilds were self-governing, and the tradition of college autonomy remains strongly entrenched in the ideology of the profession. Bureaucratic control, favoured by the increase in the size and complexity of educational institutions, is now a marked feature of college and university control in Britain and in the United States, but it is considerably tempered by what Burton Clark has called professional authority in federated form. He points out that 'as the campus moves from the characteristics of a community to the characteristics of a loosely-joined federation, faculty authority moves from the meeting of the assembled faculty and the informal interaction of a small body to the numerous dispersed units (departments, sub-schools, subcolleges) that are the foci of the disciplinary interests of the faculty and to a more formal representative government in which there is greater differentiation between those who participate and those who do not.'[1]

Within this general picture there is, of course, considerable variation. In the United States, as we have seen, there are very wide differences in the form of control of higher education, and in some colleges and universities there is very strong lay control, leaving the college teacher with very little autonomy at the level of policy-making. In English universities, faculty control is well established, but this is much less true of other types of higher education, and colleges of education, for example, like schools, are under the control of local education authorities.

It should also be noted that even where professional autonomy is strong, the democratic tradition has often been lost. Some forms of university government, for example, are essentially oligarchic with power tending to fall into the hands of departmental heads, leaving those at lower levels of the hierarchy with little formal autonomy.

---

[1] Clark, B. R. 'Sociology of Education' in Faris, R. (ed.) *Handbook of Modern Sociology*, Chicago: Rand McNally 1964, p. 759.

4 *The teacher organizations*

No account of the teaching profession would be complete without some consideration of the part played in its development by the various teachers' organizations, and it is useful for this purpose to make a comparison between the professional teachers' organizations in Britain and their counterparts in the United States, and to attempt to assess their contributions to the professional status of the teachers in the two countries.

The largest organization of educators in the United States is the National Education Association, founded in 1857 when the presidents of 10 State educational associations issued a call to the teachers of the country to form a national organization. This organization, then the National Teachers' Association, joined in 1870 with the National Association of School Superintendents and the American Normal School Association to form the N.E.A. Membership of this Association is open to anyone actively engaged in the profession of teacher or other education work.[1] This means that not only teachers, but principals, superintendents and other professional workers are all members, leading to the charge on the part of many teachers that the N.E.A. is dominated by administrators.

The main achievement of the N.E.A. has been in meeting the needs of its members for specialist information. The Research Division, which was created in 1922, provides members with information and consultative services on a very wide scale. The N.E.A. has also published an impressive list of periodicals, pamphlets, yearbooks and so on. The other main professional activity is the National Commission on Teacher Education and Professional Standards, which was established in 1946 with the declared aim of the advancement of professional standards, including standards for institutions which prepare teachers. The establishment of this Commission, 'marked the first time the N.E.A. specifically charged one of its agencies with responsibilities for spearheading the professional standards movements in education', Lieberman has argued. 'For this reason, the creation of the N.C.T.E.P.S., and of the various state and local T.E.P.S. commissions, must be regarded as one of the most encouraging developments since before World War II insofar as the professionalization of education is concerned.'[2]

[1] Lieberman, M. *op. cit.* All of this discussion on teacher organizations in the United States leans heavily upon Lieberman's study.
[2] *Ibid.*, p. 274.

On the whole, however, the N.E.A. in spite of its size and importance, has not been a particularly militant organization, largely because of its limited view of its function. Indeed, Lieberman points out that for many years it took the view that as a professional association it was not concerned with things like teachers' salaries. Consequently, its predominance has been seriously challenged by the teachers' unions, the overwhelming majority of which are affiliated with the American Federation of Teachers. This is essentially a trade union of teachers, and superintendents are excluded. The A.F.T. is itself affiliated with the trade-union movement as a whole in the form of the Combined American Federation of Labour and the Congress of Industrial Organizations. Although the first teachers' unions date from the beginning of the century, the spread of the movement was handicapped by the general opposition to trade-union activity in the United States, which led to severe opposition from local school boards including the dismissal of teachers who were union members. Since the 1940s, however, when the general opposition to trade unionism began to decline, membership of the A.F.T. has increased rapidly, although the total membership is well below that of the N.E.A.

The A.F.T. has been concerned in the main with salaries and conditions of service rather than with the wider issues of professionalism. Consequently, although active in the field of teachers' civil and professional rights, including such issues as racial discrimination, it has tended to neglect those professional functions which have been the main concern of the N.E.A.

By contrast the National Union of Teachers, the largest and most important of the English teacher organizations, is, according to Lieberman, 'a far more effective professional organization than any educational organization in the United States'.[1] The N.U.T. was founded in 1870 largely, as Tropp has related, in response to the Education Act of that year.[2] Although originally formed to protect the interests of the elementary school teacher it now includes in its membership teachers from both primary and secondary schools. Like the American Federation of Teachers the N.U.T. does not include administrators who have their own association.

Apart from the N.U.T. there are also four secondary associations, mainly representing teachers in the grammar schools. Headmasters,

[1] *Ibid.*, p. 308.
[2] Tropp, A. *op. cit.*, ch. IV.

headmistresses, assistant masters and assistant mistresses each have their own association. There is also a breakaway organization, the National Association of Schoolmasters, the members of which have been brought together mainly by their opposition to equal pay. The N.U.T. is, however, very much the dominant organization, representing as it does about 80 per cent of the whole profession, and this dominance is reflected in its position on the Burnham Committee, the joint committee of local authorities and teachers which negotiates salary scales. The N.U.T. has 16 seats on the Teachers' Panel, in comparison with only six for the Joint Four Secondary Associations.

Although the N.U.T. is not, strictly speaking, a trade union, it has from the start concerned itself with issues arising out of the conditions of employment of teachers. Foremost of these is teachers' salaries which, since the end of the First World War, have been settled by negotiations between representatives of the main teachers' associations and the local authorities, subject to government approval. Apart from salaries: superannuation, security of tenure, and the freedom of the teacher from outside interference have all been issues of central importance. In this respect the N.U.T. resembles the A.F.T. rather than the N.E.A. At the same time the N.U.T. has always been deeply concerned with the professional status of teaching, and has worked constantly to raise the level of recruitment to the profession. This was a particularly acute problem in the nineteenth century, when not only were there large numbers of uncertificated teachers, but in times of sudden demand for staff the standard of the certificate would be lowered. This happened for example after 1870 when there was a demand for teachers to meet the provisions of the 1870 Act. In an effort to prevent this serious dilution of standards, the N.U.T. worked for many years to take control of the entrance to the profession into their own hands, in imitation of the older professions like medicine or the law. Although they were completely unsuccessful in this, their efforts to resist dilution have often succeeded. For example they were able to block suggestions made in the mid-1950s for either a general lowering of the standard of entry or some kind of apprenticeship scheme. They have also been successful in resisting the large-scale recruitment of teachers' assistants.[1] Moreover, although they have failed so far in their aim of a graduate profession, their pressure for a three-year rather than a

[1] *Ibid.*, pp. 257–8.

two-year training for the non-graduate has recently been successful. On the other hand, it has proved difficult to persuade graduate entrants of the need for training.

The success of the N.U.T. as a professional organization can be attributed in part to the early development of a sense of professional awareness, clearly defined objectives and a militant and able leadership, but above all it has made itself into a powerful and influential pressure group at both the local and the national level. From the very early days of the N.U.T. every effort was made to influence the local School Boards, the Department of Education, and Parliament itself, and this tradition has continued to the present day. Moreover, as early as 1877 the N.U.T. began to plan the election of a teacher M.P., and in 1893 the first two sponsored candidates were elected. Immediately they 'began pressing the views of the union in the House of Commons. They were both able, modest, unpretentious and gifted speakers who made immediate impressions on the House. While other means of pressure were not neglected, the union was now assured that, with two of its leaders in the House, its views on educational matters would not be overlooked.'[1] By the 1950s there were 23 N.U.T. members in the House of Commons. The N.U.T. has also exercised considerable influence on local education authorities as both elected and co-opted members.

From time to time in its history the N.U.T. has also undertaken more direct action. In 1907 teachers were withdrawn from schools in West Ham, and in 1914 the N.U.T. forced the closure of schools in Herefordshire, as part of its aim of a national salary structure. More recently the N.U.T. has entered another militant phase and in 1956, as part of its fight against the Superannuation Bill, called on its members to cease collecting school savings.[2] Since then, token strikes, the refusal to supervise school meals, and to work with unqualified teachers have been employed as part of the fight for changes in working conditions and salary scales.

Undoubtedly, too, the existence of two rival organizations in the United States limits the efficacy of both the N.E.A. and the A.F.T., whereas the N.U.T. is without a serious rival. So, too, does the higher proportion of women teachers in the United States. As Lieberman points out, 'the woman teacher interested chiefly in marriage and a home is not likely to take a strong interest in raising professional

[1] *Ibid.*, pp. 142-3.
[2] Finer, S. E. *Anonymous Empire*, London: Pall Mall, 1958, pp. 65-6.

standards and in improving the conditions of teaching. Indeed, such women are frequently opposed to raising professional standards; such action runs contrary to *their* personal long term interests.'[1] On the other hand, women are in the majority in the teaching profession in Britain, too, although not, it is true, to the same extent.

Nor is the higher status of the teaching profession in Britain the responsibility of the N.U.T. alone. A less favourable market situation for the graduate and the smaller relative size of the teaching profession continue to ensure that teaching is better able to maintain the standards of recruits to the profession than in the United States, in spite of the longer training of the American teacher. Nevertheless, even in Britain the teaching profession is at a disadvantage compared with many other professions. It is, therefore, surprising that the teachers' organizations have been unwilling to consider the many suggestions that have been put forward for teachers' aids or assistants, especially since such a solution to the problem could have considerable professional advantages. Yet in recent years the N.U.T. has been firm in its opposition to such proposals. Undoubtedly, however, the opposition is a result of the constant struggles against dilution which have characterized the whole history of the N.U.T. For any such scheme to raise rather than lower the teachers' status it is necessary that it should be controlled by the teachers, both in order to gain their confidence and to ensure that it is not in practice used to flood the schools with untrained teachers. There are also many practical difficulties in its implementation. It would require, for example, not only a drastic reassessment of the teacher's role in the classroom, but in order to be fully effective, serious research into teaching methods, and changes in teacher-training. For this reason, although we are likely to see the increased use of teachers' assistants, it is unlikely that the teaching profession is yet ready for the drastic reorientation that a scheme such as Lieberman's necessarily implies.

Teachers in higher education are also organized into professional associations, but so far these have attracted very little attention from researchers into either the sociology of education or the sociology of the professions. Both the Association of American College Professors in the United States, and the Association of University Teachers in Britain are, however, important bodies which do much to safeguard

[1] Lieberman, M. *op. cit.*, p. 253.

the interests of individual members as well as to work towards professional standards and improved salaries and working conditions. There is, however, a lack of consensus as to the kind of professional association required by university teachers, as well as the kind of activity it should undertake. Neither the Association of College Professors nor the Association of University Teachers is a particularly militant body, and it is likely that in this respect they are only reflecting the views of many of their members.

Logan Wilson argued in 1942 that the academic was too individualistic to submit to collective bargaining,[1] and this may well still be true in that financial improvement is sought by means of individual preferment rather than collective action. At the same time the pull of divergent interests and disciplines may also hinder the development of a loyalty to the profession itself, and individuals may feel it more important to give their attention to the association which serves their own academic discipline than to the association which represents them as teachers. This division of loyalties is strongly reinforced by the conflict between the teaching and the research function, which has reached an acute stage in the American university. Other professional groups, which do not share in this dilemma, or share it in a less acute form, like doctors and lawyers or, indeed, school teachers, are likely to find it easier to establish a genuine professional identity. For these reasons, if for no others it would seem that the college teacher is a particularly interesting subject for study.

5 *Conclusion*

This review of the teaching profession has drawn attention primarily to the ambiguity of the teachers' position in modern society. This arises for several reasons, but mainly because the size, complexity and diversity to be found, not only amongst those who perform the teaching function, but also in the role itself. Some of the ambiguity arises from the attempt to bring unity to a profession which has, in the past, been divided in terms of function, social origin, qualifications and experience, and it is this division which creates many of the problems that arise in attempting to generalize about the teaching profession as a whole. It

[1] Wilson, L. *op. cit.*, p. 120.

may be advisable to unify the profession for tactical, political or ideological reasons, but, sociologically speaking, it confuses many of the issues that we are attempting to unravel. It is necessary, therefore, for the sociologist to consider differences within the profession as much as, if not more than, the similarities.

The diversity within teaching is also responsible for some of the controversy which surrounds the issue of professional status. There is no exact definition of a profession, but there is fairly general agreement that a professional occupation is one that involves a long period of specialized training, and a defined field of knowledge. It is usual, also, to look for a set of ethical principles, or an ethical code, relating the practitioner to the client, and a conception of service rather than simply profitability at the basis of the relationship. Control over entry, and a degree of autonomy in the practice of the profession, are usually, although not inevitably, included in the definition.

If we apply these canons strictly, no group of teachers, except possibly university teachers, can be said to be a profession. Indeed Lieberman, as we have seen, expressly denies that school teachers in America are a professional group. On the other hand, Tropp in his study of English teachers concluded that, in spite of their failure to achieve professional self-government, they had succeeded in attaining professional status.[1] Musgrave, although rather more cautious, also concludes 'that there is an arguable case for saying that there is a teaching profession'.[2] These different conclusions are a result of varying emphasis in the definition of a profession, but they also reflect the differences within the profession itself. Thus, teachers vary in terms of their educational level, their professional qualifications, the degree of control over their conditions of work and the way in which they carry out their tasks and their adherence to a professional code. It is not easy, therefore, to draw any conclusions which will apply to all teachers, even within a single country, and more difficult still if we attempt national comparisons.

So far, the discussion of the teachers' position has concerned almost exclusively the wider society, and we have considered the role of the teacher in the school only indirectly. Yet it is the relationships within the school that are central for an understanding of the teacher's occupational role. It is time, therefore, to consider, as far as the evidence

[1] Tropp, A. *op. cit.*, pp. 267-70.
[2] Musgrave, P. W. *The Sociology of Education*, London: Methuen, 1965, pp. 216-7.

will allow, the teacher in the school itself, and for this purpose the school will be treated both as a formal organization, and as a network of social relationships. This is one of the most neglected aspects of the sociology of education, and there are very few definitive conclusions to be drawn so far. In the next two chapters, however, an attempt will be made to review some of the main trends in recent research, and to discuss some of the implications of recent findings.

8 The school as a formal organization

1 *The concept of bureaucracy*

Organizations have been defined as 'social units that pursue specific goals which they are structured to serve'.[1] Typical organizations include hospitals, prisons, armies and churches as well as schools and universities. The distinctive characteristic of an organization, which distinguishes it from social structures like the family, is that it has been formally established for the *explicit* purpose of achieving certain goals. Every organization has a formally instituted pattern of authority and an official body of rules and procedures which are intended to achieve its specific goals. Alongside this formal aspect of the organization, however, are networks of informal relations and unofficial norms which arise out of the social interaction of individuals and groups working together within the formal structure. In practice the informal and formal aspect of the organization are inextricably intertwined, but for the purpose of analysis it is possible and customary to distinguish between them and this practice has been followed here. The present chapter therefore considers the school as a formal organization, and the subsequent chapter is concerned primarily with informal relationships.

One of the most important aspects of the formal structure of an organization is its system of administration, and in a modern society the typical administrative system is the bureaucracy. 'Complex organizations in American society are bureaucratized', Corwin argues, 'and schools are no exception.'[2] It is necessary, therefore, to consider

---

[1] Etzioni, A. *Modern Organizations*, Englewood Cliffs, N.J.: Prentice-Hall, 1964, p. 4.
[2] Corwin, R. G. *op. cit.*, p. 38.

the concept of bureaucracy and its meanings for the functioning of educational institutions. Weber is still the foremost authority on bureaucracy and, in spite of criticisms of particular aspects of his analysis, all discussions of the concept are derived from his treatment of the subject. According to Weber a bureaucracy is characterized by a high degree of specialization; a hierarchical system of authority; explicit rules which define the responsibility of each member of the organization and the co-ordination of different tasks; the exclusion of personal considerations from official business, and impartiality in the treatment of subordinates and clients; recruitment of experts; the existence of a career.[1]

Clearly, all of these characteristics are present to some degree in education, just as they are in political and military organizations, churches and industry. Schools, for example, increasingly employ specialized personnel recruited on the basis of expert qualifications. They have, to varying degrees, a hierarchical system of authority involving specific lines of command from the school superintendent or Director of Education downwards. At the same time there is considerable standardization with respect to such matters as textbooks, courses and examinations, although the extent to which the teachers' behaviour in the classroom is routinized varies considerably from one educational system to another and between different parts of the same system. Moreover, wherever rules exist the teacher is expected to apply them with strict impartiality.

Corwin has suggested some of the conditions favourable to the development of bureaucracy in education. These include population expansion, urbanization, increasing mobility, the knowledge explosion and the growing economic importance of education.[2] The professionalization of teaching has also done much to encourage bureaucratic tendencies by its promotion of policies with respect to qualified entrants, security of tenure, career opportunities and the pressure for control by the expert rather than the layman or amateur. Yet the process of bureaucratization also carries with it consequences that run counter to the conceptions of the teacher role held not only by the teachers themselves but by many other educators. For example, the standardization inherent in a bureaucratic system comes into inevitable conflict with the ideal of individual attention to students and pupils which is

[1] Blau, P. M. *Bureaucracy in Modern Society*, New York: Random House, 1956, pp. 29-30.
[2] Corwin, R. G. *op. cit.*, ch. 5.

basic to most current educational thinking. The hierarchical authority structure typical of bureaucracy also conflicts with the teachers' demand for professional autonomy in the classroom and a share in the decision-making process. Consequently there are strong pressures within the educational system working for what Bidwell has called de-bureaucratization. It is necessary therefore to look more closely at research on the school as an organization in order to determine the effect of these conflicting pressures on the teacher's role and the teacher's performance.

2 The teacher in the authority structure of the school

Many writers on organizational theory have pointed to the different ways in which authority is legitimated from a bureaucratic as distinct from a professional basis. In a bureaucratic system the legitimation is in terms of rank and deference, and obedience is due from those of lower to those of higher status in the organization. In professional terms, however, deference is due only to competence or expert knowledge. Consequently, the loyalty of the professional is to his professional standards, whereas that of the bureaucrat is to his superiors and to the organization itself. Moreover, whereas the bureaucrat obeys orders and carries out the tasks allotted to him, the professional fulfils his professional duties according to his own or his profession's decisions. The role of the professional in a bureaucratic organization is, therefore, of particular interest to the sociologist, involving, as it is almost certain to do, diverging role expectations and the possibilities of role conflict. It is, accordingly, of some importance to consider to what extent the teacher is in this position, and it is unfortunate that research on this topic is so limited. Bidwell has argued that 'there is no existing study of the prevalence or incidence either of bureaucratic structures or processes in school systems or of their consequences for school-systems operation'.[1] Moreover, although the study of administrative behaviour is increasingly attracting the attention of educational sociologists, the studies that have been made so far are not only small in scope but are more likely to be concerned with the setting up of a theoretical framework than with either the frequency of different

[1] Bidwell, C. E. *The School as a Formal Organization, op. cit.*, p. 992.

administrative styles in education or their consequences for the teacher.

In general, what information we have about the authority structures in schools suggests that teachers have very little control over important decisions. Corwin, for example, argues that the participation of teachers in the decision-making process 'is usually limited to either (1) interpretation of established policy, (2) advice, or (3) the execution of established policy. The actual policy decisions are usually reserved for the chief executive.'[1] Corwin is describing the American teacher but his conclusions apply in some degree to the English situation as well. Nor are bureaucratic tendencies confined to the schools. 'In higher education the increasing specialization of work and differentiation of roles extend the need for bureaucratic co-ordination, and there is a pronounced trend toward formal codification of rules, accompanied by a weaker trend toward the fixing of responsibility in a higher and wider hierarchy of administrative positions.'[2]

A number of studies have also explored the extent to which teachers actually perceive a conflict between their positions as employees and their professional standards. Washburne, for example, interviewed 20 teachers who were graduate students in education and found that 'the status of teachers is given one role by the teacher and another by the bureaucracy in which he works'.[3] Sharma also found that the percentage of teachers desiring teacher participation in decision-making was greater than the percentage reporting such participation.[4] Getzels and Guba also found evidence in interviews with teachers of a conflict between their professional role and the expectancy that they will submit to others.[5] On the other hand, a study by Seeman found many teachers reluctant to participate in decision-making.[6]

Undoubtedly, too, teachers vary in the extent to which they adhere to professional values. A number of studies have found that women teachers are less professionally orientated than men teachers, and there

[1] Corwin, R. G. *op. cit.*, p. 275.

[2] Clark, Burton R. 'Sociology of Education', in Faris, Robert E. L. (ed.) *Handbook of Modern Sociology*, Chicago: Rand McNally, 1964, p. 759.

[3] Washburne, C. 'The Teacher in the Authority System', *Journal of Educational Sociology*, vol. xxx, 1956–7.

[4] Sharma, C. L. 'Who Should Make Decisions?', *Administrator's Notebook 3* (April 1955), pp. 1–4, reported in Corwin, *op. cit.*, p. 276.

[5] Getzels and Guba, 'The Structure of Roles and Role Conflict in the Teaching Situation', *Journal of Educational Sociology*, vol. xxix, 1955–6.

[6] Seeman, M. *Social Status and Leadership: the Case of the School Executive*, Columbus: Bureau of Educational Research, Ohio State University, 1960.

is also some evidence that teachers of higher social origin are more likely to be committed to professional norms. Other factors which may well be important are the place of teacher training and the commitment of the individual to a professional organization. The raising of the educational level of teachers may also mean that younger teachers are more professionally orientated than older teachers, and the more highly qualified more so than the less-qualified. The relationship of the teacher to the community may also be of great importance. The teacher in the small town may well see himself or herself in traditional terms as a servant of the community, especially if he or she is well integrated into local life. Yet another factor of some significance is the commitment of the teacher to a professional organization and the attitude of the organization itself to professional autonomy.[1] The National Union of Teachers, for example, has shown more interest than the teachers' organizations in the United States.[2]

On the other hand, there is no evidence that schools and colleges are organized on rigidly bureaucratic lines. In practice, as Corwin points out, there are certain areas in which authority must be delegated, especially when the knowledge of an individual teacher in a particular field is greater than that of the school principal or head. Similarly Bidwell argues that 'the organizational arrangements of schools appear to be unusual in the degree of autonomy characterizing the operations of school and classroom units'.[3] In higher education particularly, the administrative hierarchy is countered by the tradition of academic self-rule, which still persists to a varying but wide extent. Moreover, there may well be important national differences, both in schools and universities, as well as differences between areas and even individual schools. As Bidwell has implied, this is an area in which more research is badly needed.

It must also be noticed that the growth of bureaucratic elements in education is not the only hindrance to the development of professional autonomy. Traditionally, elementary school teaching has had a very low status in the eyes of the community, and in spite of improvements in qualifications and education in recent years there is strong resistance to the idea that teachers are true professionals. Consequently we find that school teachers are frequently subjected to a degree of community

[1] For a discussion of these issues, see Bidwell, C. E. *op. cit.*, pp. 1006–9.
[2] See the discussion on this point in ch. 7.
[3] Bidwell, C. E. *op. cit.*, p. 996.

control that is quite incompatible with professional status but which has nothing to do with bureaucratic organization. In the United States in particular, the authority of the teacher is still severely restricted by community pressures. Clark, for example, has described the system of elementary and secondary education as 'characterized by a vulnerable bureaucracy'. This vulnerability, he suggests, 'stems in part from the decentralization of control to local lay boards, with job security of administrators closely dependent on lay approval. The vulnerability is extended by the correlated ideology of local lay control that has been a sacred component of the American conception of education *governance*. In addition, the ideologies of public school administration have adjusted to this vulnerability, with administration often guided by conceptions of service to lay demands, and efficient operation of the schools in line with community dictates.'[1] Under such circumstances the decline of lay influence and the growing significance of a professionally orientated administration could well have the effect of raising rather than lowering the professional status of teaching.

3 *Administrative styles and teacher performance*

An alternative approach to administrative leadership in education is to consider its consequences for the educational process, and a number of studies have attempted to relate administrative styles to teacher morale. For example, there have been several attempts to show that staff participation in decision-making is related to teacher satisfaction, although most such studies are limited in scope and tend in any case to rely on teacher perceptions of administrative behaviour. The general findings appear however to indicate, as we might expect, that teacher morale or job satisfaction is influenced not by the actual extent of the participation in decision-making but by the teachers' conception of its significance.[2]

The concept of authoritarian or democratic leadership is, however, only one aspect of administrative behaviour and a number of investigations have attempted to develop more sophisticated theories of admini-

[1] Clark, Burton R. *op. cit.*, p. 760.
[2] Cornell, F. G. 'Socially Perceptive Administration', *Ph. Delta Kappa*, 1955, v. 36, pp. 219–23, reported in Charters, W. W. Jnr. 'The Social Background of Teaching' in Gage, N. L. (ed.) *Handbook of Research on Teaching*, Chicago: Rand McNally, 1963, pp. 783–4.

strative styles, one of the most interesting being that developed by Halpin and his associates, although deriving initially from the work of Hemphill and Coons. This approach is based upon a series of detailed descriptions of the behaviour of leaders and factor analyses of these descriptions, leading to the isolation of two principal dimensions of administrative behaviour—*initiation of structure* and *consideration*. These two empirical dimensions are related by Halpin to the social psychological concepts of *goal achievement* and *group maintenance*; concepts which are in fact found very generally in both sociological and social psychological literature under different names. According to Halpin, measures of the frequency with which an administrator emphasized either goal achievement or group maintenance or both, lead to a profile of his administrative style. It is also Halpin's belief that effective leadership requires high performance on both dimensions of leadership behaviour. 'In short', he writes, 'the effective leader is one who delineates clearly the relationship between himself and the members of the group and establishes well defined patterns of organization, channels of communication and ways of getting the job done, and whose behaviour at the same time reflects friendship, mutual trust, respect and warmth in the relationships between himself and the group.'[1]

An attempt by Halpin to describe the behaviour of school superintendents by means of descriptions of their behaviour collected from both their staff and their boards of education showed that, although the two sets of respondents tended to agree amongst themselves, they did not agree with each other. Staff members were more likely than board members to perceive their superintendent as low on consideration or group maintenance. Nor did board members and staff members agree when asked to give their expectation of how a superintendent should behave. Staff members were more likely to stress consideration or group maintenance, and board members initiation of structure or goal achievement. Bidwell has argued that these differences 'reveal certain essential variations in their normative orientation, which differentially legitimize and thus differentially limit the administrative actions of the superintendent. These variations can be viewed as, in part, an outcome of the different tasks of board members and professionals and of variations in their background, and types of

[1] Halpin, A. W. *The Leadership Behaviour of School Superintendents*, Midwest Administrative Center, University of Chicago, 1956.

training.'¹ Differences in perceptions of actual behaviour while interesting in their suggestion of differential perception in the light of expectations do, however, make it dangerous to use the material as an objective description of administrative behaviour.

More recently Halpin has turned his attention to the construction of a typology to measure the organizational climate of schools. This typology was arrived at inductively by factor analysis of respondents' answers to a set of questionnaires. The statements in the questionnaire covered eight dimensions, four on the principals' behaviour and four on teachers' response to this behaviour. The respondents were asked to what extent each statement characterized his school. The dimensions were chosen to include behaviour directed towards goal achievement or initiation of structure as well as group maintenance or consideration. The six organizational climates that form his typology vary primarily in the way in which the school principal is seen to handle these two aspects of his leadership function. The Open Climate, for example, is characterized by a principal who is perceived as having high consideration for his staff, a high level of what Halpin calls thrust, i.e. motivations through example, and an absence of close supervision. From the point of view of the staff we have high esprit and high intimacy between staff members, who also perceive the school organization as helping in the performance of their task. At the other extreme, the Closed Climate is characterized by high aloofness, close supervision, and low consideration on the part of the principal, and a high level of disengagement on the part of the staff, who also perceive the organization of the school as hindering their task. The other organizational climates show various alternative combinations of these factors.² Nevertheless, interesting as Halpin's typology is, much more needs to be done before it will be possible to relate his measurements either to the actual behaviour of superintendents or to objective measures of teacher or pupil performance. An alternative but strikingly similar conceptualization of administrative style has been developed by Getzels and his associates, who have used a theoretical framework derived from Talcott Parsons. They describe three types of leader: the nomethic leader who is orientated towards the organization and its task at the expense of the satisfaction of the personal needs of his staff; the ideographic

¹ Bidwell, C. E. *op. cit.*, p. 1003.
² Halpin, A. W. and Croft, D. *The Organizational Climate of Schools*, Midwest Administrative Center, University of Chicago, 1963.

leader who, in contrast, tends to minimize the organizational require-ments and is orientated towards personal relationships; and the transactional leader who can reconcile the fundamental conflict between the requirements of the system and the needs of the individuals within it.

Guba and Bidwell used this framework in a study of administrative style based on the expectations held by the principal of his teachers, and teacher reports on what they believed their principals expected of them.[1] This study showed that teachers' perceptions of their principals as transactional leaders was positively related to their level of confidence in their principal and in themselves, and in their satisfaction with the teaching situation. This supports the hypothesis that transactional leadership is the most effective. When, however, the measure of administrative style was based on the principals' own reports, no such correlations were found. It is difficult, therefore, to be sure that it is the behaviour of the principal which is the causal factor in the teachers' confidence and job satisfaction.

In the main, Getzels and his associates have used their conception of leadership style mainly in order to study, not the consequences of variations in administrative style in itself, but the consequences of divergences in perceived style from desired style. Their studies show consistently that convergence of teachers' role expectations of the administrator with their perception of his behaviour was related to satisfaction, and divergence to dissatisfaction with the total teaching situation. Again, however, it is difficult to disentangle the causal chain in these studies. As Charters has pointed out, 'since most of the studies are correlational we can turn the findings around to say that subjects who report high levels of satisfaction are inclined to perceive agreement in role expectation.' The main problem is that it is customary in these studies to use the subjects' own perceptions of role agreement rather than indices of agreement furnished by methodologically independent sources. When this is done, as Charters points out, 'correlations are inclined to vanish'.[2] Consequently, in spite of the plausibility of the assumption, it has not been shown empirically that divergence of role expectation between teachers and principals causes job dissatisfaction. Nor is such divergence clearly related to types of administrative style.

---

[1] Guba, E. G. and Bidwell, C. E. *Administrative Relationships*, Midwest Administrative Center, University of Chicago, 1957.
[2] Charters, W. W. Jnr. *op. cit.*, p. 799.

Yet a further weakness of much research in this area is the tendency to assume that teachers' job performance is related to their job satisfaction or morale, rather than to subject it to empirical verification. Since industrial studies have shown that workers' morale is not necessarily related to productivity it is at least conceivable that this is also true of teachers. It is therefore of particular interest to look at Gross's recent attempt to study leadership in education, which tries to relate administrative style both to teacher morale and to teacher performance.

The context in which Gross places his study is the problem of leadership in an organization staffed by professional workers, and who therefore may be expected to demand a certain level of autonomy in their work. In such a context the executive will meet with special difficulties, especially if he attempts to conform to a role definition that 'stresses his obligation to improve the quality of staff performance'.[1] Gross calls such effort Executive Professional Leadership (E.P.L.) and puts forward the hypotheses not only that formal leaders will vary in the amount of E.P.L. they show, but that the amount will be related to the performance and morale of teachers and the behaviour of pupils.

The study itself was undertaken as part of a large-scale enquiry which involved a study of a stratified random-cluster sample of school principals in large American cities. Apart from the school principals, data were collected from immediate supervisors of the principals in the study, and a sample of teachers randomly selected from each of the schools. For the purposes of this particular study, however, only elementary schools and their principals were included. In order to measure the E.P.L. of a particular principal, the sample of teachers in his school were contacted by means of postal questionnaire and asked to describe how frequently their principal engaged in types of behaviour believed to represent executive professional leadership. The 18 items used were drawn up after a review of the literature on the potentiality of the principalship for professional leadership. They cover such aspects of the principal's role as his contribution to the morale of the teachers ('Gives teachers the feeling that their work is an important activity'); his effect on teachers' task performance ('Gets teachers to upgrade their performance standards in their classrooms'); the assistance he gives to teachers ('Helps teachers to understand the sources of important problems they are facing'); and the extent of his support

[1] Gross, N. and Herriott, R. E. *Staff Leadership in Public Schools*, New York: Wiley, 1965.

for the professional aspirations of teachers ('Takes a strong interest in my professional development').[1] The use of reports of teachers rather than of higher administrators or outside observers is justified because the definition of E.P.L. refers to the principal's attempts to influence his teachers. The reports of teachers on a particular principal did not necessarily agree, and the actual E.P.L. score for each principal was averaged from scale scores developed from the reports of each teacher in each of the schools.

The teacher-observers were also used to assess the behaviour of the principal towards his teachers. The areas of behaviour investigated included the extent to which teachers were permitted to share in decisions, the extent of his equalitarian relationships with teachers and the amount of support teachers were given in a number of different areas. Scores on all these items were cross-tabulated with the E.P.L. score, and in each case a positive relationship was found. These may all be viewed as further aspects of the principal's leadership style.

The effects of E.P.L. were also studied by means of the teacher-observers. They were asked to report on teacher morale in their school, on the classroom performance of the teachers in their school, and the academic progress of their pupils. All of these were found to be positively related to E.P.L. Finally an attempt was made to assess some of the determinants of E.P.L. It was found for example that the stronger the professional leadership offered by the principal's immediate superiors, the greater his own E.P.L.

The authors of the study are well aware of the problems involved in attempting causal inferences, using this kind of data. Nevertheless they argue, on the basis of a very sophisticated and complex statistical procedure, including amongst other methods the use of the split sample, that 'both teachers' professional performance and morale may serve as links in a causal chain between the E.P.L. of principals and the performance of their pupils'.[2]

Clearly the study has a number of important shortcomings, some arising out of the techniques of measurement, some out of the limited theoretical analysis of its most important variable, E.P.L. It is, for example, hard to justify the use of teacher-observers to assess teacher and pupil performance. Nevertheless, in its attempt to assess the effects of leadership style and in its attempts to relate teacher morale and

[1] For a full list of the items, see *ibid.*, pp. 169–70.
[2] *Ibid.*, p. 57.

teacher performance, it is an important step forward in the sociology of education, and it is to be hoped that it will encourage others to pursue this important but neglected aspect of the organization of the school.

4 The organization of learning

The concept of the school as an organization is, however, much wider than the study of administrative styles. In particular there are a number of aspects which relate primarily to administrative aspects of the teaching situation itself, and one of the most important of these is the organization of the teaching group. There are many ways of grouping pupils within a school, and only the most important of them can be described here. One of the most common is the system known as grading, which is customary both in the United States and in many European countries, including the U.S.S.R. It is a grouping system based upon the pupil's level of attainment and rate of progress. Under such a system pupils who fail to complete the work satisfactorily are made to repeat the grade. The teaching group in a graded school is, therefore, relatively heterogeneous since it will include pupils of widely different abilities and of different ages.

The main alternative to the graded school is the system known usually as streaming. This involves classifying children of the same age into two or more groups on the basis of some measure of ability. These groups are then used as the teaching unit, for all or most subjects, the rate of progress and the curriculum often being varied according to the level of ability of the group or class. A system of this kind, especially in a school with a selected intake, is often very homogeneous, both in age and in ability.

Setting, on the other hand, is the system of grouping pupils by ability for individual subjects and can be combined either with a system of grades or other forms of heterogeneous grouping, or with a system of streaming. It has, for example, long been common in British grammar schools for such subjects as languages or mathematics. Comprehensive schools, too, usually combine streaming and setting to produce homogeneous teaching groups, and heterogeneous or 'mixed ability' groups are restricted mainly to non-academic subjects, if they are used at all.

Finally there is the system known as tracking, in which pupils are allocated to particular 'sides' or 'courses'. Examples of tracking are the allocation of pupils to science or art sides in the English grammar school or to the college preparatory course in the American High School. Many comprehensive schools in Britain also organize their senior or upper school in the forms of 'sides'.

A recent survey on grouping in schools concluded that research so far has been abundant but inconclusive. 'For example, some investigations into the effect of grouping pupils in accordance with their abilities and attainments have yielded results favourable to homogeneous grouping, some have indicated that heterogeneous grouping leads to superior attainments; others show that there is no significant difference between the two.' At the same time the survey is highly critical of much of the research that has so far been carried out. In particular it points to the small samples frequently used and the short periods of time which have been included in the studies. There is a tendency, too, to ignore many important variables, including the attitudes of the teachers towards the method they are using and their ability to exploit its potentialities. The method of instruction is another important variable which is often neglected, and so is the material to be taught. The effects of streaming may also vary as between primary and secondary schools.

On the other hand, there is, the survey concludes, a growing body of evidence that the gap which separates 'able and less able children appears to widen if they are assigned to separate schools or to separate streams or tracks within a school.'[1] The reasons for this are not entirely clear, but there is no doubt that the causes are extremely complex, and include the attitude and expectations of the teachers as well as of the pupils themselves. Those in the top class quickly perceive that a great deal is expected of them, just as those in the bottom class learn fairly soon that they are the failures and the dunces. Another reason may be the tendency in some at least of the streamed schools to give the lower streams the worst teachers and the worst accommodation.[2]

In recent years there has been considerable controversy over the merits of heterogeneous versus homogeneous groupings both in

[1] Yates, A. *Grouping in Education*, New York: Wiley, 1966, p. 136.
[2] For some striking examples of this practice, see Jackson, B. *Streaming: an Educational System in Miniature*, London: Routledge & Kegan Paul, 1964.

Britain and in the United States. On the whole the use of homogeneous groups, and especially the more rigid forms of streaming, tend to be associated with the system of sponsored mobility. Consequently its opponents in Britain tend to be those who oppose early selection and a selective secondary system. It is all the more surprising therefore to find so many comprehensive schools continuing to stream. Pedley found in the early 1960s that out of 102 schools he questioned on the subject 'eighty-eight "stream" the children on entry, 11 during or at the end of the first year. The remaining three do so after two years.' The streaming, however, is often in blocks, involving perhaps three parallel classes. Fifteen of the 102 schools had some mixed ability classes but 'only four carry such "unstreamed" classes beyond the third year, and these only in such subjects as crafts, art, music, religion and physical education'.[1]

Part of the reason for this is undoubtedly the strong pressure placed upon the schools to compete in academic terms with the grammar schools. In their anxiety to prove that the comprehensive school does not lower standards, the heads are loth to experiment and possibly risk the academic progress of the abler pupils. At the same time mixed-ability groups are undoubtedly unpopular with teachers, and this is so even at the primary level. Several studies have shown that the great majority of primary school teachers favour streaming, believing it to benefit the backward as well as the more able pupils.[2] The Headmistress of Woodberry Down, one of the London comprehensive schools, has recorded the dislike of teachers for the idea of the mixed-ability group,[3] and indeed London's inspectorate, reporting on progress in London's comprehensive schools, dismissed the idea of 'teaching groups covering the whole range of ability' as impracticable.[4]

In the United States, on the other hand, the common practice of grouping relatively heterogeneous teaching groups has recently come under fire for its neglect of the needs of the able child, and there are pressures upon the schools to experiment with homogeneous groupings

[1] Pedley, R. *The Comprehensive School*, Penguin Books, 1963, p. 88.
[2] See, for example, Jackson, B. *op. cit.*, and Daniels, J. C. 'The Effect of Streaming in the Primary School', *British Journal of Educational Psychology*, vol. XXXI, 1961.
[3] Chetwynd, H. R. *Comprehensive School, the Story of Woodberry Down*, London: Routledge & Kegan Paul, 1960.
[4] *London Comprehensive Schools: a Survey of Sixteen Schools*, London County Council, 1961, p. 32.

within the framework of the American comprehensive high school. The experiments that have been carried out include so-called acceleration programmes which enable the academically talented pupil either to move faster through the grades, or enrichment courses which aim to provide the talented student with additional work. The advanced placement programmes which are now being introduced into many high schools enable the preparatory college students to pursue courses of college level in the high school and so earn college credits while still at school.[1] Such programmes, however, fall very far short of streaming as it is practised in the English context.

The tendencies working towards the bureaucratization of education have also, in general, worked towards an increase in school size. One of the main influences in this direction has been the growth in specialized knowledge, with its accompanying demand for specialized teaching and equipment. Consequently, as Conant has pointed out,[2] it has become difficult for the small high school to meet the needs of its pupils for advanced courses in mathematics, science and foreign languages, on the one hand, and non-academic training, on the other. In the British setting this problem has been less serious, since the highly selective nature of the grammar schools has meant that they could concentrate their resources on the academic needs of the abler pupils. However, the development of comprehensive schools has raised the issue in an acute form, since the schools have been expected to satisfy their critics that they could provide advanced courses to the same level as the more specialized grammar schools. In consequence there has been very strong pressure to ensure that all comprehensive schools are large enough to provide advanced teaching especially at sixth-form level.

If however a school can be too small to run efficiently it can conceivably also be too large, and there has been some anxiety expressed that the large school will be an impersonal, unfriendly place for teacher and pupil alike. Some evidence of an indirect kind is provided for this view by the researches at University of Kansas under the guidance of Barker and his associates.[3] Thirteen Kansas high schools varying in

---

[1] For a discussion of these programmes, see Copley, F. *The American High School and the Talented Student*, University of Michigan Press, 1961.

[2] Conant, J. B. *The American High School Today*, New York: McGraw-Hill, 1959.

[3] Barker, R. G. *et al. Big School—Small School*, a report to the Office of Education, U.S. Department of Health Education and Welfare, University of Kansas, Midwest Psychological Field Station, 1962.

size were studied intensively, and the results were seen in some respects at least to favour the small school. It was found, for example, that the pupils in the small school were more likely to participate in extra-curricular activities and more likely to take a leading part in them in spite of the fact that the larger schools provided a greater number and variety of such activities. The authors suggest that part of the reason for this lies in the greater opportunity to participate, and especially to lead, in a small school. For example, the same size of school orchestra will involve a higher proportion of pupils in a small school than in a large school, and so will the school football team and the school play. On the other hand, the study also suggests that in strictly academic terms the small school is at a disadvantage, especially in terms of the number of subjects it is able to offer. There is, however, little evidence directly relating school size to such measures as achievement test scores, drop-out rate and college grouping.[1] Clearly this is another area in which the amount of research is inadequate to support the conclusions that are drawn.

Size of class has aroused much less controversy than size of school. Indeed it has been regarded as almost axiomatic that small classes are more effective than large classes. Teachers' organizations in particular have worked hard to reduce the size of classes, and any success is widely regarded as a significant educational reform. It is surprising, therefore, to find that research in this field does little to support the general belief in the superiority of small classes at either the school or the college level.[2] Nevertheless, it is possible that a relationship does in fact exist but is masked by other factors in the situation. It is extremely difficult in this kind of research to set up a true experimental situation in which all but one variable is controlled. Classes which differ in size will therefore differ in other respects, some of which may be related to academic achievement. For example, rural schools may have smaller classes than urban schools, but for other reasons may also have lower academic achievement. It is also very probable that the effect of class size will vary according to the teaching method in use, so that[3] 'one would expect class size to be of minimal relevance in television teaching, of slight importance in lecturing, but of consider-

[1] Bocock, S. S. 'Toward a Sociology of Learning: a Selective Review of Existing Research', *Sociology of Education*, vol. XXXIX, 1966.

[2] *Ibid.*, p. 11.

[3] McKeachie, W. J. 'Procedures and Techniques of Teaching. A Survey of Experimental Studies', in Sanford, N. (ed.) *The American College*, *op. cit.*, p. 36.

able importance in discussion teaching'. It may also be of less relevance when the method is by rote learning rather than pupil participation.

The very firm belief in the greater efficiency of the small class as a teaching unit may also have something to do with teacher preferences. A small class may well be both more interesting to teach and easier to handle. This is particularly likely to be true for the teacher who has been trained in the child-centred approach and who tries to approach the children as individuals.

Finally, it is of interest to consider the development of what Corwin has called the bureaucratization of the search for talent. 'In the face of growing shortages of trained technicians and professionals', he argues, 'there is a natural impulse to search for misused and unused talent',[1] an impulse which is powerfully reinforced by a concern for the underprivileged, and the demand for equality of opportunity. Consequently the education system has been expected to take on the identification as well as the training of the gifted child; and the development of selection mechanisms within the educational system is a feature of modern industrial society. The function of these mechanisms is the same, but the form that they take varies considerably according to the dominant mode of mobility characterizing the society.

In Britain, where sponsored mobility is the dominant form,[2] and where early selection and segregation of the elite has dominated secondary and higher education, the process of selection for secondary education has long been bureaucratized. At the beginning of the century the awarding of scholarships was the almost exclusive prerogative of the head of the secondary or grammar school. The methods of selection most favoured were the interview and the essay type of examination, both of which allowed maximum scope for the free play of subjective impressions and the personal choice or even idiosyncrasy of individual heads. Increasingly, however, the responsibility for selection was taken over by the local education authorities, who introduced standardized procedures in order to ensure that the system operated with the maximum of objectivity. The result, known as the 11-plus, has exerted a profound influence on the primary schools.

Entry to higher education is also virtually controlled by the system of external examinations which characterizes secondary education in

[1] Corwin, R. G. *op. cit.*, p. 193.
[2] Although threatened at the present time by the development of comprehensive school.

Britain and which, because it is also used by employers as a qualification for various types of employment, has exerted considerable influence on the curriculum in the secondary schools. For example the old School Certificate with matriculation exemption became, in the years between the wars, the goal of many pupils who had no intention of entering a university, largely because it was so widely demanded for entrance to employment; and it was this, more than anything else, which stereo-typed grammar-school teaching and the grammar-school curriculum into a predominantly academic mould.[1]

There have been several attempts to free the grammar schools from the domination of external examinations, the most important being the attempts during and after the Second World War to substitute an internal examination for the General School Certificate. A Committee of the Secondary Schools Examinations Council, the Norwood Committee, suggested that, since an external examination taken at the age of 16 was difficult to reconcile with the freedom of the schools, it should be replaced, after an interval of seven years, by a wholly internal examination. An external school-leaving certificate, it was argued, should be reserved for those leaving school at 18-plus, with separate examinations for those wishing to try for a university award. In the event this idea proved unworkable[2] and the General Certificate of Education, or G.C.E., at both the Ordinary and the Advanced level, have become the entrance requirements for many types of employment, including apprenticeship, as well as serving as a qualification for higher education. The fact that it is a subject examination does, however, leave the schools more freedom than with the group system of the School Certificate. Nevertheless it is undeniable that the G.C.E. syllabuses are the dominating influence on the grammar-school curriculum, a consequence of the demand by employers and universities for a standardized assessment of the attainment of school-leavers.

Perhaps, however, the most dramatic evidence of the demand for formal educational qualifications is the spread of external examinations into the secondary modern schools in direct opposition to official policy and educational opinion. Fundamental to official thinking about the secondary modern school in the years after 1944 was its freedom to experiment, and this implied that secondary modern pupils were not to be entered for external examinations. 'Free from the pressures

[1] Banks, O. *op. cit.*, ch. 7.
[2] *Ibid.*, ch. 13.

of any external examination these schools can work out the best and liveliest forms of secondary education suited to their pupils', argued a Ministry of Education pamphlet in 1945.[1] Unfortunately, as Taylor points out, this movement of opinion against examinations in both secondary grammar and secondary modern schools 'ran counter to social and economic forces which were, and are, tending to make examinations and "paper qualifications" of more rather than less importance, and the strength of these factors has succeeded in turning the tide of much educational practice in favour of the extension of the examination system to fields previously unaffected by it'.[2] Consequently, the years since 1945 have seen the gradual but relentless spread not only of the G.C.E. but many other external examinations into the secondary modern school, until finally the Ministry of Education was forced to yield and a new lower level examination, the Certificate of Secondary Education, was designed specifically for secondary modern and comprehensive schools.

In the United States, in contrast, the ideology of context mobility and the dislike of centralization have worked to ensure that the 'talent-hunt' is far less bureaucratized. Individual schools and colleges are less standardized in terms of curriculum, organization and academic climate, and there is far more variation in college entrance requirements than is customary in Britain. Nor is there anything even approximating to the British 11-plus. Consequently it is necessary to look at the school itself and the way in which it acts as an agency of selection. Parsons has argued that 'the primary selective process occurs through differential school performance in elementary school, and that the "seal" is put on it in junior high school'.[3] This differentiation, which is made in terms of a fusion of cognitive and moral elements, 'leads up through high school to a bifurcation into college goers and non-college goers according to whether or not the pupils are enrolled in the college preparatory course in high school'. Moreover, this differentiation is made on the basis of a relatively systematic evaluation of the pupil's performance. 'From the point of view of a pupil, this evaluation particularly (though not exclusively) in the form of report card marks, constitutes reward and/or punishment for past performance; from the

[1] Ministry of Education, Pamphlet No. 1, *The Nation's Schools*, 1945.
[2] Taylor, W. *The Secondary Modern School*, London: Faber & Faber, 1963, p. 105.
[3] Parsons, T. 'The School Class as a Social System', in Halsey, Floud, Anderson, *op. cit.*, p. 436.

view point of the school system acting as an allocating agency, it is a basis of *selection* for future status in society.'[1] Within this general picture there are of course considerable variations between schools according to the background of the pupils and the social and intellectual climate of the schools. Nevertheless the important point that Parsons is making stands; the evaluation of the pupils' performance by teachers and principals becomes the basis for his future status in society.

Further information on the allocation of pupils to courses within the school is provided by a recent case study of the school-counselling service in an upper-middle-class suburb. The authors suggest that because of his control over the programming of courses and his letter of recommendation in support of college and of job applications, the school counsellor has assumed an increasing amount of authority and responsibility for the student's career within the school and his vocation choice. They found, in their case study, that students who were considered by counsellors to have low ability were automatically excluded from the college preparatory course. However, ability was not judged simply on test scores or grade point averages, but included such criteria as belonging to the in-group and not getting into trouble; the result is a system of sponsored mobility with the counsellors acting as sponsors.[2]

On the other hand, although it is possible to contrast the two systems in this way, there is much that they have in common. In Britain teachers' assessments play an important part in the allocation of primary-school children to different streams, and even enter into the 11-plus procedure in many areas. In secondary schools, too, it is the teachers' assessment which will decide the course the pupil is to follow and the examinations for which he is to be prepared. Moreover it is very probable that, with the extension of the comprehensive school system and the gradual abolition of the 11-plus, these assessments by teachers will become more, rather than less, important. It is urgent, therefore, that research should be focused on the selection procedures as they operate within the schools, as for example in streaming, setting and promotion, as well as on the more obvious selection procedures such as the 11-plus.

In order to develop a sociology of the school it has been necessary to consider the school as an organization, and this chapter has explored,

[1] *Ibid.*, p. 438.
[2] Cicourel, A. V. and Kitsuse, J. I. *The Educational Decision-Makers*, Boston: Bobbs-Merrill, 1963.

as far as possible, both administrative leadership and methods of structuring the learning process within the school. Yet clearly a school is much more than its formal structure; like all organizations it is also a social system involving a complex pattern of interaction both on the level of roles and on the level of individual personalities, and including relationships not only between teacher and pupil, but between teachers and between pupils. It is, therefore, to a consideration of the school as a social system that we now turn.

9 The school as a social system

1 *The teacher in the classroom*

'The school', Waller has pointed out in his pioneering study in the sociology of teaching, 'is a closed system of social interaction which exists wherever and whenever teachers and students meet for the purpose of giving and receiving instruction.'[1] Yet, since Waller's study, originally published in 1932, the teaching process has been neglected by sociologists, who have preferred to study the role of the teacher in the community or in the school instead of in the classroom. Studies of pupil–teacher relationships have been undertaken mainly by educationists who have attempted to describe the characteristics of the 'effective' teacher. In their earliest form such studies used rating scales and questionnaires based on traits or qualities which superintendents and supervisors considered desirable, and the criterion of teacher effectiveness was whether or not the teacher retained his job. It soon became evident, however, that 'superintendents, principals, supervisors and board members' ratings of teachers showed very little reliability and little relationship to one another's assessments',[2] and researchers turned instead to the collection of pupils' ratings of teacher behaviour. Such ratings however show little relationship with those of administrators,[3] who appear to approach the task of rating with quite different frames of reference. There is evidence both that administrators tend to stress poor discipline as the most important cause of teacher failure and that they tend to favour the 'more rigid

---

[1] Waller, W. *The Sociology of Teaching*, New York: Wiley, 1965, p. 6.
[2] Withall, J. and Lewis, W. W. 'Social Interaction in the Classroom', in Gage, N. L. (ed.) *Handbook of Research on Teaching*, Chicago: Rand McNally, 1963, p. 689.
[3] Stern, G. G. 'Measuring Noncognitive Variables in Research on Teaching', in Gage, N. L. *ibid.*, p. 421.

conforming personalities among their teachers'.[1] Pupils, on the other hand, appear to prefer teachers whose attitudes are 'receptive and permissive'.[2] Brookover, for example, in a study of the pupils of 66 male high-school history teachers, found that teachers 'who were more friendly, who most frequently joined in the recreational activities, whom the students liked to have join in such activities, in whom the students frequently confided, whom they admired personally, and who were helpful to students in their work were rated more favourably as teachers by their pupils. In the same group, teachers who frequently scolded or used sarcasm when speaking to students and those whom the pupils considered peculiar or "sissies" were rated less favourably.'[3]

The fact that pupils appear to like teachers to be friendly does not, however, mean that such teachers are the most effective. Indeed some of the evidence we have suggests that the reverse may be true. Brookover, for example, found that the teachers rated as friendly by the pupils were less successful in imparting information as measured by the pupils' gains in history.

Bush, studying primary-school pupils, found that teacher liking for pupils was seldom reciprocated by the pupils themselves.[4] On the other hand, a study by Davidson and Lang[5] found that primary-school children's perceptions of their teachers' feelings towards them could be very important indeed. The more positive the children's perception of their teachers' feelings, the higher the child's own self-image, the better the child's academic achievement, and the more desirable his or her classroom behaviour as rated by the teacher. These findings at least suggest a complex process of interaction in which the child's achievement, the teacher's approval, and the child's self-image act to reinforce one another.

An alternative to the rating method is the attempt to use observers to assess the leadership styles of teachers in the actual classroom situation. H. H. Anderson, for example, developed 26 categories for the classification of teacher behaviour, involving two main types of teacher style which he calls 'dominative' and 'integrative'. Observers in the

---

[1] Withall, J. and Lewis, W. W. *op. cit.*, p. 688.

[2] Stern, G. G. *op. cit.*, p. 421.

[3] Brookover, W. B. 'The Relation of Social Factors to Teaching Ability', *Journal of Experimental Education*, 1945, quoted in Brookover, W. B. and Gottlieb, D. *op. cit.*, p. 431.

[4] Bush, R. N. *The Teacher–Pupil Relationship*, New York: Prentice-Hall, 1954.

[5] Davidson, H. and Lang, G. 'Children's Perceptions of their Teachers', *Journal of Experimental Education*, 1960–61.

classroom recorded the contacts of the teacher with the pupils either individually, or as a group, and the teachers were differentiated on the basis of the number of their contacts in each category. Dominative contacts, as the name implied, are those involving orders, threats, reminders and punishments. Integrative contacts, on the other hand, include approving, commending, accepting, and helpful contacts. The studies of Anderson showed that teachers who used dominative techniques tended to produce in their pupils 'aggressive and antagonistic behaviours which were expressed toward both their teachers and their fellows. On the other hand, teachers who used socially integrative behaviours appeared to facilitate friendly, co-operative and self-directive behaviour in the children.'[1]

Closely related to Anderson's conceptual scheme are the many studies of authoritarian and democratic leadership styles and their effect on pupil morale and pupil performance which have developed out of Lippitt's original work with youth clubs in Iowa in 1939 and 1940.[2] This famous study utilized experimental groups of 11-year-old boys, who met for six weeks under a leader who employed either a democratic, an autocratic, or a laissez-faire leadership style. Each group was exposed to each of these leadership styles in turn, the same leaders adopting different styles. Two sets of observers kept detailed records of the behaviour of the boys in the groups. Lippitt concluded that different leadership styles produced different group and individual behaviours. Group members in a democratic social climate were more friendly to each other and showed greater initiative than they did under either authoritarian or laissez-faire leadership. Output, however, was highest under authoritarian leadership so long as the leader remained in the room.

Research on autocratic and democratic leadership in school situations has tended to make use of the concepts of teacher-centred and learner-centred teaching styles, and a large number of studies have been made within this general frame of reference, attempting to relate teaching style to cognitive achievement.[3] Unfortunately the general conclusion to be drawn from them is inconclusive. Thus, while a number of

[1] Withall, J. and Lewis, W. W. *op. cit.*, p. 693.
[2] White, R. K. and Lippitt, R. *Autocracy and Democracy: an Experimental Inquiry*, New York: Harper, 1960.
[3] For a summary of these studies and their results see Anderson, R. C. 'Learning in Discussion', in Charters, W. W. Jnr. and Gage, N. L. (eds.) *Readings in the Social Psychology of Education*, Boston: Allyn and Bacon, 1963, pp. 153–62.

studies have reported greater learning in teacher-centred groups, others have found learner-centred groups superior, and many have found no significant differences at all. Several reasons have been put forward to explain the inconclusive and indeed contradictory results of research in this field. It has been pointed out, for example, that most of the studies show a lack of methodological rigour and inadequate research design. Where, for example, students are introduced to a new method, the break from routine or 'Hawthorne effect' may in itself produce a temporary improvement in learning irrespective of the merits of the new method. This 'Hawthorne effect', as McKeachie points out, may also affect the teachers as well as the pupils. 'How many new curricula, new courses, or new teaching methods have flowered briefly and then faded as the innovator's enthusiasm waned or as new staff members replaced the originators? Unfortunately relatively few studies have made comparisons over a period longer than one semester.'[1] Other methodological problems arise in establishing a suitable control group, and in avoiding biased sampling.

Yet another problem is posed by variations in the criteria to be used in judging the effectiveness of a particular teaching style. There are many ways of measuring cognitive achievement, and the criteria in use vary from the transmission of factual knowledge to the development of problem-solving skills. There is some evidence that the techniques most suitable for transmitting knowledge may not be those most effective for developing motivation, the critical use of concepts, and skill in solving problems.

At the same time the distinction between authoritarian and democratic teaching methods not only lacks precision but is an over-simplified view of leadership style. 'To say that a style of leadership is authoritarian', Anderson argues, 'does not adequately describe the behaviour which the leader actually exhibited.'[2] He suggests that the effective style of the leader should be separated from the amount and kind of control exercised over the group. 'For example, because we have grown used to thinking of the authoritarian leader as impersonal, cool and sometimes hostile, the possibility of a leader who maintains complete control of the decisions of the group and yet is friendly and personal does not seem very real to us.'[3] As we have seen in an earlier

[1] McKeachie, W. J. 'Procedures and Techniques of Teaching: A Survey of Experimental Studies', in Sanford, N. (ed.) *op. cit.*, p. 1123.

[2] Anderson, R. C. *op. cit.*, p. 159.

[3] *Ibid.*, p. 159.

chapter it has also been found necessary to keep these two areas distinct in studies of parental control.

It should also be noted that Waller's analysis of the pupil–teacher relationship presents it as one of inevitable conflict. The teacher is seen as struggling to maintain order and discipline in the classroom. The reason for this antagonism, Waller suggests, arises because teachers need to force pupils to learn. 'If students could be allowed to learn only what interested them, to learn in their own way, and to learn no more and no better than it pleased them to do, if good order were not considered a necessary condition of learning, if teachers did not have to be taskmasters but merely helpers and friends, then life would be sweet in the classroom. These however are all conditions contrary to fact.'[1] If Waller's analysis is correct it may explain why the teachers students like best are not necessarily those who teach them most, and why in school as in industry morale does not appear to be related to productivity.

In line with his particular definition of the teaching situation much of Waller's discussion on pupil–teacher relationship is concerned with such issues as the maintenance of social distance between teacher and pupil and the methods by which the teacher retains the respect of the class. Although he recognizes the place of warmth and affection in the relationship between pupil and teacher, especially in the primary school, and the use of praise as well as punishment as a means of control, the general picture he draws is of a type of leadership by the teacher which is primarily dominative or authoritarian. Because of the antagonism which is always latent in the classroom, if the teacher lays down control the initiative passes to the class itself, and the fact that this sometimes happens, and the fear of the teacher that it will happen, is amusingly and tellingly illustrated by Waller's entertaining case-studies.

Evidence of another kind is also forthcoming in the study made by Gordon[2] of Wabash High School in 1955. Although primarily concerned with the student subculture it also contains a valuable analysis of the impact of the subculture on student–teacher relationships. The status system of the pupils gave much greater weight to extra-curricular activities than it did to academic achievement, and there

[1] Waller, W. *op. cit.*, p. 355.
[2] Gordon, C. Wayne. 'The Role of the Teacher in the Social Structure of the High School', *Journal of Educational Sociology*, 1955.

was evidence of considerable conflict as the teachers sought from the pupils a level of performance higher than they were prepared to set for themselves. There was, however, also evidence that the pupils learned how to manipulate the teachers to improve their grades. This was made easier for the pupils by the acceptance by the teachers of occupational values emphasizing nurturance and warmth. On the other hand, Henry, using an extensive programme of observation in primary-school classrooms, has shown convincingly how the use of techniques relying mainly on affective interaction between teacher and pupil can act as a powerful instrument of control, when the children, fearful of loss of love, are anxious to give the teacher what she wants.[1]

So far in this chapter the focus has been on the behaviour or charac-teristics of teachers. More recently research has focused upon the differentiation amongst the pupils and its consequences for effective teaching. Several studies have shown that student attitudes to particular teaching styles and teaching methods vary according to the students' own personality. Student-centred instruction tends to be preferred by those students who 'reject traditional sources of authority, have strong needs for demonstrating their personal independence, and are charac-terized by a high drive for academic achievement'.[2] The type of student with high authoritarian needs is likely to be unhappy in the student-centred class. It is not altogether clear how far these student preferences are related to achievement but there is some evidence to suggest that teaching is more effective if it is geared to the needs of the pupil.[3]

There has also been considerable attention paid to the differentia-tion of pupils in terms of social status, and it has frequently been suggested that teachers exhibit a good deal of unconscious discrimina-tion against working-class and especially lower-working-class children. This bias against the working-class child is assumed to arise from the adherence to middle-class values which characterizes the school teacher by virtue of his own social-class position. Teachers are, it can be argued, middle class either by virtue of their social origin in the middle classes or, in the case of those who have been socially mobile, because they have adopted middle-class values in their successful passage through school and college. In fact, however, there is little evidence

---

[1] Henry, J. 'Docility, or Giving Teacher What She Wants', *Journal of Social Issues*, vol. XI, 1955.
[2] Stern, G. G. *op. cit.*, p. 428.
[3] *Ibid.*, p. 429.

to support the assumption that a teacher's middle-class values leads to discrimination against the working-class child; not because the evidence is contrary but because the assumption is still virtually untested. It has of course frequently been demonstrated that working-class children are less likely to succeed at school than middle-class children, but this is not in itself a reason to blame either conscious or unconscious discrimination on the part of the teacher. There are, however, some studies which offer *indirect* evidence that teachers may discriminate against such children. Becker, for example, in interviews with Chicago school teachers found that lower-class children were, on the whole, considered unrewarding to teach. This was particularly true of children in slum schools. Comments were made by the teachers on such characteristics as the low level of motivation of such children, and the difficulty of maintaining control over the classroom. There were also criticisms of the habits of such children including their aggression, and their lack of cleanliness and indifference to hygiene.[1] However while some of these attitudes appear to reflect middle-class values, others are just as likely to be a reflection of the teachers' occupational needs. It is, for example, much easier to teach children who are highly motivated to learn, and who respond to the teachers' efforts.

A larger study by Kaplan into the types of pupil behaviour found disturbing or annoying by teachers reached much the same conclusions as Becker. Teachers reported that they were disturbed by such behaviour as stealing, lying, cheating, aggression and destruction of property. They also disliked inattentiveness, indifference to school work and nonconformity.[2]

There is also evidence that the career patterns of teachers in the United States are away from schools with a high proportion of working-class pupils. Becker found this to be so in Chicago in the 1950s,[3] and his findings have recently been reinforced by a much wider study by Herriott and St John. According to their survey, not only do schools with pupils of low socio-economic status contain proportionately more young and inexperienced teachers, but teachers in these schools are

[1] Becker, H. S. 'Social Class Variations in Pupil–Teacher Relationships', *Journal of Educational Sociology*, vol. xxv, 1952.
[2] Kaplan, L. 'The Annoyances of Elementary School Teachers', *Journal of Educational Research*, vol. xlv, 1952.
[3] Becker, H. S. 'The Career of the Chicago Public School Teacher', *American Journal of Sociology*, vol. xi, 1952.

the least satisfied with their teaching situation. Moreover, '42 per cent of the teachers in these schools, as compared with 18 per cent in schools of highest socio-economic status aspire to a school in a better neigh-bourhood'.[1]

Although findings such as these suggest quite strongly that teachers prefer the child who is easy to teach and so, unwittingly perhaps, discriminate in favour of the middle-class child, who is more likely to be hard-working and well behaved, we still have almost no studies of actual classroom behaviour in these terms, and especially no studies of the rewards and punishments, deprivation, and privileges accorded to the pupils. There is, however, one relevant study by Hoehn which attempts to measure the amount and kind of classroom contact the teacher has with high- and low-status pupils. Using a modified form of the Anderson Brewer observation scheme already described, the author attempted to measure not only the number of contacts made, but whether they were predominantly dominative or integrative. He found that teachers had in fact no more contacts with high-status than with low-status pupils, but argues that this is because the teachers studied tended, on the whole, to concentrate on the low achievers. They were, however more likely to have integrative contacts with high- rather than with low-status pupils and with high rather than low achievers.[2] Hoehn's study, therefore, can be taken as evidence that teachers do sometimes discriminate against lower-class children, not by giving them less attention but by giving them less approval. More research is, however, clearly needed not only to substantiate Hoehn's findings in other schools but also to discover whether the lower achievement of working-class children is reinforced by teacher attitudes and particularly by teacher disapproval.

On the whole there has been little research into how pupils from different social classes perceive and react to teacher behaviours, although the study by Davidson and Lang already referred to found that working-class children tended to perceive their teachers as less approving than middle-class children.[3] Brookover has drawn attention to the extent to which the teacher acts as a model of behaviour with which the child may or may not identify, and this may be influenced

[1] Herriott, R. E. and St John, N. H. *Social Class and the Urban School*, New York: Wiley, 1966.
[2] Hoehn, A. J. 'A Study of Social Status Differentiation in the Classroom Behaviour of Nineteen Third-Grade Teachers', *Journal of Social Psychology*, vol. XXXIX, 1954.
[3] Davidson, H. and Lang, G. *op. cit.*

by the discrepancy between the teacher as model and the parents, neighbours and often adults in the local community.[1] The middle-class teacher may therefore appear as a more acceptable model to the middle-class child. Bernstein has also drawn attention to the problem of communication between middle-class teachers and working-class pupils. Little research has been done in this field either, but a recent study by Piesach found that when children were asked to restore words deleted from samples of teachers' speech, middle-class children performed better than working-class children, and these differences were more marked in the fifth than in the first grade. Performance was also related to I.Q., although whether as a cause or a consequence is not clear from the study.[2]

The need for genuine interaction studies would therefore appear inescapable if any progress is to be made in studies of teacher effectiveness. Moreover, it is clear that the attempt to view effective teaching in terms of relatively permanent characteristics of the teacher must give way to a concept of classroom interaction as a dynamic process. So far, however, studies which actually focus upon the interaction process within the classroom are extremely rare. Nevertheless, there have recently been some important developments in the techniques of the systematic observation of classroom behaviour. For example, Flanders has introduced a matrix technique which attempts to provide a picture of the total interaction occurring in a classroom.[3] It is possible, therefore, that considerable advances in knowledge may come in the near future.

2 *The peer group and the student sub-culture*

Although the interaction between pupil and teacher is, perhaps, the most important set of relationships within a school, the pupils themselves form significant social groupings such as cliques, gangs and the like, which are in part a reflection of the community, in part related to the structure of the school itself. These social groupings, moreover,

[1] Brookover, W. B. and Gottlieb, D. *op. cit.*, p. 443.

[2] Piesach, E. C. 'Children's Comprehension of Teacher and Peer Speech', *Child Development*, vol. XXXVI, 1965.

[3] For a description of this and other techniques see Medley, D. M. and Mitzel, H. E. 'Measuring Classroom Behaviour by Systematic Observations', in *Handbook of Research on Teaching, op. cit.*, pp. 247–328.

are characterized by a distinctive youth culture which is to a large extent distinct from, and can even be in opposition to, the adult world of the teacher and the school.

Waller was one of the first to draw attention to the existence of this separate student culture, but its more systematic analysis has not been undertaken until more recently. Gordon, in the study already referred to of Wabash High School, reported that, for boys, athletics and, for girls, popularity were the chief determinants of status, rather than academic achievement, which appeared to be considerably less important as a source of prestige.[1] Coleman's findings, a few years later, and using 10 high schools varying in size and type of community, was in substantial agreement with Gordon.[2] The student subculture for both boys and girls was centred upon predominantly non-academic issues, in which athletics for boys and looks and personality for the girls were the most important ingredients. Good grades and academic achievement had relatively low status in all the schools, although it is interesting to notice that the 'leading crowd' tended to get better grades than the student body as a whole. On the other hand, Coleman was also able to show that the achievement of students of high I.Q. varied according to the value climate of the school. Where it supported achievement the students of high I.Q. were more likely to perform at a high level. Indeed in the schools with the strongest anti-intellectual bias, the students showing the highest performance were not the most intellectually able students, but those with motivation to stand out against the prevailing value climate.

Interesting as Coleman's findings are, they appear to raise as many problems as they solve. Why for example should the 'leading crowd' consistently get higher grades than other students? It would appear that value climate is at most only one factor in achieving behaviour. Other studies, moreover, have come to rather different conclusions. Turner, for example, in a large questionnaire study of high-school seniors in the Los Angeles area found little evidence in most schools of 'an effective youth conspiracy against academic excellence'. There was, for example, no general relationship between endorsement of youth-culture items on a questionnaire and either level of ambition or lower-class background. Moreover, there was a 'higher degree of conformity to youth-culture values in response to a question asking for the kind

---

[1] Gordon, Wayne. *op. cit.*
[2] Coleman, J. S. *The Adolescent Society*, Glencoe, Illinois: Free Press, 1961.

of person one preferred to have as a friend than in response to questions asking for personal goals or admiration'.[1] Similar findings are also reported by Riley, Riley and Moore.[2] These contradictions suggest 'that the query concerning the relative impact of the adult and the peer group and the amount of conflict between these influence agents has not yet been satisfactorily answered'.[3]

An interesting and unusual approach to the problem of peer-group influence is to be found in the comparative studies carried out by Bronfenbrenner and his associates at Cornell University. In a small cross-national attempt to evaluate the part played by peers vis-à-vis adults in the socialization process, and using an ingenious experimental design, they found important differences between the United States and the U.S.S.R. In order to measure reaction to peers, the children were asked to respond to questionnaire items dealing with a series of conflict situations under three different conditions: a neutral condition in which they were told that no-one except the researchers would see their replies; an adult condition in which they were informed that their responses would be shown to parents and teachers; and a peer condition in which the children were told that the responses would be shown to the class itself. In both countries children gave more socially approved responses under the adult than under the neutral conditions, although the shift was more pronounced for Soviet children. When told that their classmates would see their answers there was a national difference in direction as well as degree. 'American pupils indicated greater readiness to engage in socially disapproved behaviour, whereas Soviet children exhibited increased adherence to adult standards. In other words, in the U.S.S.R., as against the United States, the influence of peers operated in the same direction as that of adults.'[4] In England, on the other hand, the peer group seems to operate in the same direction as in the United States, although the evidence suggests that the influence is even stronger.[5]

[1] Turner, R. The Social Context of Ambition, New York: Chandler, 1964, p. 223.

[2] Riley, M. W., Riley, J. Jnr. and Moore, M. E. 'Adolescent Values and the Riesman Typology', in Lipset, S. M. and Lowenthal, L. (eds.) Culture and Social Character, Glencoe, Illinois: Free Press, 1961, pp. 370–88.

[3] Campbell, J. D. 'Peer Relations in Childhood', in Hoffman, M. L. and Hoffman, L. W. (eds.) Review of Child Development Research, New York: Russell Sage Foundation, 1964, p. 315.

[4] Bronfenbrenner, U. 'Response to Pressure from Peers versus Adults amongst Soviet and American School Children', Cornell Soviet Studies Reprint No. 16, Committee on Soviet Studies, Cornell University, p. 5.

[5] Ibid., p. 1.

At the college level, studies of Vassar College students under the general direction of Nevitt Sanford have also found evidence of a student value climate. Although this climate is certainly not anti-intellectual and high marks are generally respected, 'the one reservation voiced by most students is that scholastic excellence should not be the sole virtue. If there is an ideal Vassar girl, she is the one who receives consistently high grades without devoting her whole time to the endeavour.'[1] Similarly, studies of student society in a medical school show vividly the extent to which the students themselves reinterpret the demands made on them by their teachers. For example, the students believed that 'the patients whom it is really important to study thoroughly are those who have common diseases—whether simple or complicated—for which there are available treatments a general practitioner could utilize'. They regarded anything they did not expect to do as general practitioners as a waste of time. Moreover, 'matters of this kind are widely discussed among the students and have important consequences for the way they interpret their experience in school and distribute their effort and time among their many competing interests'.[2] This is not to assert, however, that student values are always in opposition to those of their teachers, or that college-going has no effect on values. The influence of college on values is indeed a complex and difficult area of study, which is discussed in some detail in the following chapter, and where evidence is presented that under certain conditions important changes in attitude do occur.[3] There is, however, sufficient evidence of the importance of distinctive student cultures to justify the attention the subject is now beginning to receive.

An alternative and perhaps more fruitful approach to college value climates is to consider them in terms of sub-cultures within a single institution. Not all students necessarily go along with the values of the 'leading crowd', and these students may not be isolates, but may instead form their own well-integrated group. Martin Trow,[4] for example, has suggested that there are at least four types of college culture or climate: the collegiate, the vocational, the academic and the

[1] Bushnell, J. H. 'Student Culture at Vassar', in Sanford, N. (ed.) *op. cit.*, p. 507.
[2] Hughes, E., Becker, H. and Greer, B. 'Student Culture and Academic Effort', *ibid.*, p. 527.
[3] See pp. 210–4.
[4] Trow, M. 'The Campus Viewed as a Culture', in Sprague, H. T. (ed.) *Research on College Students*, University of California, 1960.

nonconformist or bohemian. The collegiate culture is anti-academic and anti-achievement orientated; it stresses football, dates, drinking and campus fun. In this sense it resembles the high-school climate described by Gordon and Coleman. The vocational climate is also anti-academic although not anti-achieving. It is clearly the predominant climate in the medical school described above. Trow believes that the vocational culture is gaining ground in American colleges, largely because of the expansion of higher education and its role in social mobility.

The typology suggested by Trow is obviously useful for classifying both schools and colleges, and for describing differences between institutions as well as differences within them. Moreover, as interest grows in this field, it is likely that our knowledge of value climates is likely to expand quite quickly. At the moment, however, we still need to know much more, not simply at the descriptive or classificatory level, but on the consequences of different value climates on individual behaviour, and—of even greater interest to the sociologist—the reasons for the differences we find. So far, evidence on this point remains fragmentary. Nevertheless it is worth considering the few studies we have, and making an attempt to assess the significance of their findings.

There have been several attempts to relate pupil aspirations and pupil achievement to school milieu, defined in terms not of value climate but of the social-class composition of the school. Wilson,[1] for example, showed not only, as we might expect, that the level of educational and occupational aspirations varied with the class composition of the school but that, within each social class, educational and occupational aspirations varied according to the social composition or social-class milieu of the school. For example, in the predominantly working-class schools, only a third of the sons of working-class parents wished to go to college, whereas in predominantly middle-class schools half of the working-class boys had college aspirations. Moreover, the social-class milieu of the school also affected middle-class children. In predominantly middle-class schools as many as 93 per cent of the sons of professional workers aspired to college, but this proportion dropped to below two-thirds in predominantly working-class schools. Academic achievement, as well as aspirations, was affected by the school milieu, so that it was lower for both working-class and middle-class boys in

[1] Wilson, A. B. 'Residential Segregation of Social Classes and Aspirations of High School Boys', *American Sociological Review*, vol. XXIV, 1959.

predominantly working-class schools. Indeed the achievement of the middle-class boys was affected even more than their aspirations. High achievers were also found to be less likely to want to go to college if they had attended a predominantly working-class school, and low achievers had higher aspirations in a predominantly middle-class school.

Wilson's study does not tell us which aspect of the school milieu was the operative one, and clearly a number of factors might have been responsible, not just singly but in interaction. These factors include more effective teaching, higher expectations on the part of the teacher leading to greater pressure on the pupils to achieve, the imposition of higher standards by the teacher, and the operation of the value climate and the pressure of peer-group norms. There is of course the possibility that working-class parents who live in predominantly middle-class areas differ in terms of their own values and aspirations from other working-class parents. Wilson, however, was able to show that, in his area of study at least, the working-class parent living in middle-class areas was not likely to be better educated or more highly skilled than other working-class parents.

A later study by Michael, using a national sample of schools, came to very much the same conclusion as Wilson. Indeed, in Michael's study the differences in achievement according to the school milieu are very great indeed. The achievement scores of those from a high-status background in a predominantly working-class school were lower than those of a low-status background in predominantly middle-class schools. Moreover school milieu has more effect on attainment than on aspirations.[1]

Studies in Britain are less easy to interpret because of the complication introduced by the selective system of secondary education, which appears to act as an independent and highly important factor in determining aspiration levels. A study by Himmelweit and her associates[2] showed that working-class boys in grammar schools have vocational aspirations above middle-class boys in secondary modern schools. Moreover, these middle-class boys are likely to see themselves as downwardly mobile. Other writers have drawn attention to the very

[1] Michael, J. 'High School Climate and Plans for Entering College', *Public Opinion Quarterly*, 1961.
[2] Himmelweit, H. T., Halsey, A. H. and Oppenheim, A. N. 'The Views of Adolescents on Some Aspects of the Social Class Structure', *British Journal of Sociology*, vol. III, 1952.

'realistic' ambitions of the secondary modern pupil.[1] Although part of these differences almost certainly arises out of factors in the home background of the pupils, it is likely that 11-plus success or failure and the school milieu itself also play their part both in reinforcing and sustaining previous aspirations, and also in raising and lowering them.

It is clear, however, that such studies of school milieu can in themselves throw no light on the actual processes by which the school society influences the aspirations or the achievement of its pupils. Genuine interaction studies are as necessary at this level as at the level of pupil–teacher relationships. Some attempts have however been made to fill this gap by means of peer-group studies which focus on the level of the friendship group, or clique, rather than on the school climate or school culture as a whole.

3 Peer groups, reference groups and social mobility

Implicit in the concept of the reference group is the idea that the individual will employ the perceived, or possibly imagined, behaviour of his group of reference as a criterion for his own behaviour. In certain cases he may also attempt to be accepted as a member of the group. Parsons has suggested that within the school class 'the individual headed for higher occupational status will choose peer groups that tend on the whole to facilitate his progress in this direction'. In these groups he will not only have the opportunity to learn the appropriate values and behaviour but will actually be required to do so in order to gain acceptance. The acceptance by the achievement orientated peer group of the candidate for higher status, can also, Parsons argues, 'be a major factor in reinforcing the child's predispositions in terms of his own ability and its encouragement in the school, to transcend the expectations of his class origin'.[2]

It is, however, necessary to consider how far Parson's largely theoretical formulations are supported by empirical evidence. A large number of studies have pointed out that potentially mobile working-class boys are more likely to have middle-class friends. Simpson, for example, in a questionnaire study of high-school boys, found that

---

[1] See the summary in Taylor, W. *The Secondary Modern School, op. cit.*, pp. 69–71.

[2] Parsons, T. and White, W. 'The Link between Character and Society', in *Culture and Social Character, op. cit.*, p. 127–8.

ambitious working-class boys tended to have more middle-class friends than unambitious boys from both the middle and the working class. They were also more likely than the unambitious boys to be members of extra-curricular clubs.[1] Similarly, Ellis and Lane, in a four-year panel study of working-class boys entering a high-status university found that these boys had close associations with middle-class boys while they were at high school.[2]

Parsons' position is also in line with the findings reported by Turner in the Los Angeles study which has already been described. He found that, amongst high-school seniors, stratification in terms of aspirations, or *stratification by destination* as Turner calls it, was more important than stratification by parental background, that is to say there was no tendency for cliques to form on the basis of a class *background*. There was, however, a 'marked cleavage according to ambition. In more than two-thirds of the classrooms there is an apparent tendency for students to select as friends others with ambitions like their own.'[3] At the same time, 'some of the classic "middle class" values were uncorrelated with stratification of origin but were correlated with stratification of destination.'[4]

A study by McDill and Coleman also found that, by the end of the senior year at high school, status in the social system of the school contributed more to variation in college plans than father's or mother's education. The authors suggest that a plausible explanation for this finding lies in the influence of the cliques themselves, which are differentiated not only by status but by attitude to college. Consequently, those in high-status cliques who had not, in their freshman year, planned to attend college are orientated towards college by the rest of the clique. In the low-status cliques on the other hand, 'there is socialization away from college plans'. The plausibility of this explanation is reinforced by the finding that 'in those high schools where college attendance is highly valued, social status in school is a more important source of variation in such plans than in those schools in which college going is not highly valued'.[5]

[1] Simpson, R. L. 'Parental Influence, Anticipatory Socialization and Social Mobility', *American Sociological Review*, vol. XXVII, 1962.

[2] Ellis, R. A. and Lane, W. C. 'Structural Support for Upward Mobility', *American Sociological Review*, vol. XXVIII, 1963.

[3] Turner, R. *The Social Context of Ambition*, op. cit., p. 118.

[4] *Ibid.*, p. 212.

[5] McDill, E. L. and Coleman, J. 'Family and Peer Influences in College Plans of High School Students', *Sociology of Education*, vol. XXXVIII, 1965.

It should be noted that because neither McDill and Coleman, nor Turner, are able to include high-school drop-outs, it is possible that they have under-estimated the total effect of parental background. This is not, however, to deny the importance of their findings for the understanding of the role of the peer group in the anticipatory socialization of the mobile working-class boy.

In Britain, too, such studies as we have, tend to suggest that peer-group or friendship cliques are associated with both attitudes and behaviour. An early study by Hallworth, using sociometric techniques in a study of grammar-school pupils, found that cliques were bifurcated, as Parsons has suggested, in terms of their agreement with or their opposition to the values of the school staff. Those cliques with opposing values contained a higher proportion of both absentees and early leavers.[1]

Sugarman, in a more recent study, administered questionnaires to fourth-year pupils in two secondary modern, one grammar and one comprehensive school. The pupils in all the schools, but particularly in the grammar school, contained a relatively high proportion from non-manual homes. He found that high teenage commitment, as measured by such criteria as smoking, going out with girls, wearing teenage fashions, etc., was associated with unfavourable attitudes to school, to poor conduct according to teachers' ratings, and to 'under' achievement relative to I.Q. as measured at the age of 11.[2]

Hargreaves has successfully combined the approach of both Hallworth and Sugarman in an intensive study of the fourth-year pupils at a secondary modern school using participant observation, questionnaires and sociometric data. An analysis of the friendships and status systems of the boys revealed two value climates, the academic and what Hargreaves calls the delinquescent. The academic subculture as Hargreaves describes it is characterized by hard work, a high standard of physical hygiene and dress, the avoidance of 'messing' in class, and of copying work from another pupil. The delinquescent subculture is its exact counterpart. Dress is deliberately nonconformist, ties are taboo, and long hair and jeans, both of which are against the school rules, are encouraged. At the same time 'messing' in class becomes a substitute for work, truancy is frequent and copying is the rule.

[1] Hallworth, H. J. 'Sociometric Relations among Grammar School Boys and Girls', *Sociometry*, vol. XVI, 1953.

[2] Sugarman, B. 'Involvement in Youth Culture, Academic Achievement, and Conformity in School', *British Journal of Sociology*, vol. XVIII, 1967.

Smoking in the school yard and fighting are signs of status. Moreover, a number of factors such as staff allocation, the structure of the time-table and the schools promotion/demotion system combine to associate these two subcultures with the system of school streams. As Hargreaves points out, 'the higher the stream, the greater degree of pupil commitment to school, satisfaction with school life, and conformity to the expectations of the teachers'.[1] At the same time the higher the stream, the greater is the tendency for high status within the peer group to be associated with academic values. In the lower streams by contrast, the academically orientated boys are deviants from group norms, and the boys of high status are those who conform to the delinquescent culture.

These studies taken together provide fairly impressive evidence that both in Britain and in the United States, it is more fruitful to consider differences within the student culture rather than to postulate an all-inclusive student society. Moreover these differences within the student culture appear to be associated, in some school settings at least, not only with student values but also with several aspects of behaviour. At the same time it is still not clear how far this bifurcation is itself a causal factor or how far it is a reflection of student values and student friendship choices. It is true that Turner shows that social origin is of less importance in student clique formation than ambition or stratification by destination, but he presents no evidence to show either that the peer group is itself a factor in changing values, or that the values of these students needed to be changed. It may be that the potentially mobile child from a working-class family comes to high school with middle-class values already acquired from the pressures of the family itself, and finds in the high-status clique a congenial because familiar frame of reference. It is true that both experimental studies in the formation of group norms and industrial studies of group pressures on output, suggest that peer groups can and do influence both aspirations and performance,[2] but the process itself has yet to be adequately demonstrated in the school setting. Although the methodological difficulties in the way of such a demonstration are considerable, interest in the topic is high at present and it seems likely that this will prove to be one of the growth-points of the subject in the future.

[1] Hargreaves, D. H. *Social Relations in a Secondary School*, London: Routledge & Kegan Paul, 1967, p. 67.
[2] Campbell, J. D. *op. cit.*, pp. 307–8.

4 *The teacher in the staff-room*

So far in this chapter we have considered the teacher only in terms of the pupil–teacher relationship. Yet the concept of the school as a social system implies that the teacher is enmeshed in a whole system of social relationships which include not only his pupils but also his colleagues on the school staff. Yet curiously enough very little attempt has been made to study informal colleague relationships. Brookover has, however, suggested a number of factors which underlie clique formation amongst teachers. These include age, length of service, sex, values and interests both inside and outside school.[1] Corwin points out that 'segregation between sexes, and between college and non-college graduates is nearly complete in many school faculties. In some schools coaches who teach social studies part-time are excluded from the informal activities of the social studies department because their primary identification is with the physical education department. The structure of these cliques and their cohesiveness is influenced by the school's physical structure, by considerations such as whether there are segregated smoking lounges for male and female teachers, whether there is a place for coffee, and whether or not smoking is permitted in the building.'[2]

Informal cliques of this kind will often compete with each other for power within the school system and influence with administrators, parents or pupils. Frequently conflict will arise between older and younger teachers, or senior and junior teachers, over the introduction of new methods, or new organizational forms or procedures. Other controversial areas include the allocation of funds to particular departments or for particular subjects or activities; the relative importance of subjects within the time-table; 'poaching' of students; the allocation of particular duties or responsibilities amongst the staff; and so on.

Teacher colleagues may also be expected to play a significant part in the socialization of the teacher into the organization. This will include the transfer not only of official values and objectives but informal goals, ideologies and procedures. Newcomers may learn, for example, that even though it is officially outlawed, corporal punishment is customarily used in some schools. Webb has described some of the methods used to bring a new colleague in line with the dominant

[1] Brookover, W. B. and Gottlieb, D. *op. cit.*, pp. 260–5.
[2] Corwin, R. G. *op. cit.*, p. 12.

THE SCHOOL AS A SOCIAL SYSTEM

ideology in the school. 'If a teacher lets playground chaos into his class, it may spill over into a colleague's, so threatening him with increased fatigue. Ridicule is used to stop this threat. (Hell of a row from your room this morning, Mr. Penguin. Thought you'd left them for a minute, and the little blighters were taking advantage. Just going to go in and step on them, when I saw you were there.)'[1]

A study by Finlayson and Cohen suggests that this process of socialization may begin while the teacher is still a student. In a comparison of student and head-teacher expectations for teachers' behaviour in four role sectors, they found that a consistent pattern of change towards less authoritarian classroom behaviour was found to reach its peak in the second-year students' responses. The third-year students were closer to the head teachers and more authoritarian in expectations than the second-year teachers. The authors suggest that it is during the second year that students are most detached from the everyday workings of school, and more likely therefore to come under the influence of the liberal views of college of education lecturers. During the third year of training, however, the student teachers are in closer contact with the schools and in consequence they seek 'to narrow the gap in the conception of what is thought to be desirable teacher behaviour by the college and what they see will be expected of them in schools'.[2]

An interesting approach to informal relationships in the school is made by Corwin in a study of staff conflict in seven high schools, ranging from 'jealousies over promotions to concern about the side of the typewriter on which the typing book should be left after class. In such a setting certain face-saving devices or strategies are commonly utilized in order to preserve the face-to-face formalities and prevent incipient interpersonal breakdowns from crystallizing.' These strategies include the avoidance of the individuals involved, the use of intermediaries and what Corwin calls polite rituals, discretion, or the art of ignoring an embarrassing situation, secrecy and joking relationships. Corwin argues that, although his discussion of these strategies is only illustrative, 'the basic relevance of this type of analysis to understanding the vocation of the public school teacher is undeniable. It is at the level

[1] Webb, J. 'The Sociology of a School', *British Journal of Sociology*, vol. XIII, 1962, p. 269.
[2] Finlayson, D. S. and Cohen, L. 'The Teacher's Role: a Comparative Study of the Conceptions of College of Education Students and Head Teachers', *British Journal of Educational Psychology*, vol. XXXVII, 1967, p. 29.

of day to day personal relations that teachers actually function. It is, therefore, at this level that the teaching roles and expectations are forged out and compromised.'[1]

We are left, therefore, with the same conclusion that was reached from the survey of research into pupil–teacher relationships. In both cases the immediate necessity is for research into the actual relations within a school, whether these occur within the classroom, the headmaster's office, or the staff common rooms. Only when these studies have been successfully carried out can we expect to have an adequate sociology of the school. At the same time there is enough evidence to show that informal relationships between staff and student, colleagues and peer groups, are as important in their way to the functioning of the school as the more formal relationships described in the previous chapter.

[1] Corwin, R. G. *op. cit.*, pp. 301–40.

10 Education and social change

1 *The problem stated*

In the past, education has had primarily a conservative function, transmitting a relatively unchanging culture and traditional skills to the new generation. Only in a changing society, or one seeking to change, does it make sense to enquire into the part that educational institutions play in the introduction of change. Yet this question has proved to be extremely difficult to answer. Of considerable practical as well as theoretical interest, it has aroused considerable and often passionate controversy, yet we are still far from any real agreement as to the answer. One reason for this is undoubtedly the complexity of the relationship between education and social change in modern industrial societies.

In the first place, the education system is still expected to play a part in the preservation of the cultural heritage by means of its transmission to the next generation. Consequently schools are expected to teach the dominant value system of the society. Schools in the United States, Brookover has argued, are expected 'to preserve the capitalist system, to demonstrate that the enemy is always to blame for war, to prevent the intervention of government in business, to maintain permanent patterns of family relations, to teach respect for private property, and to protect the middle class by perpetuating the belief that the poor are inherently lazy "no-count" people for whom nothing can be done.'[1]

At the same time, schools may also be expected to serve as agencies of social reform or social improvement, to build, that is to say, a new social order rather than perpetuate the old. In post-revolutionary Russia, for example, the schools were given the task of destroying the

---

[1] Brookover, W. B. and Gottlieb, D. *A Sociology of Education, op. cit.*, p. 74.

old bourgeois values and creating new values appropriate to a socialist society.

Finally the educational system may be charged with the task of encouraging innovation in the material and technological sphere. This may involve the process of innovation itself, or the training of the labour force in the new skills required by an expanding technology. Education may also be required to smooth the path of innovation by breaking down traditional attitudes, and so lessening the resistance to change. It may also be encouraged to promote social mobility and to allow new elites to threaten and overcome the old.

Clearly these expectations are, to a large extent, contradictory. The radical or innovatory functions of education are hard to reconcile with its role in the transmission of culture. For example, schools may be expected to teach traditional values alongside a belief in the inevitability and desirability of technical change, as well as the skills and knowledge which make such change possible.

Further and more serious complications arise from the fact that schools and universities are themselves a part of society, subject to pressures from other parts of the social system. In a highly stratified society, for example, it is unrealistic to expect the schools to inculcate strongly equalitarian principles. Those controlling the school system are likely in such a society to hold strongly to elitist principles, and to ensure that these principles are taught in the schools, so that teachers who seek to challenge them may be silenced or dismissed. Moreover the schools themselves are likely to function as important agencies within the stratification system, training the young for adult status, and, accordingly, elitist principles will be built into the educational system itself. Only where equalitarianism is accepted as part of the dominant value system of a society is it likely either to influence the organization of education or to be part of the moral and social training given by the school.

Developments within education are also influenced considerably by economic and technological factors. The extreme economic determinist position would deny education any but a purely adaptive role, but there is no need to go as far as this to admit that the economic and technological systems set often quite severe limits on the type of educational provision. Education may, however, influence social and economic change directly as a consequence of its role in the discovery and dissemination of new knowledge.

Finally, we must draw a distinction between planned and unplanned change. The spread of education, and changes in its content, the organization of schools and the training of teachers may have important social and economic consequences. Planned social or economic change is another and far more complex issue. It is necessary, however, to consider how far social reform can be brought about by changes in the educational system.

Although many of these issues have been raised in previous chapters they have not, so far, been given more than a passing mention. Nor, in the present state of the subject, is any really systematic treatment possible. All that the present chapter can attempt to do is to delineate certain areas which have received attention in recent years and discuss them in terms of the most relevant research findings.

2 *Education and economic development*

There has long been a widespread faith in both academic and government circles that education is the main determinant of economic growth. This belief is reflected, for example, in the increasing proportion of the United States Technical Co-operation Programme devoted to educational assistance.[1] In fact, however, planning policies which have given priority to investment in educational expansion have often had disastrous consequences, and increasingly the simple view of the primacy of educational institutions in economic development has lost ground.[2] Moreover, a closer look at the empirical data available suggests that in its relationship to the occupational structure, education is likely to be a dependent rather than an independent variable. It is interesting, therefore, to consider why education has been deemed to be of such overriding importance.

One of the reasons, undoubtedly, is the misleading analogy with highly developed and rapidly growing economies. 'It should be noted', Hoselitz has pointed out, 'that those who have stressed the productive aspects of education have, on the whole, drawn their examples and their empirical evidence from such countries as the United States or Western European nations.' These are all countries with, amongst

[1] Coleman, J. S. (ed.) *Education and Political Development*, Princeton University Press, 1965, p. 522.
[2] Hurd, G. E. and Johnson, T. F. 'Education and Development', *Sociological Review*, vol. XV, 1967, p. 59.

other relevant factors, 'a high degree of specialization in many occupations and hence with a substantial need for elaborate training programmes for many of the skilled occupations'. Hoselitz goes on to point out that these conditions apply only to a limited extent, if at all, in many developing countries. Nor did they apply during the initial stages of industrialization in Europe. Consequently, although some returns from investment in education may be expected at all stages of economic development, investment in educational facilities may produce much lower returns at certain earlier stages of economic growth than the application of equal amounts of investment in other forms of capital.[1] For example, the development of roads and power stations may yield higher returns in terms of economic development than an equal investment in education.

A further problem relates to what economists call the optimal mix for a particular economy, in terms of the proportion spent on widespread or universal primary education as against highly selective secondary or higher education. This issue is still largely a controversial one. Moreover the decision in any particular case will depend not only upon economic consideration but upon various social and political pressures, and the spread of populist ideologies.

All this is not to suggest that the failure of an educational system to meet the needs of its labour market will be anything other than harmful to the economy, generally, and to the possibilities of economic development. Indeed there is some evidence to suggest that an educated population is an asset of considerable importance to the country anxious to 'catch up' with a more advanced economy. In Germany, for example, the educational system was developed as a tool of political control, which from the start 'was seen as providing educated men for the upper levels of the labour force. It was not difficult to build on this ideal after the industrial revolution came to Germany and to see the educational system as a whole as serving all levels of the labour force.'[2] Musgrave has suggested that the efficiency of her educational system enabled Germany to catch up with Britain after an initially late 'take-off' into industrialization. Dore, too, has claimed that a high literacy rate in the 1870s was an important factor in the swift development of Japan as a highly industrialized nation.[3] Moreover both Musgrave and Dore rest

[1] Hoselitz, B. F. 'Investment in Education', in Coleman, J. S. *op. cit.*, pp. 542–3.
[2] Musgrave, P. W. *Technical Change, the Labour Force and Education, op. cit.*, p. 262.
[3] Dore, R. P. *Education in Tokagava Japan*, London: Routledge & Kegan Paul, 1965, ch. 10.

their case mainly on the greater efficiency and adaptability of an educated labour force. This applies not only at the managerial and higher technical levels, but at all levels of the economy. The literate factory operative, for example, is not only better able to follow instructions and undertake new tasks, but has been trained in the school in habits of order and discipline.

On the other hand, educational expansion which outstrips occupational need results in educational 'devaluation'. This has happened, and is continuing to happen, in a very striking way in the United States where high-school graduation is now the norm, and college graduation has itself ceased to be linked to elite status. This process of devaluation can also be shown to have occurred in a number of developing countries where investment in education has outstripped the comparatively limited growth in the economy. 'The result, now a commonplace, is a vast and nearly uncontrollable increase in the number of unemployed and under-employed school leavers, whose political orientation toward the policy is marked by disaffection and alienation.'[1] This discontent arises primarily because education has become linked with the expectation of elite status. This is particularly likely to occur in ex-colonial territories where education has been given an exaggerated importance, and where social advancement has been closely tied to educational achievement. At the same time the speed of the educational expansion has undoubtedly made the adjustment harder to make.

The content of education is also seen as relevant to economic growth, and the traditional literary education inherited from colonial days is contrasted sharply with a more practical and scientific approach. In higher education in particular, but also at the secondary level, there has been an emphasis on the humanities, law and arts subjects rather than on science and engineering. A number of reasons have been put forward to explain this, including the lower cost of a liberal education, the continuing influence of the European tradition, and the attraction of the civil service. In Africa, for example, 'not only did the civil service continue to enjoy the high prestige it had had in the colonial period, but independence meant that many new posts were opened up to young Africans. For ten years or more, the new universities were able to look forward to a period during which abundant employment opportunities were available to their liberal arts graduates.'[2] A number

[1] Coleman, J. S. *op. cit.*, p. 29.
[2] Cowan, L. G., O'Connell, J. and Scanlon, D. G. (eds.), *Education and Nation Building in Africa*, 1965, p. 31.

of developing societies have, accordingly, attempted to move towards a more practical education and African educational schemes in particular are 'full of provisions for manual work, especially agricultural, for all, and specialized technical education for as many as can be afforded'.[1]

To a large extent this move away from traditional arts subjects is necessary, particularly if secondary and higher education is to be expanded. In Egypt, for example, 'about 70 per cent of the university enrolment is in the Faculties of Art, Law and Commerce, and for the vast majority of these graduates there is no demand; there is meanwhile a pressing need for scientists, doctors and engineers and the 20 per cent enrolment in these fields absorbs the best student talent'.[2] On the other hand, the swing towards science and technology carries its own dangers. It is just as easy to over-estimate the demand for scientists and technologists as it is for lawyers, and it is even more expensive. Foster, for example, has suggested, taking Ghana as his example, that there is a real danger that technicians will be produced before they can be made use of by the economy.[3] Nor is it enough to provide training programmes if students do not choose to undertake the training, or if they do not make use of it afterwards. Whether or not they do so will depend ultimately upon their perception of the opportunities provided by different types of career. Only if technical and scientific employment can compete with law and administration in terms of social and economic rewards is it likely to appeal to the college graduate.

Moreover, as Hurd and Johnson point out, the same argument applies at lower levels of the educational ladder. 'School graduates, whether prepared as general farmers or as agricultural technicians have proved unwilling to return, so equipped, to the land of their fathers, or to the land of anyone else's fathers for that matter. It is argued that this unwillingness stems from the content of education in many under-developed societies, which stresses an elitist attitude towards manual work of all kinds, thus prejudicing students against farming life. It is true that a prejudice against manual work may exist, but in a number of societies it has been observed that such school graduates are more willing to face urban unemployment or accept labouring jobs

[1] Coleman, J. S. op. cit., p. 73.
[2] Ibid., p. 187.
[3] Foster, P. J. Education and Social Change in Ghana, London: Routledge & Kegan Paul, 1965.

in the city than return to the villages.'[1] This was, indeed, very much the situation prevailing in England between the wars, when grammar schools were tied, so it was asserted, to a bookish and irrelevant curriculum which served to divert the best brains of the country into clerical occupations. In fact, however, it is probable that it was the organization of industry rather than the curriculum of the school which was the decisive factor in turning boys away from industrial employment. Not only was industry largely organized to recruit elementary school boys at the age of 14, but prospects within industry were uncertain and haphazard.[2] Clerical work not only had higher status in the eyes of pupils and their parents, but offered, or appeared to offer, greater opportunities for advancement.

It would seem, therefore, that however imperative it is for the educational process to keep pace with the demands made by economic and technical development on the labour force, there is a very real sense in which educational expansion is a consequence rather than a cause of economic development. On the other hand it may also be argued that to concentrate upon the relationships between education and occupation is to overlook the possible significance of changes in attitudes and values. From this point of view education is seen as introducing the developing society to new needs, and new expectations, and even to the idea of change itself. In short, education helps to wean the developing society away from the old, and towards the new; it inspires a belief in progress, in efficiency, in achievement and in rationality. At the same time education may be seen as creating the conditions for political as well as economic development by laying the foundations of a democratic form of government. Since a belief in the power of education to change attitudes and values is found in developed as well as developing societies, it is of great interest to consider how far the evidence we have available justifies this faith.

3 Education and democracy

It may be appropriate to begin this section with a review of the findings on the relationship between education and democracy. It can be shown, for example, that the higher the education level of a country, the more

---

[1] Hurd, G. E. and Johnson, T. F. *op. cit.*, p. 62.
[2] Banks, O. *op. cit.*, ch. 12.

likely is it to be a democracy. Within countries, moreover, there is an even stronger relationship between education and democratic attitudes. In a summary of the main research findings Lipset argues that 'data gathered by public opinion research agencies which have questioned people in different countries about their beliefs on tolerance for the opposition, their attitudes toward ethnic or racial minorities, and their feelings for multi-party as against one-party systems have showed that the most important single factor differentiating those giving democratic responses from the others has been education. The higher one's education, the more likely one is to believe in democratic values and support democratic practices. All the relevant studies indicate that education is more significant than either income or occupation.'[1] Particularly impressive in this connection is Lipset's evidence that the working classes, and the less-educated, tend to be more authoritarian in their attitudes, and to be more likely to favour extremist political and religious groups.[2] There is also some, although by no means conclusive, evidence that students at college become more liberal 'in the sense of being more sophisticated and independent in their thinking, and placing greater value upon individual freedom and well-being'.[3]

Lipset's picture of the working class as authoritarian has however been criticized as over-drawn. It has been pointed out for example that another characteristic of the working-class respondents is the tendency to give uncertain or no opinion responses, and that in fact the proportion holding extremist or anti-democratic views in the working classes is probably fairly low.[4] Nor is a tendency towards authoritarian views found only amongst the working classes. As Lipset himself has pointed out, 'data from numbers of countries demonstrate that classic Fascism is a movement of the propertied middle classes'.[5]

At the same time there is evidence to suggest that there is no *necessary* connection between education and democracy, and both Germany and Japan are examples of nations which have combined a high level of literacy with a totalitarian form of government. Moreover Coleman has argued that the content of education is itself a factor of

[1] Lipset, S. M. *Political Man*, London: Heinemann, 1960, p. 56.
[2] *Ibid.*, ch. IV.
[3] Webster, H., Freedman, M. B. and Heist, P. 'Personality Changes in College Students', *The American College, op. cit.*, p. 828.
[4] Miller, S. M. and Riessman, F. 'Working Class Authoritarianism? A Critique of Lipset', *British Journal of Sociology*, vol. XII, 1961.
[5] Lipset, S. M. *op. cit.*, p. 174.

considerable importance, and suggests that there may be something of an affinity between a predominantly scientific and technological emphasis in education and totalitarian government. He points, for example, to the 'comparatively slight attention given to the humanities, law, the arts, and the social sciences in Communist totalitarian countries'.[1] Jacob, however, found that the 'values and outlook of students do not vary greatly whether they have pursued a conventional liberal arts programme, an integrated general education curriculum or one of the strictly professional-vocational options. The more liberally educated student may take a somewhat more active interest in community responsibilities and keep better informed about public affairs. But the distinction is not striking and by no means does it occur consistently among students at all colleges.'[2] Nor, according to Jacob, do social science courses appear to exert influence on students' beliefs and values. These findings, on the other hand, relate only to the United States.

The content of education may however be important in another way. Most totalitarian régimes attempt to use their schools to inculcate conformity, submissiveness and uncritical loyalty to the state. In Japan, for example, before the war the schools were expected to encourage submissive acceptance of the existing order. The principal instrument for the inculcation of these principles was the teaching of morals. 'A minimum of one hour per week of morals was mandatory in all schools, from elementary through the secondary schools. But apart from the formal morals course, the ideas were worked into the curriculum and into school life in any way the ingenuity of the educators could devise.'[3] Moreover inside the classroom, 'self-expression was discouraged and disagreement with teachers and elders severely frowned on'.[4]

In Russia, too, emphasis in the schools has been on the indoctrination of the pupil in conformity and obedience as well as in love for the Soviet system. In the school itself, 'the atmosphere was pervaded by a spirit of discipline and hierarchy', and teachers were warned 'not to coax students but rather to demand obedience, for only in this way would students develop the desired moral qualities'.[5]

[1] Coleman, J. S. op. cit., pp. 531–2.
[2] Jacob, P. E. Changing Values in College, New York: Harper & Row, 1957, p. 5.
[3] Passin, H. 'Japan', in Coleman, J. S. op. cit., p. 308.
[4] Ibid., p. 310.
[5] Ibid., pp. 243–4.

Moreover in considering the developing countries of Asia, Africa and South America, we cannot overlook the possibility that democratic government is, as Max Weber suggested, unique to the countries of North America, Western Europe and their English-speaking offspring. According to this explanation both democracy and capitalism were the products of a historically unique development in which Protestantism and its emphasis on individual responsibility played a major role. Indeed, in his more pessimistic moments Weber seems to have doubted whether democracy would continue in the future. Instead, he suggested that the 'dictatorial potential implicit in mass appeals added to the desire for a secure subsistence would result in a centralized bureaucracy under a dictator'.[1]

We must conclude, therefore, that the influence of education upon political attitudes is very much more complex than has sometimes been supposed, and that although it may be correct to argue that a high level of education is necessary for effective participation in democratic government, there is no guarantee that education and democratic attitudes are necessarily related.

4 *Education, value transmission and value change*

On the other hand if, as we have seen, totalitarian governments can use the educational system to attempt to inculcate a docile and submissive belief in authority it is relevant to ask how far it is also possible to educate for democracy. It is useful, therefore, to look more closely at the education process as a means of value transmission, and to consider not only the extent to which such indoctrination is possible, but also the conditions under which it is likely to operate most effectively.

There is every indication that the educational system of the U.S.S.R. has not only transformed a largely illiterate and traditionally orientated population into both a literate and industrialized work force, but it has also managed to produce a generation who are in the main ideologically committed to the social order. At the same time observers have noted some signs that the process of indoctrination is by no means complete. There is evidence of a small number of young people who are disenchanted with the system, and a much larger number who are

[1] Bendix, R. *Max Weber: An Intellectual Portrait*, New York: Doubleday, 1960, p. 453.

not only politically apathetic but to some extent opportunist as well.[1] Students in particular have been accused of a dislike of manual labour, of elitist attitudes, and of putting their own career before service to the State. The 1958 school reforms with their introduction of the concept of 'polytechnical education'[2] were designed to teach the dignity of labour, and to prevent the development of a new upper class. Khrushchev, for example, spoke bitterly of the distinction that still exists in the Soviet Union between mental and manual work. 'This is fundamentally wrong and runs counter to our teaching and aspirations. As a rule, boys and girls in secondary school consider that the only acceptable path in life for them is to continue their education at higher schools. Some of them even consider (work) beneath their dignity. This scornful and lordly attitude is to be found in some families. If a boy or girl does not study well and fails to get into college, the parents frighten him by saying that if he does not study well and fails to get into college he will have to work in a factory as a common labourer.'[3]

Moreover, it should not be overlooked that the schools, as such, have only been expected to play a small part in the total process of indoctrination. Indeed, the aim of a totalitarian system is to ensure that every agency of socialization is involved in the process. Directly and indirectly, Grant points out, 'the communist viewpoint is put over at every stage of schooling, and reinforced by other media of communication outside the schools, such as the theatre, films, radio, television and the Press, while the youth organizations act as a link between the school and the world outside.'[4] This is in striking contrast to most democratic systems where the various media of socialization are only loosely controlled. This is not to suggest that democratic societies do not attempt to indoctrinate their children in the religious, moral and political values dominant in the society. The process, however, is normally less conscious and less thorough, partly because there is less emphasis on the production of *new* values, and concern instead is with the maintenance of traditional religious and moral beliefs and attitudes, partly because democratic societies are usually *pluralistic* and different and even opposing value systems may be

[1] Coleman, J. S. *op. cit.*, pp. 254–71.
[2] See the discussion of polytechnical principles above, on p. 51.
[3] Khrushchev, N. S. 'Memorandum approved by the Presidium of the Central Committee of the Communist Party of the Soviet Union', September 1958, quoted in Grant, N. *Soviet Education, op. cit.*, pp. 101–2.
[4] Grant, N. *op. cit.*, p. 25.

transmitted by different institutions. An exception, however, is the deliberate and largely successful 'Americanization' of immigrant children which has been an important function of the American school.

It is, therefore, important to consider some of the possible reasons for the partial failure of the Soviet system's indoctrination programme. One of the most important handicaps would appear to be the failure to indoctrinate the parents, who are, in consequence, unwilling to accept the consequence of Soviet policy as it affects their children. Even more significant, however, are the contradictions which have clearly arisen between the official ideology and actual experiences and observations in everyday life. The existence of a privileged elite group, and income and status differences between manual and non-manual workers, are the source of parental and student anxieties as well as of their ambitions, and are likely to serve as a serious handicap to the full acceptance of the official doctrine of the equality of all forms of service to the State.

Indeed it would appear that indoctrination through the educational system is by no means a simple process, and that propaganda, even in the conditions of a totalitarian system, is limited in its scope. For this reason it would appear unreasonable to expect a school system alone to achieve major changes in attitudes, especially when the changes expected cut across strongly entrenched interests, traditional values or everyday experience.

For the same reason we may be somewhat sceptical of the more optimistic claims to reform society by somewhat limited changes in school reorganization. It is unlikely, for example, that either the changeover to the comprehensive system in secondary education, or the abolition of the independent schools, will succeed, *on their own*, in introducing any radical change in the nature of British society.

This somewhat pessimistic conclusion should not, however, lead us to suppose that education can have no effect on values. In his now classic study of Bennington, Newcomb[1] showed that, given the right conditions, the experience of college could change student values. The students concerned, who came in the main from upper-middle-class conservative families, became more radical in their attitudes as a result of their stay at Bennington. According to Newcomb's analysis, the

[1] Newcomb, T. M. *Personality and Social Change: Attitude Formation in a Student Community*, New York: Dryden Press, 1943.

teachers' interest in and attitude to social and political issues appears to have been the crucial factor. Because the student leaders were strongly influenced by their teachers, liberal opinions enjoyed popularity and prestige, and incoming students were consequently exposed to such opinions not only from the teachers but as part of the student culture. Significantly, it was the students who were most involved in peer-group activities who were the least conservative.

The situation at Bennington does not appear to be typical and it seems that a great many students, in the United States at least, pass through college 'without experiencing significant changes in basic values, or without becoming much involved in problems that interest teachers'.[1] There is evidence, however, that certain colleges, at least, appear to have what Jacob calls a 'peculiar potency' that seems to be the result of a combination of factors, which produce a distinctive institutional atmosphere or a 'climate of values' in which students are decisively influenced.[2] Although the precise combination of factors is not known, Jacob suggests that it is more likely to be found in the 'liberal arts' private college with a sense of special educational mission.[3]

On the other hand there is some evidence that different types of institution attract different kinds of students, and that the effectiveness of certain colleges in changing values may in part be due to the greater readiness of the students to be influenced. It has been found, for example, that the highly productive colleges in terms of future scholars and scientists, 'attract highly motivated students who are more inner-directed, socially independent, receptive to learning, non-authoritarian, theoretical, aesthetic, unconventional and creative'.[4]

We are left, therefore, with very little direct evidence on the part played by education in changing values. Nevertheless, our greater awareness of the problems of research in this area, including the difficulties of measuring values themselves, and the greater interest taken in such issues as the school and college 'climate' may well offer some hope for the future. It is, however, unlikely that we will make any major progress until we know much more about the effect of the peer group on the learning situation and the consequences for different

[1] Webster, H., Freedman, M. and Heist, P. 'Personality Changes in College Students', in *The American College, op. cit.*, pp. 840–1.
[2] Jacob, P. E. *op. cit.*, p. 99.
[3] *Ibid.*, p. 115.
[4] Stern, G. G. 'Measuring Noncognitive Variables in Research on Teaching', in Gage, N. L. (ed.) *Handbook of Research on Teaching, op. cit.*, p. 431.

pupils of variations in the teacher–pupil relationships. The study of the effect of education on values is therefore very much a part of the still undeveloped general sociology of learning.

5 Education and the under-privileged

One of the dominant themes in educational reform in both the nineteenth and the twentieth century has been the extension of educational opportunities to wider sections of the community. In general this has taken the form of free schooling, scholarships, and maintenance grants for needy students, all with the objective of providing equal educational opportunity for all classes in the community. Increasingly, however, we have come to realize that the provision of formal equality does surprisingly little to eliminate educational privilege. Whatever changes we make in our selection mechanisms, or in the scope of our educational provision, many children, because of their home background, are still unable to take advantage of the opportunities opened up to them. Accordingly, attention is now being turned, not simply to the removal of formal barriers to equality, but to the provision of special privileges for those who would otherwise be handicapped in terms of educational achievement.

Such provision is not, of course, new. The fact that a hungry child cannot learn was officially recognized at the beginning of the present century, and the provision of school milk and meals and the school health services early became established features of the British education scene. Yet it has taken a long time to see beyond the purely physical needs, and to grasp the concept of what has come, perhaps misleadingly, to be called 'cultural deprivation'. Moreover although the idea of equal educational provision for all classes in the community is now accepted, it has by no means been translated into everyday practice. Even today, children from slum homes are all too often educated in slum schools quite untypical of schools elsewhere. The Plowden Report has described the gaunt-looking buildings, the cramped and often overcrowded conditions inside them, the inadequate and old-fashioned lavatories, the lack of staff rooms and similar facilities, and 'sometimes, all round the ingrained grime of generations'.[1]

[1] Report of the Central Advisory Council for Education (England), *Children and their Primary Schools*, vol. I, p. 51.

Yet, increasingly, it is being recognized that, for these children, even equality is not enough, and the Plowden Report has emphasized the need for 'positive discrimination' in favour of slum schools. It is argued that 'schools in deprived areas should be given priority in many respects. The first step must be to raise the schools with low standards to the national average, and second quite deliberately to make them better. The justification is that the homes and neighbourhoods from which many of their children come provide little support and stimulus for learning. The schools must supply a compensating environment.'[1]

In the United States, where slum areas face problems certainly as severe as anything in Britain, the idea of providing compensatory education for the culturally deprived child is further advanced. In New York City an experiment known originally as the Demonstration Guidance Project was started in 1956. Originally involving one junior high school and one senior high school the intention was to 'identify and stimulate able students from a culturally deprived area, and from generally low income families without any educational tradition, to reach higher educational and vocational goals'.[2]

The success of the original experiment led to its extension in a less intensive form to 65 schools, and it became known at this stage as the Higher Horizons Programme. The scheme involved remedial teaching, an intensive counselling service, and trips to museums, theatres, libraries and laboratories. In 1960 the Great Cities School Improvement Programme, sponsored by the Ford Foundation, extended the experiment into other cities, and into the elementary school. Apart from the intensive work with the children inside and outside the school, there are also attempts to bring the parents into the scheme.[3] At the same time, New York has started to experiment with pre-school education for Harlem children.[4]

Some of these experiments have been highly successful. Academic grades have improved, more children have gone on from school to college, school attendance figures have improved and parents have become more closely involved with the school. On the other hand, there are some critics of the scheme, who doubt whether it is in fact radical enough. Riessman, for example, points out that in the early

---

[1] *Ibid.*, p. 57.
[2] Krugman, M. 'Educating the Disadvantaged Child', in Kerber, A. and Bommarito, B. (eds.) *The School and the Urban Crisis*, New York: Holt, Rinehart & Winston, 1965, p. 241.
[3] For a description of the scheme in several American cities, see *ibid.*, pp. 239–76.
[4] *Ibid.*, p. 348.

years of the Project enormous resources of money and energy were poured into a relatively small area, and consequently in view of the previous neglect of these schools, it was not surprising that the results were positive. He argues that what we really need is to 'develop approaches that will be effective on a large scale in the everyday school setting, where teachers are not working day and night and 14 Sundays per term. We need techniques that can be applied by the average teacher, hopefully with a fair amount of devotion, but not necessarily the short-lived zeal fostered by a unique experiment.'[1] His own suggestions involve a more radical change in teaching methods to bridge the gap between the teacher and the deprived child and, in particular, a broadening of the curriculum based on an understanding and respect for the culture of the under-privileged.

Gordon in a recent review of special programmes of compensatory education is also critical of the absence of a really radical approach. He blames the failure of the behavioural scientists to provide sufficiently convincing theories on which the educator can act.[2] Wolf and Wolf have also warned against expecting more from the schools than they can be expected to achieve. They argue that compensatory education cannot in itself solve problems of health, housing and discrimination, and that these must be tackled by agencies outside the school.[3] None of these criticisms, however, is an argument against some form of compensatory education, and they all acknowledge that formal equality of opportunity is an inadequate basis for an equalitarian policy. They do, however, underline the interdependence of education with other aspects of the social structure.

Finally, in this same context, it is necessary to pay some attention to the issue of school integration, since this has proved to be a particularly intractable aspect of the problem, especially in the United States. Since the Supreme Court of the United States declared that equality in education could not be attained in segregated schools, desegregation has proceeded gradually, although often slowly, and not by any means always peacefully. It is useful, therefore, to consider some of the consequences of desegregation particularly as they affect the school system and the under-privileged child. There is already,

---

[1] Riessman, F. *The Culturally Deprived Child*, New York: Harper & Row, 1962, p. 104.

[2] Gordon, E. W. 'A Review of Programmes of Compensatory Education', *American Journal of Orthopsychiatry*, vol. xxxv, 1965.

[3] Wolf, E. P. and Wolf, L. 'Sociological Perspectives on the Education of Culturally Deprived Children', *School Review*, vol. lxx, 1962.

for example, evidence of the extent to which white pupils leave schools where desegregation has brought in a high proportion of negro students. This has occurred more particularly in the big cities, and many examples can be found in Detroit, Chicago, New York and Los Angeles. In these areas, desegregation often means an influx of pupils whose educational standards are extremely low, in part because of the poverty of their home surroundings, in part because of the inadequacy of their previous schools; and this situation is particularly acute in areas where there has been much recent immigration from the South, from Puerto Rico and from Mexico. In such circumstances parents may move house, or they may move their children to a parochial or other non-public school.[1] The result is an increase in the racial and ethnic imbalance in the schools, with consequences not only for the policy of integration, but on the standards in the schools themselves. Attempts have been made to overcome the problems of residential segregation by means of a transfer programme between schools, by rezoning, or by reclassifying schools to handle fewer grades and thus serve larger areas, but none of these solutions can be effective on anything but a small scale. The development of compensatory education programmes becomes, therefore, one of increased urgency.

6 *Conclusion*

The precise relationship of the educational systems to social and economic change can therefore be seen to be one of extreme complexity, and it is almost impossible to draw any conclusions that are not misleading. It is possible, however, that at least part of the problem lies in the way the question is framed. The concept of education as producing or impeding social change is enormously complicated by the fact that the educational system is itself a part of the society which is changing. Consequently the real issue is one of the actual interrelationship between educational institutions and other aspects of society. Moreover it is this interrelationship which makes it so difficult to use the educational system to produce conscious or planned social change. The present chapter contains numerous examples of such

[1] Sheldon, E. B., Hudson, J. R. and Glazier, R. A. 'Administrative Implications of Integrative Plans for Schools', in Reiss, A. J. Jnr. (ed.) *Schools in a Changing Society*, Glencoe, Illinois: Free Press, 1965, pp. 153–89.

efforts which have come to grief just because the educational system has been seen in isolation from its social context. This is not to suggest, on the other hand, that change in education is never important or necessary. An educational system that fails to adapt to the needs of the economy can, for example, seriously handicap economic development, and an elitist ideology can restrict educational development and waste a very considerable amount of working-class ability. Moreover education, in so far as it increases knowledge and understanding, both of man himself and of his environment, creates the conditions necessary for the development of both the individual and society. The discovery that educational reform is not a universal panacea should not therefore lead us to minimize the importance of knowledge about the educational institutions in society. The very complexity of the issues involved suggests rather that we need not only more but better and more sophisticated research into the interrelationship between education and society.

Select Bibliography

Banks, O. *Parity and Prestige in English Secondary Education*, London: Routledge & Kegan Paul, 1955.
Ben-David, J. 'Professions in the Class System of Present-day Societies', *Current Sociology*, vol. XII (3), 1963–4.
Bereday, G. *et al. The Changing Soviet School*, London: Constable, 1960.
Bidwell, C. 'The School as a Formal Organization', in March, J.G. (ed.) *Handbook of Social Organization*, Chicago: Rand McNally, 1965.
Blyth, W.A.L. *English Primary Education*, London: Routledge & Kegan Paul, 1965.
Brim, O. *Sociology in the Field of Education*, New York: Russell Sage Foundation, 1958.

Charters, W.W. Jnr. and Gage, N.L. (eds.) *Readings in the Social Psychology of Education*, Boston: Allyn & Bacon, 1963.
Cicourel, A.V. and Kitsuse, J.I. *The Educational Decision-makers*, Boston: Bobbs-Merrill, 1963.
Clark, Burton R. *The Open Door College. A Case Study*, New York: McGraw-Hill, 1960.
Coleman, J.S. *The Adolescent Society*, Glencoe, Ill.: Free Press, 1961.
Conant, J. *Slums and Suburbs*, New York: McGraw-Hill, 1961.
Cotgrove, S. *Technical Education and Social Change*, London: Routledge & Kegan Paul, 1958.
Crowther Report, Central Advisory Council for Education, *15–18*, London: H.M.S.O., 1959.

Douglas, J.W.B. *The Home and the School*, London: MacGibbon & Kee, 1964.
Durkheim, E. *Education and Sociology*, Glencoe, Ill.: Free Press, 1956.

Floud, J. and Halsey, A.H. 'The Sociology of Education. A Trend Report and Bibliography', *Current Sociology*, vol. VII (3), 1958.

Gage, N.L. (ed.) *Handbook of Research on Teaching*, Chicago: Rand McNally, 1963.
Grant, N. *Soviet Education*, Penguin Books, 1964.
Gross, N. *Who Runs Our Schools?*, New York: Wiley, 1958.
Gross, N. and Herriott, R.E. *Staff Leadership in Public Schools*, New York: Wiley, 1965.

Halsey, A.H., Floud, J. and Anderson, C.A. (eds.) *Education, Economy and Society*, Glencoe, Ill.: Free Press, 1961.

Hargreaves, D.H. *Social Relations in a Secondary School,* London: Routledge & Kegan Paul, 1967.
Herriott, R.E. and St. John, W.H. *Social Class and the Urban School,* New York: Wiley, 1966.
Hoffman, M. and Hoffman, L.W. (eds.) *Review of Child Development Research,* New York: Russell Sage Foundation, 1964.

Jackson, B. *Streaming: an Educational System in Miniature,* London: Routledge & Kegan Paul, 1964.
Jacob, P.E. *Changing Values in College,* New York: Harper & Row, 1957.

Kerber, A. and Bommarito, R. *The Schools and the Urban Crisis,* New York: Holt, Rinehart, 1965.
Klein, J. *Samples from English Cultures,* vol. 2, London: Routledge & Kegan Paul, 1965.

Lieberman, M. *Education as a Profession,* Englewood Cliffs, N.J.: Prentice-Hall, 1956.

McKinley, D.G. *Social Class and Family Life,* Glencoe, Ill.: Free Press, 1964.
Miller, T.W.G. *Values in the Comprehensive School,* Edinburgh: Oliver & Boyd, 1961.
Musgrave, P. W. *Technical Change, the Labour Force and Education,* Oxford: Pergamon, 1967.

Newsom Report, Central Advisory Council for Education, *Half Our Future,* London: H.M.S.O., 1963.

Peschek, D. and Brand, J. 'Policies and Politics in Secondary Education: Case Studies in West Ham and Reading', *Greater London Papers, No. 11,* London School of Economics, 1966.
Plowden Report, Central Advisory Council for Education, *Children and their Primary Schools,* London: H.M.S.O., 1967.

Riessman, F. *The Culturally Deprived Child,* New York: Harper & Row, 1962.
Robbins Report, *Committee on Higher Education,* London: H.M.S.O. Cmnd 2154, 1963.

Sanford, N. (ed.) *The American College,* New York: Wiley, 1962.
Sexton, P. *Education and Income,* New York: Viking, 1961.

Taylor, W. *The Secondary Modern School,* London: Faber and Faber, 1963.
Tropp, A. *The School Teachers,* London: Heinemann, 1956.
Turner, R. *The Social Context of Ambition,* San Francisco: Chandler, 1964.

Vidich, A.J. and Bensman, J. *Small Town in Mass Society* (Garden City, New York), New York: Doubleday, 1960.

Yates, A. *Grouping in Education,* New York: Wiley, 1966.

Index

Ability, measurement of 49, 59
  wastage of 59–61
  environmental influence on 67
Achievement, measurement of 68, 86
  motivation 85–7, 88–92, 107–8
  values 71–86, 88, 91–2, 95, 97–8, 101–4, 107–8
Acton Society Trust 43–4
Adolescent peer groups, and reference groups 194–6
  and social class 192–4
  and social mobility 194–7
  and student culture 19, 105, 184–5, 188–92, 196–7
American High School 25, 47, 58, 177–8
Anderson, C. Arnold 26, 42–3
Anderson, H.H. 181–2
Anderson, R.C. 182–3
Argyle, M. and Delin, P. 96
Ashby, Sir E. 29–30, 32

Bamford, T.W. 132
Banks, O. 23–4, 35, 47, 123, 176, 207
Barker, R.G. 173
Baron, G. and Tropp, A. 121–2, 127
Becker, H.S. 141, 186
Becker, W.C. 91
Ben-David, J. 26, 29–30, 34, 36, 54, 57, 63–4
Bereday, G. 37, 50
Bereday, G. and Lauwerys, J. 123
Berelson, B. 137
Bernstein, B. 87, 96–101, 107, 108, 188
Bendix, R. 14, 210
Biddle, B.J., Rosencranz, H.A. and Rankin, E.F. 121
Bidwell, C.E. 16, 118, 120, 124–5, 161, 163, 165–6.
Blau, P.M. 160
Blyth, W.A.L. 144
Bocock, S.S. 174
Bowman, M.J. 21
Bowman, T.R. 125
Brim, O. 7
Brittan, S. 127

Bronfenbrenner, U. 89, 93–5, 190
Brookover, W.A. and Gottlieb, D. 16, 58, 68, 104, 116, 129, 140–1, 145–6, 181, 188, 198, 201
Brunner, E. de S. and Wayland, S. 40
Bureaucracy 14, 16, 128, 159–64, 173, 175
Bush, R.N. 181
Bushnell, J.H. 191

Campbell, J.D. 190, 196
Campbell, R.E. and Bunnell, R.A. 73
Cannon, C. 123
Caplow, T. and McGee, R.J. 137
Carlson, R.O. 140
Caro, F.G. 78
Caro, F.G. and Pihlblad, C.T. 77–8
Centers, R. 42
Charters, W.W. Jnr. 118, 164, 167
Chetwynd, H.R. 172
Child-rearing, and achievement 86–7, 89–90
  and achievement motivation 88–93
  and achievement values 91–5
  and linguistic development 97–101
  and social class 93–5, 98–100, 104–5
  techniques of study 67, 95–6
Chinoy, E. 78
Cicourel, A.V. and Kitsuse, J.I. 178
Clark, Burton R. 48, 150, 162, 164
Cognitive development 87, 96–101, 108, 188
Cohen, E.C. 106–8
Coleman, J.S. 189, 203, 205–6, 209–11
Compensatory education 214–7
Comprehensive schools 24–5, 48–52, 123, 135, 170–3
Conant, J.B. 8, 13, 73, 136, 143, 147–8, 173
Copley, F. 173
Cornell, F.G. 164
Corwin, R.G. 7, 9, 14, 16, 159–60, 162–3, 175, 198, 200
Cotgrove, S. 30–6, 56
Counts, G.S. 25
Cowan, L.G., O'Connell, J., and Scanlon, D.G. 205
Crowther Report 32, 49, 55–9, 71, 106